PETROLEUM CONSERVATION IN THE UNITED STATES

Petroleum Conservation in the United States: An Economic Analysis

by STEPHEN L. McDONALD

Published for **Resources for the Future, Inc.**
by **The Johns Hopkins Press, Baltimore and London**

RESOURCES FOR THE FUTURE, INC.
1755 Massachusetts Avenue, N.W., Washington, D.C. 20036

Resources for the Future is a nonprofit corporation for research and education
in the development, conservation, and use of natural resources and the improvement of the quality of the environment. It was established in 1952 with the
cooperation of the Ford Foundation. Part of the work of Resources for the
Future is carried out by its resident staff; part is supported by grants to universities
and other nonprofit organizations. Unless otherwise stated, interpretations and
conclusions in RFF publications are those of the authors; the organization takes
responsibility for the selection of significant subjects for study, the competence of
the researchers, and their freedom of inquiry.

This book is one of RFF's studies in energy and mineral resources, which are
directed by Sam H. Schurr. The research was supported by a grant to the
University of Texas at Austin. Stephen L. McDonald is professor of economics
at the university. The manuscript was edited by Sheila Barrows. The index was
prepared by Margaret Stanley.

RFF editors: Henry Jarrett, Vera W. Dodds, Nora E. Roots, Tadd Fisher.

Copyright © 1971 by The Johns Hopkins Press
All rights reserved
Manufactured in the United States of America

The Johns Hopkins Press, Baltimore, Maryland 21218
The Johns Hopkins Press Ltd., London

Library of Congress Catalog Card Number 71-149242
ISBN 0-8018-1261-5

Foreword

The system by which petroleum is "conserved" in the United States is far more complex than is generally realized. Each producing state has its own system. Although the technical realities of petroleum occurrence and production and other factors result in some general similarities of the systems of control, the variations are important, partly because the systems were formed at different times but also because the organization of the industry differs among the producing states. As a result, the task of describing the system in terms that facilitate the economic analysis of its effects is difficult.

Professor McDonald's execution of this task is an outstanding example of applied economic analysis, a result flowing not only from long acquaintance with and reflection on the conservation system but also from the skill with which he uses the relevant economic theory.

The standard with which the conservation system is compared is that of maximum present value of net benefits. This criterion is used to evaluate the various characteristics of the system. If they result in inefficiency, they will cause social product to be diminished, either by altering the time flow of product and inputs in a way that fails to take proper account of the alternative use of productive services (which receives concrete expression as the cost of capital) or by stimulating wasteful outlays that do not result in an equivalent amount of product.

An impression of the complexity of the conservation system can be conveyed by a mere listing of some of the control measures whose effects are analyzed. Perhaps less well known outside the industry is the detailed regulation of many aspects of drilling and oil well operation to prevent "waste"; these include the gas-oil ratio, reservoir energy, disposal of brine, fire hazards, plugging of wells, and so on. The better known control devices are the various systems of production control and the regulation of well spacing. An especially interesting calculation is made to show the full range of factors—including both regulatory and market forces—that play on decisions on whether to drill and the depths at which to drill.

McDonald gives the conservation system high marks for avoiding a very large quantity of economic waste as compared with no regulation at all. At the same time, the system has serious defects and falls far short of what could be achieved by way of reducing or eliminating economic waste.

Such unitization as has resulted in those states with voluntary and/or compulsory unitization laws has brought substantial gains, but much more could be achieved, especially in view of the fact that important producing states have no compulsory unitization law. McDonald's view is that compulsory unitization is the route to efficient exploration and production of oil. His discussion is distinguished by a recognition of many subtle facets of this remedy that ordinarily receive little attention, such as the need for continued regulation of many types affecting drilling and production, the need to control reservoir development and operation prior to unitization, and the need for supplementary regulations to prevent inequities among producers.

While a few readers will come to their task with an adequate background in both economic theory and the intricacies of the conservation system, most will find themselves lacking in one or the other respect. These are fortunate, for if they persevere, they will find that ideas somewhat new to them are explained in logical progression and in simple yet adequate language.

Orris C. Herfindahl
Associate Director
Energy and Minerals Program

September, 1970   Resources for the Future

Preface

This book is not addressed to my fellow professional economists, although I hope that some of them will read it for what they may learn about regulatory practices. It is addressed, rather, to all those who have an interest in, or curiosity about, the petroleum industry and the efficiency with which it exploits the nation's oil and gas resources: oilmen, regulators, legislators, students, and conscientious citizens generally. I hope that it will be read by many oilmen, for they stand to benefit most directly from improvements in efficiency, and their influence is crucial in shaping the further evolution of the regulatory system.

The study was made possible by a generous grant from Resources for the Future, Inc. through its energy and minerals program under the direction of Sam H. Schurr. This support is most gratefully acknowledged.

I am indebted also to the conservation officials of thirty-two states (listed in table 1), who supplied me with copies of statutes, regulations, and other material on which much of my research is based, and who made themselves available to me for personal interviews. James L. Carlton, Dan R. Dunnett, Cleon B. Feight, M. C. Hoffman, Carlton V. Hudson, Ray C. Jones, James F. Neely, A. Fred Peterson, A. L. Porter, Jr., John P. Roberts, Douglas V. Rogers, William Smith, and Fred H. Young were especially generous with their time. Particular thanks go to the late Lawrence R. Alley, former executive secretary of the Interstate Oil Compact Commission, who opened the library and files of the commission to me and otherwise extended helpful courtesies.

I am grateful for the help of two able research assistants, A. Gordon Everett and Ernest P. Werlin.

Valuable comments on an earlier draft of the study were received from Morris A. Adelman, Lawrence R. Alley, Richard J. Gonzalez, Richard L. Gordon, the late Robert E. Hardwicke, James O. Haynes, Orris C. Herfindahl, S. Frank Holmesly, Alfred E. Kahn, Richard J. Kruizenga, Onnie P. Lattu, James W. McKie, Charles S. Overmiller, and W. Earl Turner. I thank them all and absolve them completely from responsibility for any errors which may remain.

Austin, Texas. May 1970   Stephen L. McDonald

Contents

Tables

Figures

PETROLEUM CONSERVATION IN THE UNITED STATES

1. Introduction

Purposes and background

This study of conservation regulation in the petroleum industry of the United States has two major, interrelated purposes. The first is to present a comprehensive and balanced explanation of a complex, still evolving system. The resulting coverage and emphasis differ in several respects from those of predecessor studies. The technical basis of petroleum production, the concept of waste prevention underlying most regulation, the prevention of external damages, and the economics of well spacing are given unusual attention; the regulatory programs of all the significant producing states, not just the "market demand" states, are surveyed; and, in connection with the analysis of each major type of regulation, the more important new developments in the postwar period—specifically since 1948—are traced. The second purpose, also differentiating this study from earlier ones, is to develop in detail an economic framework of analysis and to apply this framework in interpreting, evaluating, and proposing changes in the existing regulatory system. Three chapters are devoted to the economics of petroleum conservation, from the role of conservation in the general economic process to the price-lowering and price-stabilizing effects of universal unit operations in a competitive petroleum industry. The resulting framework permits some unusual interpretations and evaluations—for instance, of controlling external damages and regulating well spacing—but it has, perhaps, a more important function; it provides a broadened basis for the old and familiar recommendation that all petroleum reservoirs be developed and operated as units.

Throughout the study attention is focused primarily on the conservation of crude oil and associated gas. Only occasional paragraphs are necessary to relate the analysis to nonassociated gas. As far as possible, the discussion avoids problem policy areas other than conservation, such as differential taxation, import restriction, and gas price regulation.

The pervasive concern of the study is the economic efficiency with which we exploit our petroleum resources. This concern is based on the presumption that the purpose of conservation is to raise present and/or future levels of material well-being, and that only success in this purpose

1

justifies some system of regulation in the name of conservation. Of course, the selection of a particular system or its modification is conditioned by other, perhaps conflicting, goals of public policy, but can be made more intelligently if we fully understand the economic merits of alternative systems and appreciate the economic costs of pursuing competing goals. This study is intended to contribute to such an understanding and appreciation.

The economic efficiency with which we exploit our petroleum resources is of interest to everyone in the United States, for it helps determine the level of well-being of each of us. It is of more immediate and compelling interest to oilmen, however, for it helps to determine the size and growth rate of the industry, and hence the range and profitability of investment opportunities. This latter interest has been heightened by recent and prospective conditions in the domestic industry.

The American petroleum industry entered the postwar period with virtually no excess capacity, a small export surplus, a burgeoning demand (partly at the expense of coal), and abundant exploration opportunities. The result was an unprecedented growth of drilling, sustained, it appears in retrospect, several years too long. By 1956 crude oil capacity exceeded output by about a third; and the immediate prospect was for additional increases in the capacity-output ratio as existing discoveries were drilled up, as net imports rose rapidly relative to domestic demand, and as crude oil's share in total energy consumption in the country leveled off. The future was further darkened by the rising cost of drilling to the depths and in the (often offshore) locations where the best remaining prospects lay, by the decline in crude oil prices after 1957, and by the uncertainties accompanying the subjection of natural gas prices to federal control. Drilling, particularly exploratory drilling, consequently went into a slump, beginning in 1957, which had not clearly ended at the time of writing (mid-1970). Despite the imposition of mandatory oil import quotas in 1959, excess capacity continued to rise and prices continued to exhibit weakness into the early sixties. The ranks of contract drillers and independent producers thinned, and those remaining looked hopefully to possible future price increases. Some modest increases occurred as the country's deeper involvement in Vietnam stimulated demand and reduced excess capacity; still others are probable if drilling remains depressed. But now, even though excess capacity is declining, expectations of further price increases are restrained by two considerations: first, import restrictions might be relaxed if the margin between domestic and foreign prices were significantly enlarged; and second, production of oil from shale or other unconventional sources might become a commercial reality if crude oil prices rose much higher.

Thus, even as it struggles with the consequences of over-expansion in the first decade after World War II, the industry faces a difficult future. It enters the seventies with the prospect of rising replacement costs, as the search for oil and gas extends to greater depths and less accessible locations, and at more slowly rising prices. The implication is clear. Oil and gas must be produced ever more efficiently if the industry is to continue growing at even the same rate as total energy consumption. Technological progress in exploration, drilling, and production will no doubt continue to help; but in prudence the industry will look for all opportunities to reduce costs, including those offered by the regulatory system. Already, as we shall see, significant cost reduction has recently been achieved through markedly wider well spacing in new oil and gas fields. This study is intended to show that still more opportunities in the realm of regulation remain to be exploited.

The argument will be easier to follow with the guidance of a brief outline of the presentation.

Outline of the presentation

Part I of the study, "The Setting of the Problem," is designed to provide a factual background for the theoretical and analytical sections to follow. The first of the two chapters in this part, chapter 2, provides a discussion of the natural occurrence, discovery, production, and marketing of petroleum, stressing the technical and institutional peculiarities which give rise to conservation and related problems. Chapter 3 begins with an identification of those problems with which regulation attempts to deal, continues with an account of the historical development of regulation, and concludes with a survey of the principal forms of regulation in use in the significant producing states.

In part II, "The Economics of Petroleum Conservation" (chapters 4 through 6), the analytical framework for the remainder of the study is developed. The role of conservation in the general economic process is discussed in chapter 4. Here the meaning of economic efficiency is explained, the role of the price system in promoting efficiency is described, and conservation as a tool of efficiency is defined. Having associated conservation with the allocation of resource use over time, I discuss the optimum time-distribution of use in chapter 5. Here it is shown that only under unit operations would the operators of a reservoir tend to select the optimum time-distribution of use (production) from the point of view of society. The interaction between the optimum rate of production and the optimum rate of exploration for new petroleum deposits is also explained in this chapter. Finally, in chapter 6 the demand for, supply, and price of crude oil are discussed, and it is shown that under universal unit operations, price tends to be lower and more stable than under unrestrained competitive[1] operation of reservoirs.

Chapters 7 through 10 make up part III, entitled "Evaluation of Conservation Regulation." In this part the principal forms of regulation are explained in detail and then evaluated in terms of the framework developed in part II. Chapter 7 is concerned with the concept of prohibited waste that underlies most state regulation. Chapter 8 is addressed to the control of external damages; that is, regulation of petroleum activities designed to avoid or limit damage to other resources, such as fresh water and hard mineral deposits. Chapter 9 covers two interrelated forms of regulation, control of production rates and regulation of well spacing. Much of this chapter is devoted to a quantitative analysis of well spacing incentives embodied in the depth-acreage allowable schedules in use in the states that regulate production on the basis of market demand. Finally, unitization and unit operation of reservoirs are discussed in chapter 10. Here the emphasis is on the benefits of unitization, obstacles to voluntary unitization, and provision in many state laws for a degree of compulsory unitization.

Part IV, "For the Future," consists of a single chapter containing proposals that seem to grow out of the preceding analysis. Several suggestions for modifying the present regulatory system are made, including a rather fundamental one: the substitution of universal mandatory unitization for most specific regulation—e.g., of well spacing and production rates—now practiced by the producing states.

Briefly, the argument of the study is this: Where private ownership of mineral rights is the rule, as in the United States, certain unique problems of conservation arise in connection with the drilling for and production of oil and gas. The states have attempted to cope with these problems, while protecting equities, by restraining operators in their pursuit of profit, requiring positive acts chiefly in connection with the prevention of external damages. The result is a very complex system of regulation, the details of which differ among states. To evaluate this system, an explicit analytical framework is needed. The framework offered is based upon the concept of conservation as an integral part of the general economic process, one designed to promote an allocation of resource use over time that would maximize the capital value (to society) of resource endowments. Private operators, motivated by the

---

[1] "Competitive" here refers to competition among operators within a reservoir for the oil in that reservoir, which occurs in the absence of unitization or regulatory restraint. To avoid confusing this "bad" competition with "good" market competition among firms, it is henceforth referred to as "unrestrained operation of reservoirs."

prospect of profit and guided by the price system, would tend to practice (thus conceived) conservation of oil and gas provided that two conditions were met: (a) operators were required to avoid or compensate for external damages and (b) petroleum reservoirs were required to be developed and operated as units. Cost and benefit allocation formulas in unitization agreements would protect equities, and universal unit operations would lower costs (hence prices), stabilize prices, and assure the optimum resource life for oil and gas. The existing system of conservation regulation is based upon the concept of conservation as the prevention of certain physical wastes. The specific implementing regulations, including those designed to prevent external damages, are rarely conditioned by economic considerations. Although generally beneficial in comparison with no regulation at all, they fall short of assuring optimum well spacing, production rates, use of associated gas, and exploration. Costs (and prices) remain unnecessarily high, and the resource life of petroleum is unnecessarily shortened. The prevailing regulatory system is still evolving, however, and in ways that must be regarded as improvements. Notably, statutory provisions for a degree of compulsion in unitization are rapidly spreading through the producing states. Further improvements can be made in the existing system, but ideal conservation regulation requires a more fundamental change in approach—the substitution of universal unit operations for all restraining regulations save those to prevent external damages. With such a change, profit-motivated enterprise guided by the price system would become consistent with—indeed, a positive instrument of—conservation of oil and gas.

Before proceeding to the study proper, a comment on the normative implications of the frame of reference may be useful.

A note on the frame of reference

The question of conservation is considered here as a problem of efficiency in the use of resources. As for the economy, profit motivation and a reasonably competitive market system of allocating resources, organizing production, and distributing income are taken for granted. My proposed standard of efficiency and definition of conservation are derived from the logic of such a market system. (That logic is outlined in chapter 4.) I identify those regulatory conditions in the petroleum industry that would allow conservation as defined to be one of the products of the free working of the system. These conditions are labeled "ideal," and the associated state of conservation is taken as the standard for evaluating the results of prevailing regulatory practices.

I shall speak of the optimum allocation of resources and of maximizing satisfactions. These ideas of "the best" are conceived within the context of the assumed market system; their significance is limited by the terms and conditions of the system. I do not mean them to represent normative conditions without reference to the system. More particularly, I do not claim that the general allocative results of the free working of a competitive market system, including the allocation of natural resource use over time under "ideal" regulatory conditions, are the best of all possible results independently of the system. My strongest claim is that under the "ideal" regulatory conditions the decisions determining the allocation of natural resource use over time are properly integrated with other allocative decisions (e.g., those governing investment), so that the resulting general allocation is efficient. Efficiency within the system is my norm.

It is of course possible to posit norms that have no necessary reference to a particular allocative system. For example, recognizing that conservation decisions affect the distribution of income among generations over time, we might choose as our norm the desired distributive effect.[2] We might decide on (presumably) ethical grounds to make our grandchildren X percent better off per capita than ourselves[3] and so modify the allocative system as to bring about the desired result. Since we could achieve the desired intertemporal distribution of income through many different possible combinations of investment, technological progress, education, and restrained use of natural resources— indeed, through many different possible combinations of investments in particular assets, of specific kinds of technological progress, etc.—we would have some specific economic choices to make, and we might choose the combination that was in some sense least costly. Efficiency would thus play a role, but it would be subordinated to an ethically based distributive norm.

I choose efficiency within the market system as my norm, then, not because there is no other conceivable norm, but because it seems most appropriate to the problem at hand and the skills at my disposal. My problem is how best to use our petroleum resources, given our general arrangements for allocating resources and distributing income over time. This is an efficiency problem, and the skills of the economist are specifically designed to deal with its type.

[2] For a cogent discussion of issues in the intertemporal distribution of income, see Orris C. Herfindahl, "Goals and Standards of Performance for the Conservation of Minerals," *Natural Resources Journal*, vol. 3 (May 1963), pp. 78–97.

[3] Since it is impossible to make interpersonal comparisons of utility or satisfactions, particularly over time, it would not be possible to choose an optimum intertemporal distribution of income on economic grounds.

PART I

THE SETTING OF THE PROBLEM

2. Petroleum Production and Marketing

The distinctive problem of conserving petroleum resources stems from certain unique characteristics of petroleum production and marketing. It is essential to understand these characteristics in order to appreciate fully either the economics of petroleum conservation or the various conservation regulations employed in the different producing states. The following description, which is intended also to familiarize the reader with pertinent terminology, is necessarily limited to the bare essentials. Those desiring a fuller treatment are referred to several excellent sources.[1]

The nature of petroleum deposits

Although it is often equated with crude oil only, "petroleum" is a

[1] Stuart E. Buckley, ed., *Petroleum Conservation* (Dallas: American Institute of Mining and Metallurgical Engineers, 1951); Ralph Cassady, Jr., *Price Making and Price Behavior in the Petroleum Industry* (New Haven: Yale University Press, 1954); Norman J. Clark, *Elements of Petroleum Reservoirs* (Dallas: American Institute of Mining and Metallurgical Engineers, 1960); Thomas C. Frick, ed., *Petroleum Production Handbook*, vols. I and II (New York: McGraw-Hill Book Co., 1962); Institute on Economics of Petroleum Exploration, Development, and Property Evaluation, Southwest Legal Foundation, *Economics of Petroleum Exploration, Development, and Property Evaluation* (Englewood Cliffs: Prentice-Hall, 1961); Interstate Oil Compact Commission (IOCC), Governors' Special Study Committee, *A Study of Conservation of Oil and Gas in the United States, 1964* (Oklahoma City: IOCC, 1965); IOCC, Engineering Committee, *Oil and Gas Production: An Introductory Guide to Production Techniques and Conservation Methods* (Norman: University of Oklahoma Press, 1951); IOCC, Research and Coordinating Committee, *Well Spacing* (Oklahoma City: IOCC, 1952); U.S. Department of the Interior, Office of Oil and Gas, *An Appraisal of the Petroleum Industry of the United States* (Washington: U.S. Dept. of the Interior, 1965); U.S. Department of Justice, *Third Report of the Attorney General Pursuant to Section 2 of the Joint Resolution of July 28,1955, Consenting to an Interstate Compact to Conserve Oil and Gas* (Washington: Government Printing Office, 1958).

generic term denoting all natural hydrocarbons[2] except those in the coal family. Petroleum so defined is normally found in underground reservoirs as a fluid mixture of chemically distinct hydrocarbon compounds ranging in number from a few to many. The physical properties of a given mixture in the reservoir vary with temperature and pressure but, as delivered to the surface, any mixture is classifiable as crude oil, natural gas, or a combination of the two. The liquid hydrocarbons often obtained from surface condensation or special processing of natural gas, such as natural gasoline, propane, and butane, known collectively as natural gas liquids, are implicitly included in raw natural gas. Hence the common technical practice,[3] followed here, of using "petroleum" synonymously with crude oil and natural gas. For convenience where no ambiguity would result, we refer to these substances in the familiar shortened forms, "oil" and "gas."

The exact origin of petroleum is unknown; but according to the most plausible and widely accepted hypothesis, the constituent hydrocarbons were created from marine life buried off the shores of ancient seas beneath sedimentary deposits and decomposed by pressure, temperature, and bacterial action.[4] As sedimentary layers accumulated in the millions of years during which the earth's crust as we know it evolved, the deeper layers of silt, sand, and calcium carbonate were progressively compacted, forming, with the aid of mineral cementation, strata of shale, sandstone, and limestone saturated with (saline) sea water and any hydrocarbons present. The hydrostatic pressure (and temperature) in these strata increased with increasing depths below sea level.[5] From time to time in the evolutionary process, uneven stresses produced by shifting

---

[2] The molecules of hydrocarbon compounds consist of hydrogen and carbon atoms in various proportions and arrangements. In general, specific gravity, vaporizing temperature, and viscosity of hydrocarbon compounds vary directly with the number of carbon atoms in the molecule. Thus methane, the chief constituent of natural gas and the lightest of the hydrocarbon compounds, has only one carbon atom in its molecule.

[3] As in Buckley, *Petroleum Conservation* and Clark, *Elements of Petroleum Reservoirs.*

[4] Clark, *Elements of Petroleum Reservoirs*, pp. 1–17, gives a lucid account of the process by which petroleum is believed to have been formed and collected into concentrated deposits.

[5] The pressure in water-filled porous sedimentary rocks tends to increase by 430 to 460 pounds per square inch for each 1,000 feet of depth beneath the surface. The larger figure is the approximate weight at rest of a column of sea water one inch square and 1,000 feet high. (Hence "hydrostatic" pressure.) Subsurface temperatures are not so simply explained. However, they tend to increase by 6° F. to 20° F. for each 1,000 feet of depth. Buckley, *Petroleum Conservation*, pp. 111–12; and Clark, *Elements of Petroleum Reservoirs*, p. 67.

land and water masses caused the earth's crust to buckle and fracture, thus tilting, folding, and faulting the accumulated strata. Subsequent sedimentary layers were deposited horizontally over the deformed older strata to form angular intersections. Compaction and cementation of the finer-grained sedimentary layers largely eliminated pore space and connecting channels in them, making the resultant rock strata (e.g., shale) effectively impermeable to fluids. Hydrocarbons squeezed out of the "tighter" strata joined those formed in the coarser-grained, permeable strata (e.g., sandstone). Being lighter than the salt water dominantly occupying the pores of these strata, the hydrocarbon particles floated upward, migrating with the tilt of the strata through tiny channels connecting pore spaces until trapped by some impermeable layer or section of rock blocking further upward movement. Here the individual particles gradually accumulated to form concentrated deposits of petroleum under hydrostatic pressure. The portion of a permeable stratum containing a trapped concentration of petroleum is known as a reservoir.

There are many recognized types of reservoir traps,[6] but nearly all of them may be interpreted as combinations or variations of three basic types: the *anticlinal,* the *fault-sealed,* and the *stratigraphic.* These are illustrated schematically in figure 1. The *anticlinal trap* results from an upfolding of strata, which produces a structure resembling an overturned bowl. Petroleum migrates to the highest portions of the structure and is retained there by its buoyancy in water and the ceiling imposed by an overlying impermeable stratum. Often the upfolding affects several permeable strata in a vertical section, so that separate petroleum reservoirs may be encountered at different depths under a given surface area. The *fault-sealed trap* results from a deep fracture in the earth's crust and slippage of one segment so that the upper end of a severed permeable stratum is sealed off by the opposing end of an impermeable stratum. Essentially the same sort of trap is formed when a dome of (impermeable) salt thrusts up through a permeable stratum, tilting it and sealing off its upper end. When several permeable strata in a vertical section are affected by a fault or a piercement salt dome, separate petroleum reservoirs may be formed at different depths along the fault or the flanks of the dome. The final type, the *stratigraphic trap,* results from gradual or abrupt loss of permeability in a segment of a given stratum caused by change in composition of the original sedimentary deposits. Similar in significant respects to the stratigraphic trap is the kind of trap formed

[6] For schematic illustrations of numerous types of reservoir traps see IOCC, *Oil and Gas Production,* pp. 115–22.

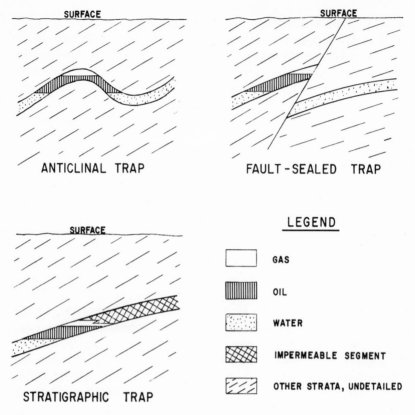

Figure 1.   Schematic illustrations of reservoir trap types (cross section).

by the angular intersection of a tilted permeable stratum with a horizontal (or less tilted) impermeable stratum. Since the stratigraphic trap does not arise from structural features that may involve several strata in a vertical section, the presence of such a trap at one depth offers no suggestion of others at different depths under a given surface area.

For reasons already indicated, reservoir traps almost universally contain salt water in addition to petroleum. "Free" water typically saturates the rock below the petroleum zone. Within the petroleum zone, additional water normally coats the walls of pore spaces with a thin film. This water, known as "connate" or "interstitial" water, was retained in place by surface tension when migrant petroleum particles displaced the rest of the original water in the uppermost portions of the trap. The petroleum itself may consist of oil and gas (both conceived in terms of surface conditions) in any proportions. Oil is usually found with some gas present, either entirely dissolved in the oil or, if the reservoir pressure is insufficient to force all the gas into solution, partly in solution and partly as a "cap" above the oil in the trap. Gas, in contrast, is frequently found unassociated with oil; and many gas deposits are capable of yielding only negligible quantities of natural gas liquids. Both oil and gas vary widely in chemical and physical properties, including content of such impurities as sulphur and such valuable rarities as helium.

Discovery and development of petroleum reservoirs

Petroleum exploration is the search for subsurface structural and stratigraphic conditions conducive to the entrapment of petroleum, followed by the drilling of one or more wells to the prospective trap. The predrilling search consists of study of surface features, such as faults, outcroppings, and uplifts, to detect signs of underlying structural formations; geophysical testing, such as seismographic analysis,[7] to gain more direct indication of deep structural characteristics; and correlation of data secured from the logs[8] and rock samples of wells already drilled in the area to find those strata that possess qualities favorable to the accumulation of petroleum. Surface study and geophysical testing frequently are successful means of locating faults, anticlines, and salt domes, but they rarely are successful in finding stratigraphic traps. The latter are usually found on evidence gained from actual drilling in the immediate environment.[9]

The petroleum explorer seldom owns outright the land on which he wishes to drill. Almost always he secures the right to drill, and to produce for his own benefit any petroleum found, by leasing the land for his limited purposes from the owner or prior lessee. In consideration of the rights acquired, he typically makes an immediate cash payment (a

[7] The seismograph indicates the depth, density, and shape of subsurface strata and masses by measuring the behavior of reflected or refracted shock waves artificially produced at the surface. The gravity meter and the magnetometer, two other major geophysical devices, sense gravitational and magnetic anomalies often associated with trap-producing structures. Ibid., pp. 20–21.

[8] There are many types of well logs, or records of the characteristics of strata through which a well is drilled. Two of the most important logging devices sense the electrical and radioactive properties of strata, indicating such qualities as permeability and fluid content. H. G. Doll, M. P. Tixier, M. Martin, and F. Segesman, "Electrical Logging"; and John L. P. Campbell, "Radioactivity Well Logging"; in Frick, *Petroleum Production Handbook*, ch. 43 and 44.

[9] A. I. Levorsen, "Exploration for Stratigraphic Traps," in Institute on Economics of Petroleum Exploration, *Economics of Petroleum Exploration*, pp. 17–37.

"lease bonus"), promises periodic "delay rentals" until a well is commenced or the primary term of the lease expires, and further promises a royalty on any production realized, commonly one-eighth or more of the total petroleum captured or its value equivalent.[10] Thus two distinct property interests are created—the royalty interest and the operating (or "working") interest, each having its own relationship to the problem of petroleum conservation.

In drilling a well, the operator bores through numerous strata, some of which may be permeable and contain fresh water (especially near the surface), salt water, or other mineral brines under pressure. Counterpressure exerted by the drilling fluid[11] may adequately exclude these liquids from the well bore during actual drilling operations; but upon cessation of drilling, more specific measures must be taken to exclude them and avoid damage to valuable resources. If the well is "dry" (no commercial petroleum deposit found), the basic problem is to keep salt water and other brines from rising in the bore, entering the relatively low-pressure fresh-water strata, and flooding the surface. This kind of pollution can be prevented by casing the fresh-water zone with pipe solidly cemented to the walls of the well, leaving the well filled with drilling fluid, and plugging the hole at the surface with cement. Surface plugging also protects against humans or livestock falling into the hole, of course. If the well is productive, the problem is not only to avoid pollution of fresh water and surface soil, but also to exclude all foreign liquids from the producing zone and to keep the well bore clear for the installation, operation, and maintenance of lifting equipment. Thus, in productive wells appropriate casing all the way to the bottom of the hole is ordinarily required for full protection of petroleum, fresh water, and other resources.[12]

A producing well is "completed" with the installation of casing, a smaller-gauge string of pipe through which fluids are conducted to the

---

[10] Although leases have been written to terminate unconditionally after the passage of a specified time, nearly all modern leases provide that if production occurs before expiration of the primary term the contract remains in force until the lessee voluntarily ceases production. For a full discussion of leases and other property interests in oil and gas, see J. B. Clarke, Jr., "Oil and Gas Leases," in Frick, *Petroleum Production Handbook*, ch. 49.

[11] The drilling fluid is ordinarily a mixture of water and earth materials known in the industry as "mud." The fluid, forced under high pressure down the drill pipe, around the drill bit, and back to the surface, lubricates the bit and flushes rock particles to the surface.

[12] In some areas, special measures may be required to protect coal, potash, or other mines from hazards (e.g., gas leakage and flooding) created by petroleum operations.

surface and the necessary control valves. Completion often also includes stimulation of the well by artificially increasing the permeability of the reservoir rock in the immediate vicinity of the well bottom. This may be done by means of acid treatment, which scours out pore spaces and connecting channels, or by fracturing the rock with explosives or hydraulic pressure. Finally, on the surface, a well is equipped as needed with flow lines; devices to separate gas, liquid hydrocarbons, and water from each other; and oil storage tanks.

When sufficient performance data are obtained from a discovery well to indicate the presence of a commercial deposit, operators holding leases in the immediate vicinity proceed to "develop" the reservoir by drilling additional wells and equipping the productive ones as just described. The primary intent of those drilling the wells is to gain additional means of access to the petroleum in the reservoir. Where leases are small and numerous, and operators are free to pursue their own interests, a discovery may be followed by intensive drilling as each operator seeks to avoid drainage from beneath his land to the wells on nearby leases. But development drilling is also a final-stage exploratory activity, yielding information on the areal extent of the reservoir, variations in rock permeability and thickness within the reservoir, the total oil and gas in place, and the dominant natural "drive," or expulsion mechanism. As this information accumulates, it forms the basis of all subsequent development and operating decisions, including those relating to cooperative actions by means of which the several operators in a reservoir may further their common interest.

Types of natural drives—oil reservoirs

An oil or gas well "produces" because the hole creates a point of low pressure in a reservoir. In response to a pressure loss at some point, all the fluids in a reservoir tend to rearrange themselves so as to restore the equilibrium of forces—gravity, surface tension, and hydrostatic (and sometimes hydrodynamic[13]) pressure—holding the fluid particles in place. Particles immediately adjacent to the well move into it, those just behind move in to occupy the voided pore space, those farther be-

---

[13] Hydrodynamic pressure is the force exerted by a flowing liquid. Often this pressure, arising from water currents in subsurface strata, helps trap petroleum behind barriers that otherwise would not be impermeable to oil and gas. G. A. Hill, W. A. Colburn, and J. W. Knight, "Reducing Oil Finding Costs by Use of Hydrodynamic Evaluations," in Institute on Economics of Petroleum Exploration, *Economics of Petroleum Exploration*, pp. 46–52.

hind move forward in their turn, and so on throughout the continuously permeable portions of the reservoir. With steady flow into the well, a smooth pressure gradient tends to be formed, sloping upward from the well to whichever is closer—the limits of the reservoir or the intersecting pressure gradient formed by a competing well. There is abundant evidence of pressure interference and drainage extending for several miles in oil as well as in gas reservoirs.[14]

The pressure gradient extending out from a well is affected by the rate of production, the producing age of the reservoir (under natural drives), and the means employed to lift oil from the bottom of the well to the surface. The higher the rate of production, other factors given, the greater is the draw-down of pressure in the immediate vicinity of the well and the steeper is the gradient. Since pressure drops throughout the reservoir as unreplaced fluids are removed from it, the pressure difference between reservoir and well declines with depletion and eventually becomes so small that further production of hydrocarbons is unprofitable. This decline of reservoir pressure with depletion largely accounts for the typical decline of an oil well's producing capacity from completion to abandonment in a pattern often adequately described by a negatively sloping exponential curve. As for the lifting mechanism, the weight of a column of oil rising to the surface in the production tubing creates a back-pressure. So long as this back-pressure does not eliminate the gradient between bottom-hole and reservoir pressures, the well is capable of natural flow to the surface. Eventually, as reservoir pressure declines with depletion, the back-pressure must become excessive, necessitating some form of artificial lift if production is to continue. Either pumping or injection of gas to lighten the oil column will create or restore a gradient in low-pressure reservoirs.

For pressure to be maintained in the oil zone of a reservoir, the pore space voided by oil moving toward the well must be occupied by volumetrically equivalent fluids. In effect, the oil must be displaced by fluids under slightly greater pressure. Three basic displacement mechanisms, or drives, are recognized: *dissolved-gas* drive, *gas-cap* drive, and *water* drive.[15] Two or more of these may function in combination, although one usually dominates. Gravity supplements all of them and, in some situations, is a major force in oil recovery.

The *dissolved-gas* drive arises in situations where reservoir pressure

[14] R. C. Craze, "Development Plan for Oil Reservoirs," in Frick, *Petroleum Production Handbook*, ch. 33, pp. 8–14.

[15] The following discussion of oil reservoir drives is based on Buckley, *Petroleum Conservation*, pp. 117–40; Clark, *Elements of Petroleum Reservoirs*, pp. 66–83; and IOCC, *Oil and Gas Production*, pp. 36–50.

has forced so much gas into solution with the oil that the expansive force of the dissolved gas dominates the process of oil displacement. After a well creates a low-pressure point, oil (with its dissolved gas) is displaced at first by expansion of the solution and then, when reservoir pressure has dropped sufficiently, by liberation of the gas into voided pore space. There the gas continues to accumulate and expand as fluids are removed from the reservoir. The remaining oil shrinks with loss of gas content and becomes more viscous, while the accumulating free gas progressively occupies the available pore space and flow channels to the well. Consequently, the ratio of produced gas to produced oil, the "gas-oil ratio," rises steeply; and continued withdrawal of fluids rapidly depletes the reservoir pressure.

A *gas-cap* drive results when the oil displacement process is dominated by expansion of gas existing as a free fluid between the oil and the reservoir ceiling. If a well is completed deep in the oil zone and is cased off from the gas zone, the flow of oil into the well is accompanied by movement of all the reservoir fluids down and toward the well. The upper limit of oil saturation moves lower, and the force of gravity tends to keep this limit in a horizontal plane. Expanding gas in the cap occupies the pore space voided by the receding upper limit of oil saturation and thus minimizes the pressure drop in the oil zone. The volume of gas in the cap may be augmented by gas coming out of oil solution as pressure declines. Since reservoir strata may be tilted only a few degrees and rarely approach the vertical, the fluids in a reservoir under gas-cap drive migrate not only downward but also laterally. Consequently, a well located on the upper portion of the reservoir may experience a rapidly rising gas-oil ratio quite early in its life. Such a well tends to lose oil to wells located lower in the reservoir, but its gas production accelerates the depletion of reservoir pressure and limits the oil recovery of all wells taken together.

In a *water* drive reservoir, oil is displaced primarily by the encroachment of water from below. Water is only slightly compressible; but where the volume of water is very large relative to the volume of reservoir fluids and the initial pressure is great, water expansion may be sufficient to occupy pore space voided by the migration of oil toward a well. Often natural recharge of the water-bearing portion of a reservoir stratum helps to maintain pressure in the oil zone. Moreover, by means of capillary action, water invades relatively impermeable sections of reservoir rock, flushes out oil into the more permeable sections, and thus permits recovery of oil that would be left in place under other drives. The direction of fluid migration in a water drive reservoir is, of course, the opposite of that in a gas-cap drive reservoir. The lower limit of oil saturation moves upward and laterally with the tilt of the reservoir stratum, the force of gravity tending to keep the water-oil contact in a horizontal plane. A well located on the lower end of a water drive reservoir loses some migrant oil to wells located higher on the structure and at an early age experiences a rapidly increasing produced water-oil ratio. The (salt) water produced not only accelerates depletion of reservoir pressure but also creates a problem of disposal in order to avoid pollution of soil and fresh water at or near the surface.

Ultimate recovery and the "maximum efficient rate" of production

As measured under surface conditions, the oil initially in place per unit of rock volume in a reservoir depends on rock porosity, space occupied by connate water, and shrinkage of oil as it is cooled and dissolved gas is removed. For instance, a cubic foot of oil-zone rock with 30 percent porosity and 20 percent connate water saturation would contain 0.24 cubic feet of oil [.30(1 − .20)] under reservoir conditions. Assuming a one-third shrinkage from reservoir to surface, the contents of the rock would be 0.16 cubic feet (approximately 0.029 barrels) of oil under surface conditions.[16] Such a figure multiplied by the volume of oil-zone rock sets the upper limit of oil physically recoverable from a reservoir.

Not all of the oil initially in place can be recovered through the use of any natural drive. Because of the natural limitations of the respective displacement mechanisms, the recoverable portion of oil initially in place rarely exceeds 30 percent with dissolved-gas drive, 50 percent with gas-cap drive, and 75 percent with water drive.[17] Given such factors as rock permeability and oil viscosity, the recoverable percentage also depends on the rate of production.

Ultimate recovery is not sensitive to the rate of production in a reservoir subject to a dissolved-gas drive. But often conditions will permit shifting dominance from a dissolved-gas drive to a water or a gas-cap drive, either of which is capable of effecting greater ultimate recovery. Thus, if a subordinate water drive is present, restriction of the rate of oil withdrawal to the natural rate of water encroachment allows the water drive to become effective; or, if structural features are suitable, sufficient

---

[16] A 42-gallon barrel contains 5.61 cubic feet of oil at 60° F. and atmospheric pressure. For an interesting history of the 42-gallon barrel conventional in the oil industry see Robert E. Hardwicke, *The Oilman's Barrel* (Norman: University of Oklahoma Press, 1958).

[17] Clark, *Elements of Petroleum Reservoirs*, pp. 71–78.

production restraint allows much of the gas liberated from solution to be segregated by gravity into a cap, where it may be retained as a displacing agent until the oil zone is nearly depleted.

Ultimate recovery in both water drive and gas-cap drive reservoirs is sensitive to the rate of production. For a water drive to be most effective, the removal of oil and the advance of water must be slow enough both to permit water to invade the "tighter" sections of rock by capillary action and flush out the oil there and to permit gravity to segregate oil from water and maintain a uniform front of water advance. At higher production rates, the more mobile water tends to form flow channels to wells through the relatively permeable sections of the oil zone, bypassing oil in the less permeable sections and, with removal to the surface, depleting reservoir pressure as much as a volumetrically equivalent amount of produced oil. The most effective utilization of a gas-cap drive requires that oil production be slow enough to permit gravity to segregate gas from oil and maintain a uniform plane of gas-oil contact. Otherwise, the highly mobile gas channels through the oil zone to the wells, bypassing oil and rapidly depleting reservoir pressure.

From these considerations it is concluded that, if other measures are taken to limit withdrawal of displacing fluids, there is for each reservoir some maximum rate of oil production at each stage of depletion consistent with the fullest exploitation of the expulsive forces present. A higher rate of production would result in some avoidable reduction of ultimate recovery. This critical rate, known as the maximum efficient rate, or MER, naturally varies from one reservoir to another and from one state of depletion to another in the same reservoir.

Although the MER is usually associated with *no* technically avoidable loss of ultimate recovery, some authorities suggest that sensitivity to the rate of production is so low over a significant range of rates that economic considerations necessarily enter the determination of an operative MER. Thus Buckley writes:

> Operation of a reservoir at an infinitesimally low rate of oil production would not in itself assure efficient recovery unless other necessary conditions were met. However, if all other conditions are fulfilled, the ultimate oil recovery from most pools is directly dependent on the rate of production. The nature of this dependence is such that for each reservoir there is for the chosen dominant mechanism a maximum rate of production that will permit reasonable fulfillment of the basic requirements for efficient recovery. Rates lower than such maximum may permit still higher ultimate oil recovery, but once the rate is sufficiently low to permit the basic requirements to

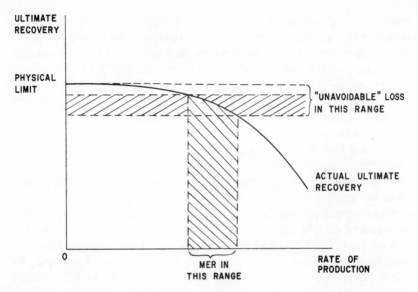

Figure 2.   Illustration of the MER concept (given stage of reservoir depletion).

be met, the incremental ultimate recovery obtainable through further reduction of the rate of production may be insufficient to warrant the additional deferment of a return and the additional operating expenses that would result from a prolongation of the operation. A rate of production so low as to yield no return would obviously be uneconomic, of no advantage to the operators, and of no ultimate benefit. However, increase of the rate of production beyond the maximum commensurate with efficient recovery will usually lead to rapidly increasing loss of ultimate recovery. From these considerations there has developed the concept of the *maximum efficient rate* of production, often referred to as the MER. For each particular reservoir it is the rate which if exceeded would lead to avoidable underground waste through loss of ultimate recovery.[18]

Taken as a whole, this passage seems to indicate that an operative MER would be somewhere in the range of producing rates associated with the transition from slowly to "rapidly" increasing loss of ultimate recovery. The MER so conceived is illustrated in figure 2.

Ultimate oil recovery is not functionally dependent on the number of wells (hence the average distance between wells) in a reservoir. Once a sufficient number of wells have been drilled to reveal the limits and oper-

---

[18] Buckley, *Petroleum Conservation*, pp. 151–52.

ating characteristics of a reservoir and to place wells in the locations required for most effective use of the chosen expulsive mechanism, further increase in the number of wells serves only to speed up the rate at which the reservoir may be depleted.[19] Of course, the number of wells consistent with the MER determined on either purely technical or technical-economic grounds may be larger than the minimum indicated.

Supplemented natural drives and secondary recovery

Except in the case of a naturally recharged water drive, oil production under natural drives is necessarily accompanied by declining reservoir pressure. The pressure drop must eventually allow any dissolved gas to come out of solution, shrinking the remaining oil and making it more viscous (hence more rapidly bypassed by water or gas); and it may bring profitable production to a halt after only a small fraction of initial oil in place has been recovered. However, the oil operator is not necessarily limited to relying on natural reservoir pressure. He may maintain reservoir pressure at some desired level by injecting water or gas from another source or by reinjecting water or gas produced with oil. He may create an artificial gas cap with gas acquired from another source, continuously renew the pressure in the cap with reinjection of produced gas, and thus retain dissolved gas in solution for its favorable effect on oil mobility. Pressure maintenance injections usually must be confined to selected areas of the reservoir, below the oil zone if water is injected and above the oil zone if gas is injected. Injection is costly, and ultimate recovery benefits extend throughout the oil zone. Consequently, where two or more operators are involved, some form of cooperative action is nearly always essential.

Secondary recovery is the use of artificial means to increase recovery after the primary (natural) drive has been completely or almost exhausted. Secondary recovery may be accomplished by various means, chiefly by injecting water, steam, gas, or gas preceded by a solvent; by heating the oil zone with one of several possible devices; or by burning

---

[19] Craze, "Development Plan," ch. 33, p. 17. There is some dissent by a very small minority to the view that ultimate recovery is independent of the number of wells, but the arguments of the dissenters appear to be refuted by theoretical, experimental, and field evidence. For a review of the evidence, see ibid., ch. 33, pp. 5–17; and IOCC, *Well Spacing*.

in situ a part of the residual oil.[20] With water or gas injection, the general principle of oil displacement is the same as with natural drives; however, the usual practice in old reservoirs is to inject one of these fluids in a geometrical pattern throughout the reservoir, rather than in a restricted area below or above the oil zone, increasing pressure around the injection wells and driving oil to the immediately surrounding producing wells. A bank of solvent, or miscible fluid (such as propane), in advance of injected gas serves to break down the capillary forces which prevent residual oil from flowing freely through narrow pore channels. Heating the residual oil expands it and decreases its viscosity. Steam injection both heats the oil and provides a pressurized displacement fluid. In situ combustion consumes only a small part of the residual oil while heating the remainder and driving it toward producing wells ahead of expanding gases and steam generated by the combustion process. Thermal methods are especially effective in recovering the high-viscosity oils so difficult to displace by natural water and gas drives. All of the methods discussed can be made more effective and less risky to individual operators if carried out under a plan of cooperative action governing each reservoir as a whole (unit operation).

The additional recovery possible through pressure maintenance and secondary recovery depends on the efficiency of the primary displacement mechanism and the nature of the supplementary or secondary mechanism employed. Formation of a gas cap and pressure maintenance in a natural dissolved gas reservoir may easily double the recovery possible.[21] Recovery of 80 percent of residual oil in place is reported from secondary recovery by means of in situ combustion.[22] The economic attractiveness of these operations is enhanced by the fact that they require no additional lease acquisition and exploration expense, while the

---

[20] Buckley, *Petroleum Conservation*, pp. 182–95; Clark, *Elements of Petroleum Reservoirs*, pp. 195–228; T. W. Nelson and J. S. McNeil, "Oil Recovery by Thermal Methods," *Oil and Gas Compact Bulletin*, vol. 17 (December 1958), pp. 56–70. The use of hydraulic fracturing in old wells also may be considered a secondary recovery technique. A possible future method of assisting either primary or secondary recovery is the explosion of a nuclear device at the bottom of wells, thus extensively fracturing the producing zone and heating the contained hydrocarbons. J. W. Watkins and C. C. Anderson, "Potential of Nuclear Explosives for Producing Hydrocarbons from Deposits of Oil, Natural Gas, Oil Shale and Tar Sands in the United States," *Information Circular 8219* (U.S. Department of the Interior, Bureau of Mines, 1964), reprinted in U.S. Congress, Joint Committee on Atomic Energy, *Peaceful Applications of Nuclear Explosives—Plowshare*, 89th Cong., 1st sess., January 1965, pp. 519–38.

[21] IOCC, *Oil and Gas Production*, p. 51.

[22] Nelson and McNeil, "Oil Recovery," p. 66.

anticipated increment to income is usually more certain than a similar increment anticipated from exploratory activity. Also, little additional development drilling may be required, since old producing wells often can be used for injection purposes.

Production from unassociated gas reservoirs

When gas is found in association with oil, disposition of the gas is conditioned by the fact that it is both a potentially marketable product and a displacing fluid in oil production. If a reservoir can be operated as a unit, it is usually both technically and economically desirable to utilize gas primarily as a displacing fluid, reinjecting the gas unavoidably produced, until recoverable oil is nearly exhausted. Without unit operation, in contrast, each competitive operator is motivated to produce gas freely in the scramble to lay claim to either oil or gas before it is drained away by some other operator. To the individual operator in competitive pursuit of oil, venting or flaring may be the most economical disposition of gas incidentally produced.

Unassociated gas reservoirs present a different range of choices. If the gas is "dry" (i.e., it contains no commercially recoverable natural gas liquids), it represents a single potentially marketable product that has no alternative utility in the reservoir. If the gas is "wet," it represents two potentially marketable products, but neither can be had without bringing the gas to the surface. There the liquids may be extracted by condensation or more elaborate processing, leaving the dry gas to be flared, marketed, used as fuel on the lease, or returned to the reservoir to aid in further recovery of wet gas. The value of the last alternative is enhanced by unit operation of the reservoir, since, to avoid excessive early dilution of the wet gas, it is desirable to locate producing wells at one end of the reservoir and injection wells at the other.[23]

Natural gas is highly compressible, and the basic displacement mechanism in gas reservoirs is simple expansion of the gas as pressure is released at one or more wells. As it is quite mobile in permeable rock, gas continues to flow to wells until reservoir pressure equals bottom-hole pressure. Reasonably expectable recovery is 90 percent or more of original gas in place, even with an abandonment pressure as high as 100 pounds per square inch.[24] With the exception noted in the following paragraph, a water drive makes no significant contribution to physical

[23] Buckley, *Petroleum Conservation*, p. 246.
[24] Ibid., p. 176.

recovery efficiency in gas reservoirs. However, since water encroachment reduces the pressure drop resulting from a given withdrawal of gas, a water drive may contribute to the total gas economically recoverable by increasing the volume withdrawable before abandonment pressure is reached.[25] The up-structure direction of fluid migration in water-drive gas reservoirs presents the same problems of efficient well location and equity between owners as it does in water-drive oil reservoirs.

Normally, a gas liquefies under sufficient pressure and revaporizes upon release of that pressure. But at the very high temperatures and pressures encountered at depths of 5,000 feet or more, gas and light liquid hydrocarbons merge into a single phase that has the essential properties of a gas. When the pressure in the reservoir drops to a critical level, the liquids emerge as a separate phase. This partial condensation of a gas phase, called retrograde because of its inverse relation to pressure change, distributes liquids throughout the reservoir in such low concentration that they become unrecoverable. If reservoir pressure is maintained above the critical level, however, these liquids may be conducted to wells in the gas phase and condensed under conditions permitting full recovery.[26] The required pressure maintenance may be provided by a natural or artificial water drive, but it is usually accomplished by cycling (reinjecting) produced gas that has been stripped of its liquid content. For reasons already indicated, efficient recovery of hydrocarbons from a retrograde condensate gas reservoir by means of cycling requires unit operation of the reservoir.

Unitization of petroleum reservoirs

It should be evident from the description of petroleum production to this point that the reservoir, and not the well or the lease, is the natural petroleum producing unit. The operative expulsive mechanism in the reservoir is common to all wells. A change in pressure in the neighborhood of any well, caused by either withdrawal or injection of fluids, affects the pressure in the neighborhood of every well. Production through any well reduces by at least an equivalent amount the petroleum that may be produced by all other wells in the reservoir. Expulsive drives cause fluids to migrate within the reservoir without respect to lease lines or areas served by particular wells.

In recognition of these facts, and in the desire to increase ultimate recovery and decrease costs while protecting private property interests,

[25] Ibid., pp. 177, 243–44.
[26] Clark, *Elements of Petroleum Reservoirs*, pp. 44–45, 183–84.

operators and royalty owners often enter into an agreement under which a reservoir may be operated as a unit. The unitization agreement provides for pooling of the affected property interests (at least property in the petroleum produced), acceptance of a plan for future operation of the reservoir under a single management, and allocation of costs and benefits among the participants.[27] Such an agreement requires knowledge about the reservoir and its environment that can be acquired only after substantial development; so unless early development is carried out with very wide spacing of wells, the opportunity to reduce development and operating costs through unitization is limited. It is difficult to secure agreement for equitable allocation of costs and benefits when some operators and royalty owners find that the reservoir contents tend to migrate toward their wells, giving them an opportunity to recover more petroleum than was originally in place beneath the surface area of their property. (The advantage is known as "structural advantage.") Consequently, entirely voluntary unitization is most feasible when its basis is a prospective increase in ultimate recovery so large that even those with structural advantage stand to gain from pooling interests. Secondary recovery and pressure maintenance operations most frequently satisfy these conditions. In retrograde condensate gas reservoirs, unitization may be accompanied by agreement for joint construction and operation of a cycling plant to separate gas liquids and reinject dry gas into the reservoir.

Petroleum marketing

Oil is usually marketed in the field[28] at prices posted by the principal buyers, who nearly always are refining companies or their affiliates. At the direction of buyers, pipeline companies (nearly always affiliates of refining companies) typically collect purchased oil from lease tanks through gathering lines and ship it through feeder and trunk lines to a refinery, or to a marine or rail terminal for further transportation to a refinery. Sometimes oil is collected from lease tanks by independent gathering companies or by the oil field operators themselves, utilizing trucks, barges, or pipelines as the circumstances permit. In such cases, the oil is usually marketed at the nearest buyer-affiliated pipeline terminal at prices posted there by buyers. Although long-distance pipelines

---

[27] Buckley, *Petroleum Conservation*, pp. 281–86.
[28] The term "field" is often used synonymously with "reservoir," particularly in assigning names. As a technical term, however, field denotes a general area in which are found one or more reservoirs related to some common geological feature.

are always constructed to serve particular refinery centers and can transport oil in one direction only, their typical common-carrier status and their numerous interconnections and contacts with other modes of transportation permit buyers, whether affiliated with a refinery or not, to ship oil from the field to almost any major refining center.[29] To save unnecessary transportation, however, buyers affiliated with refineries frequently make exchanges, or swaps, permitting the affected oil to move to the nearest refinery capable of processing it. The present flexibility of the transportation system, achieved largely since World War II, assures a wide range of alternatives to both buyers and sellers and creates a nearly nationwide market in which local field prices are mutually dependent.[30]

The number of buyers in a field may range from one to many, and the number of gathering pipeline systems from one to a few, depending on the size of the field and its distance from trunk lines and refineries capable of processing the oil. In the usual arrangement, transactions between a given seller and given buyer may be terminated on short notice by either party; but once a relationship is established, particularly if it involves a gathering pipeline "connection," it is seldom broken. A continuing relationship is economically beneficial to both parties so long as the price offered is equal to the best available alternative[31] and the volume of production remains large enough to be profitable to both seller and gatherer.

The demand for oil is derived from the aggregate of demands for refined products. Therefore, given competitive circumstances, the prices posted by buyers reflect the unit value of refined products, less cost of transportation and refining, expected to result from a projected refinery product mix and volume of crude oil runs.[32] Relative posted field prices reflect variations from field to field in crude oil characteristics and dis-

---

[29] The statement holds for the United States east of the Rocky Mountains. There is very little pipeline communication between the areas east and west of the Rocky Mountains.

[30] IOCC, *Conservation of Oil and Gas*, pp. 141–48; U.S. Department of Justice, *Third Report of the Attorney General*, pp. 45–56, 72–87; Cassady, *Price Making and Price Behavior*, pp. 109–40.

[31] The "best available alternative" is, of course, an alternative price adjusted for any cost incidental to a change in buyer-seller relationship. Often there is a substantial initial cost in breaking an old relationship and forming a new one, such as removing one gathering line and installing another, which must be weighed against the present value of the expected gain from a higher (seller) or lower (buyer) price.

[32] Even where buyers are the producers of the affected oil, this appears to be the basis of individual field prices. However, so as to maximize the benefits of percentage depletion, which applies to the gross value of oil at the wellhead, producer-buyers may compress the transportation and refining margins used in constructing posted prices. This matter is discussed more fully in ch. 9.

tance to the nearest suitable refinery.[33] Posted oil prices may be regarded as tentative equilibrium prices[34] corresponding to target product prices and outputs for some planning period. Rarely are posted prices changed more frequently than once in several months. Changes are often preceded by growing discounts or premiums offered by nonposting buyers.

The described transportation and marketing arrangements stem logically from a set of circumstances which, taken as a whole, are peculiar to the petroleum industry. The set includes the relatively low cost of transporting oil in large-diameter pipelines which have no other simultaneous uses; the high overhead costs of both refineries and pipelines; the high cost of surface oil storage; and the numerous, widely dispersed sellers dealing with a relatively few, more geographically concentrated group of refineries. Under the first three circumstances, a buyer-refinery seeks a steady flow of oil in near-capacity volume. This it can best assure, given the remaining circumstance, by means of owned or affiliated pipelines constructed with its specific needs in view, stable connections with numerous sellers, and initiative in establishing field prices.

Another circumstance is of particular relevance to the problem of petroleum conservation. Although independent producers are far more important at home than abroad, most domestically produced oil is produced by integrated companies.[35] Consequently, in many fields integrated companies are at once sellers, buyers, and transporters of oil. Where other producers have no close alternative buyer-transporters, a single integrated company is in a position to discriminate with respect to both price and purchased volume in favor of its own production, within and between reservoirs. Such discrimination with respect to purchased volume within a reservoir would allow the company (as producer) to drain oil from beneath the leases of other producers, not only creating an inequity but also perhaps violating the pattern of withdrawal consistent with efficient drainage of the reservoir as a whole.[36] Even where

---

[33] Not all refineries are equipped to process crude oils of extreme characteristics, such as those with high sulphur content ("sour" crudes) or those with a heavy asphaltic base. Consequently, a field may be near one or more refineries but quite distant from a suitable refinery.

[34] An equilibrium price is one at which the quantity demanded is equal to the quantity supplied in a specified market.

[35] Thirty-two of the largest integrated companies produce about two-thirds of the oil produced in the United States. U.S. Department of the Interior, *An Appraisal of the Petroleum Industry*, p. 28, citing Chase Manhattan Bank, *Financial Analysis of Thirty-two Petroleum Companies* (New York: 1959 and 1963).

[36] Price and purchasing discrimination between fields raises issues not directly related to efficient reservoir drainage. However, in ways to be discussed later in this study, these issues are related to the broadly conceived problem of petroleum conservation.

there is no conscious discrimination but two or more buyers independently purchase oil from a common reservoir using separate gathering facilities, inequity and inefficient drainage may result from the unplanned pattern of fluid withdrawal from the reservoir.

In contrast with the case of oil, gas is normally marketed at negotiated prices under long-term contracts with liquids plants, local utilities, or pipeline transmission companies. Field prices of gas destined for resale in interstate commerce are subject to utility-type regulation by the Federal Power Commission (FPC).[37] Of necessity, gas transportation from field to ultimate consumer is by means of pipelines. The pipelines are almost always owned by buyers in the field. Often gas buyers are also producers, a circumstance which motivates such buyers, and sometimes enables them to discriminate with respect to price or purchased volume against other producers in the same reservoir. Often two or more buyers using separate gathering systems take gas at disparate rates from different sectors of a reservoir. These circumstances create the same problems of equity found under similar conditions in oil reservoirs. However, because of the simple expulsion mechanism in gas reservoirs, relative rates of withdrawal from different sectors do not of themselves affect physical recovery efficiency.[38]

[37] For a concise statement of the origins and present nature of FPC regulation of gas prices in interstate commerce see IOCC, *Conservation of Oil and Gas*, pp. 194–97.

[38] In retrograde condensate reservoirs, it is only in association with pressure maintenance that a planned pattern of gas withdrawal increases ultimate recovery (of liquids).

3. The States' Approaches to Conservation Regulation: A Survey

Acting under their general police powers, the several producing states assume primary responsibility for petroleum conservation regulation in the United States. The federal government contributes chiefly by supporting the states' regulatory efforts. It sanctions limited cooperation of the producing states under the Interstate Compact to Conserve Oil and Gas;[1] assists the regulatory agencies that impose statewide production restrictions by publishing monthly forecasts of oil demand in each state; helps enforce state production restrictions by outlawing interstate shipment of oil produced in violation of state regulations;[2] and, as a matter of policy where applicable, subjects operations on federal lands to the production restrictions of the states in which these lands lie.[3] Through lease provisions and supervision, the federal government directly regulates petroleum drilling and operating practices on federal lands, but it does so in active cooperation with the affected state conservation agencies.[4]

All of the thirty-two producing states, plus six other states, have

[1] The general nature and purposes of the compact are explained on pp. 39–40.
[2] The prohibitive legislation is the Connally "Hot Oil" Act of 1935 (49 Stat. 33; 15 U.S.C.A. 715 *et seq.*), which replaced a similar prohibition in Section 9(c) of the National Industrial Recovery Act of 1933.
[3] In the case of the offshore lands under federal jurisdiction, the production restrictions of the contiguous states (e.g., Louisiana and Texas) apply.
[4] For a comprehensive treatment of the federal government's role in petroleum conservation, see Northcutt Ely, "The National Government and the Conservation of Oil and Gas," in B. M. Murphy, *Conservation of Oil and Gas: A Legal History, 1948* (Chicago: American Bar Association, Mineral Law Section, 1949), pp. 599–716. Ely's treatment is extended under the same title in Robert E. Sullivan, *Conservation of Oil and Gas: A Legal History, 1958* (Chicago: American Bar Association, Mineral Law Section, 1960), pp. 295–346. Developments at the federal level since 1958 are reported annually by Ely in IOCC, Legal Committee, *Legal Report of Oil and Gas Conservation Activities* (Oklahoma City: IOCC, annual).

petroleum conservation statutes of some sort.[5] Although the various
statutes differ widely in scope, emphasis, and detail, each recognizes one
or more general conservation problems and authorizes one or more forms
of regulation employed in common by at least a few of the states. In this
chapter, which is intended only to provide background for the subsequent economic analysis, the recognized conservation problems will be
defined and, following a brief historical sketch, the states employing
each of the principal forms of regulation will be listed. For these purposes, "conservation" is interpreted broadly to embrace the objectives
and methods of state regulation. An analytical definition of conservation
will be supplied in chapter 4.

The conservation problems defined

Taken as a whole, the state petroleum conservation statutes identify and
seek to cope with four general problems that tend to arise in connection
with unregulated petroleum production: damages external to the industry, wastes[6] internal to the industry, instability of production and prices,
and inequities among producers. Although these problems are closely
related, in some dimensions merging into the single problem of wastes
internal to the industry, each alone is of sufficient importance to justify
separate identification.

External damages

As explained in the preceding chapter, a well bore may connect
permeable strata containing fresh water, salt water (or other mineral brines), and petroleum. The brines and petroleum, often under
very high pressure, tend to rise in the well bore, invade the fresh
water strata, and flow out onto the surface. Brines often are produced in
quantity with oil, particularly in the older, more nearly depleted fields,
and must be separated and disposed of as waste material. Consequently,
in the absence of deliberate protective measures in both abandoned and
producing wells, subsurface fresh water and surface soil and streams

---

[5] The producing states are listed in table 1. The nonproducing states with petroleum conservation statutes are Georgia, Idaho, Iowa, North Carolina, Oregon,
and Washington. Washington produced a small volume of oil in the period
1957–60.
[6] The problem of defining waste in a meaningful sense is discussed at length in
chapter 6. Here we simply adopt the terminology of the conservation statutes,
which generally define waste as an avoidable physical loss of oil or gas.

may be contaminated by brines or uncaptured petroleum.[7] Drilling and producing activities may also interfere with mines and nearby surface land uses, creating special fire and other hazards to life and property.

Internal wastes

The internal wastes resulting from unregulated petroleum production arise from three principal sources: the fluid (hence potentially migratory) nature of petroleum deposits; the multiplicity of property interests in and around the typical reservoir; and the common presence of associated gas, which may, but need not, be fully utilized to displace oil from reservoir rock. Confronted with the tendency of petroleum to migrate within the reservoir in response to pressure differentials early in the history of the industry, the courts developed a doctrine of property in petroleum deposits based on the analogy with wild game and consequently known as the "rule of capture."[8] According to this rule, which still prevails as basic law, petroleum ultimately belongs to the landowner (or lessee) who captures it through wells located on his land, regardless of its original location as a natural deposit.[9] The owner (or lessee) of the original location can protect his initial title only by drilling wells and taking possession of the petroleum in place before it is drained away by wells on neighboring land. In consequence of the rule of capture, the process of unregulated development and exploitation of petroleum deposits tends to be a race for possession by competitive operators. The results are dense drilling, especially along property lines; capacity production of both oil and associated gas; rapid dissipation of reservoir pressure; irregular advance of displacing fluids

---

[7] Conversely, a petroleum-bearing formation may be damaged by uncontrolled invasion of water from other strata. Some of the statutes, by requiring the casing and plugging of wells to prevent interchange of fluids among strata, protect petroleum deposits; others protect fresh water and other resources. Usually, the same protective measures serve either purpose.

[8] Key cases in the development of the rule of capture are: *Westmoreland and Cambria Natural Gas Co.* v. *DeWitt*, 130 Pa. 235, 18 Atl. 724 (1889); *Kelly* v. *Ohio Oil Co.*, 57 O.S. 317 (1897); *Barnard* v. *Monongahela Natural Gas Co.*, 216 Pa. 362, 365, 65 Atl. 801, 802 (1907).

[9] While the cited decisions had the stated effect, they were couched in more negative terms: a landowner loses title to any underlying petroleum which migrates away before being reduced to possession, and such landowner has no valid claim to damages against a neighbor who may have caused the migration by drilling and operating wells on his own land. The language of *Kelly* v. *Ohio Oil Co.* and *Barnard* v. *Monongahela Natural Gas Co.* indicates that the basic source of the rule is uncertainty as to the original location of petroleum captured through given wells.

through the reservoir oil zone; and, therefore, loss of ultimate recovery.[10] Production of oil and gas may outrun the construction of pipelines and gas processing facilities, so that oil produced to avoid adverse drainage must be stored in makeshift tanks or open pits, where it is subject to loss through leakage, overflow, fire, and evaporation, and gas must be vented or flared as produced. The density of activity and the haste to complete wells and get oil to the surface also increase the likelihood of damages external to the industry. Finally, the certain prospect of high development costs due to dense drilling in new reservoirs restricts the number of exploratory prospects worth pursuing under given price expectations and thus, in the long run, reduces the quantity of petroleum economically recoverable from available natural deposits.

Instability of production and prices

Under the rule of capture unmodified by regulation, production from a newly discovered oil deposit rises quickly to a peak and then, with progressive loss of reservoir pressure, recedes almost as quickly to a fraction of the peak level.[11] Consequently, if an oil discovery is large in relation to existing total reserves or is developed simultaneously with several other discoveries, prices tend to be depressed during the phase of relatively high production and elevated during the subsequent phase of relatively low production.[12] The resulting pattern of wide and irregular price fluctuations, occasionally aggravated by cyclical shifts in demand, may limit the recovery of petroleum from known and discoverable reservoirs. Depressed prices not fully offset by the (discounted) expectation of elevated prices in the future force the early abandonment of some marginal wells, reservoirs, and exploratory prospects. By add-

---

[10] In retrograde condensate gas reservoirs, the dissipation of pressure itself causes loss of ultimate recovery (of liquids).

[11] The Spindletop (Texas) field, discovered in 1901, provides an extreme example. As ultimately developed, the field had an average well density of approximately three to the acre. Production peaked at 17.4 million barrels in 1902 and declined at a rate in excess of 50 percent per year to a level of only 1.7 million barrels in 1905. This and other examples are given in Erich W. Zimmermann, *Conservation in the Production of Petroleum* (New Haven: Yale University Press, 1957), pp. 281–90, citing various original sources.

[12] The effect is due in large part to the fact that, in the short run at least, the demand for oil is rather inelastic with respect to price; i.e., the quantity demanded is only slightly responsive to a difference in real price. The price elasticity of the demand for oil is discussed in some detail in chapter 6. Suffice it here to observe that if the price elasticity of demand for a good is low, a large decrease (increase) in real price is required to induce buyers to take a slightly increased (decreased) quantity of the good.

ing to business risks, wide and irregular price fluctuations may tend to discourage the entry of new firms, reduce the availability of credit, and increase the degree of concentration in the industry. They may thus dampen exploratory activities and in the long run reduce the quantity of petroleum recoverable from available natural deposits.[13]

Inequities among producers

The conditions of unregulated development and exploitation of petroleum deposits are highly conducive to inequities among producers and consequent internal wastes. With unrestricted output, those producers who are first connected to gathering lines can drain substantial amounts of petroleum from the properties of neighbors awaiting connections. Buyers who are also producers and affiliated with pipeline companies therefore have the strongest of motivations to discriminate in favor of their own wells in making purchases and providing gathering line connections. To take advantage of their opportunities, buyer-producers in a new reservoir may temporarily cease purchasing in reservoirs where they have no producing interest, leaving their former suppliers subject to drainage by neighbors whose market outlets remain unaffected. Separate purchasers in distinct sectors of a new reservoir may be unwilling or unable to buy in proportion to sector capacities, so that the suppliers of the heavier purchasers are permitted to drain petroleum from the lands of others. Whatever the cause, the injured producers have the choice of submitting to inequity—in which case the resultant pattern of withdrawal from the reservoir may also contribute to loss of ultimate recovery—or of producing for makeshift and wasteful storage until transportation and market outlets become available. Because of the time required for managerial decisions and construction of facilities, competition among pipelines and buyers, even if quite vigorous by normal standards, cannot be expected fully to avert these problems of inequity and waste in the brief periods of flush production characteristic of unregulated new reservoirs.

These, then, are the problems to which petroleum conservation regulation is addressed. After briefly sketching the historical background, I shall survey the major forms of regulation currently employed in the various states.

---

[13] This is not to imply that only rigid price stability is compatible with petroleum conservation. In part II, it will be shown that price flexibility plays an important role in conservation; but also that the price fluctuations characteristic of unregulated production are invariably wider than those consistent with conservation.

Brief historical background[14]

In the fifty years of the industry's development prior to 1909, petroleum conservation regulation in the producing states was concerned
almost entirely with preventing external damages and certain apparent
wastes of natural gas. Typical legislation in this period prescribed the
manner of casing and plugging wells (so as to prevent interchange of
fluids among strata, pollution of fresh water, and damage to coal
mines); restricted the venting of gas from gas wells (but not from oil
wells); and prohibited the burning of gas for illumination in flambeau
lights.[15] First to break the pattern was Oklahoma. In the development of
its first extensive discoveries, that state had witnessed enormous losses
of oil (and severely depressed prices), apparently caused by makeshift
storage because producers had unequal access to pipeline connections
and market outlets. Consequently, in a series of pioneering enactments
from 1909 to 1915, Oklahoma outlawed discrimination by oil and gas
purchasers and pipelines, prohibited various kinds of waste (including
"economic waste") in oil production,[16] and authorized the Corporation

[14] This section is based on American Bar Association, Mineral Law Section, *Legal
History of Conservation of Oil and Gas—A Symposium* (Chicago: American
Bar Association, 1938); Murphy, *Conservation of Oil and Gas*; IOCC, *Legal
Report of Oil and Gas Conservation Activities* (annual, 1958–68); Robert E.
Hardwicke, *Antitrust Laws et al. v. Unit Operation of Oil and Gas Pools* (New
York: American Institute of Mining and Metallurgical Engineers, 1948); and
Northcutt Ely, "The Evolution of the Interstate Compact to Conserve Oil and
Gas," *IOCC Committee Bulletin* (December 1959).

[15] Such was the character of legislation in the following states in the indicated
years: Pennsylvania, 1878, 1881, 1885, and 1891; New York, 1879, 1882, 1893,
and 1898; West Virginia, 1891 and 1897; Kentucky, 1892 and 1903; Ohio, 1883,
1889, and 1893; Indiana, 1891, 1893, 1903, and 1909; Illinois, 1905 and 1911;
Kansas, 1891, 1901, 1905, and 1913; Texas, 1899, 1905, and 1913; Oklahoma,
1905; and Louisiana, 1906 and 1910. This early legislative record loosely follows the spread of the petroleum industry from Pennsylvania throughout the
Upper Appalachian and North Central regions, then into the Gulf-Southwest,
1859–1900.

[16] The wastes prohibited in the 1915 act included "economic waste, underground
waste, surface waste, and waste incident to the production of crude oil or petroleum in excess of transportation or marketing facilities or reasonable market
demands." The term "economic waste" appears from the textual and historical
context to mean, among other possible things, the sale of oil at a price lower
than its "value." In section 2 of the act, the Corporation Commission was authorized to determine this value and to prohibit production when the going
price was lower. The commission had attempted in 1914, without statutory
authority, to do just this, finding 75 cents per barrel (a recent price) in one
field "to be just to prevent waste." However, no orders were ever issued under

Commission, as regulatory body, to limit production and allocate it among wells in a reservoir if necessary to prevent waste. When in 1917 Texas declared pipelines common carriers, hence forbidden to discriminate among shippers, and then in 1919 enacted a general waste prevention statute[17] giving broad regulatory powers to the Railroad Commission, conservation regulation entered a new and critical phase of development.

The new phase of development was significantly shaped by events growing out of the conservation proposals of Henry L. Doherty.[18] Appalled by the wastes characteristic of petroleum production under the rule of capture and concerned over the adequacy of prospective oil supplies for national defense, Doherty proposed compulsory unit operation of petroleum reservoirs under federal law. He first urged his plan in 1923 before the board of directors of the American Petroleum Institute (API), of which he was a member. Meeting hostility there,[19] Doherty appealed in 1924 to the president of the United States. Four months

---

the 1915 authorization, the commission holding in 1916 that "the fixing of a price of crude oil under sec. 2 of this act is absolutely impossible and impractical." The authorization was repealed in 1933. (W. P. Z. German, "Legal History of Conservation of Oil and Gas in Oklahoma," in American Bar Association, *Legal History of Conservation of Oil and Gas*, pp. 120–27.) The concept of "economic waste," the effort to prohibit which was widely equated with price fixing, was to play a major role in the nationwide struggle over an acceptable approach to conservation regulation in the early thirties.

[17] The wastes prohibited in the Texas statute of 1919 were less comprehensive than those prohibited in the Oklahoma statute of 1915. No mention of "economic waste" was made in the Texas statute; and, except for waste in its "ordinary meaning" and "underground waste," the wastes prohibited were related to natural gas.

[18] Doherty was president of H. L. Doherty and Company, fiscal agent for the Cities Service Companies. He is now recognized as a major prophet of modern conservation practice. The volumes by Buckley, Clark, and Hardwicke previously cited in this study were published by the American Institute of Mining and Metallurgical Engineers in a series named for Doherty. The definitive account of the evolution of attitudes toward unit operations is given in Hardwicke, *Antitrust Laws*.

[19] The American Petroleum Institute (API) led the fight against Doherty's proposals in subsequent years. It based its opposition on denial of significant waste in the industry, optimism about future petroleum supplies, and alleged unconstitutionality of federal conservation regulation. See Committee of Eleven of the Board of Directors of the API, *American Petroleum—Supply and Demand* (New York: McGraw-Hill, 1925). Between 1929 and 1933, the API supported various supply-limitation and quota schemes, including that embodied in the National Industrial Recovery Act. In 1932, it finally endorsed unit operations and urged state laws to authorize them.

later, President Coolidge created the Federal Oil Conservation Board, consisting of the Secretaries of War, the Navy, the Interior, and Commerce, to supervise continuous study of the waste-prevention and supply-adjustment problems of the petroleum industry in their relation to the national interest. There immediately ensued nearly two years of fact finding, including lengthy hearings in which Doherty and his opposition were heard. In its first (1926) report, the board recognized both the problem of waste under the rule of capture and the validity of the principles of reservoir mechanics on which Doherty based his proposal for unit operation; but it viewed the federal government as constitutionally powerless to regulate petroleum operations outside the public domain, except in a national defense emergency. It recommended cooperation among the states, even to the extent of forming an interstate compact, in developing uniform conservation laws. In subsequent reports, the board warmly endorsed unit operation as a principle of production and urged permissive state legislation, but it gave growing emphasis to controlling supply by means of import limitations and domestic production quotas. Its final report in 1932 contained a specific proposal for an interstate compact under which a state-federal agency would forecast demand for oil,[20] subtract the volume of imports to be permitted under federal restraint, and allocate the remainder among the producing states as domestic production quotas. Somewhat similar supply-control measures were put into effect the following year through the Code of Fair Competition for the Petroleum Industry adopted under the National Industrial Recovery Act.

The Federal Oil Conservation Board's growing preoccupation with control of supply after 1926 reflected a similar preoccupation in the industry and the producing states. A series of major discoveries in California and the Southwest from 1926 to 1931, combined with cyclical decline in demand after 1929, sent capacity soaring and prices plummeting.[21] From 1926 onward, voluntary agreements among operators to restrict production in individual reservoirs, tacitly or explicitly approved by state conservation authorities, were common in Oklahoma, Texas, California, Kansas, and New Mexico. Acting under the 1915 statute, the Oklahoma Corporation Commission in 1927 issued the first of a number of individual field "proration" orders (orders limiting pro-

---

[20] In 1930, the Secretary of the Interior inaugurated a program of preparing periodic demand forecasts for the use of state conservation agencies. The program, directed by the Bureau of Mines, has been continued in effect to this day. Under the National Industrial Recovery Act, the forecasts by state formed the basis of assigned state production quotas.

[21] The average price of crude oil in the United States declined by about one-third between 1926 and 1929, and further by about one-half between 1929 and 1931.

duction and allocating the total pro rata among wells). It issued its first statewide proration order (in which a total state allowable production based on market demand was allocated among fields) in 1928. The Texas Railroad Commission, acting under the 1919 statute, issued its first individual-field proration order in 1928 and its first statewide proration order (based on market demand) in 1930. In 1931, Kansas enacted a statute under which the regulatory authority (after 1933, the Corporation Commission) quickly proceeded to issue proration orders.[22] In the same year, a voluntary committee of governors, known as the Oil States Advisory Committee, was formed to coordinate the supply-control activities of the major producing states and promote an interstate compact.[23]

The validity of the 1915 Oklahoma statute and orders under it was upheld by the courts in the Julian and Champlin cases.[24] In its landmark 1932 decision in the Champlin case, the United States Supreme Court held that production restriction based on market demand was a reasonable method of preventing physical wastes, and that the effect on price, if any, was incidental. The legal going in Texas was much rougher. When in 1929 the legislature amended the 1919 statute to redefine prohibited waste, it specified that the term was not to be construed to mean "economic waste." It thus provided part of the basis of two suits challenging some early market-demand proration orders of the Railroad Commission. In the first, the Danciger case,[25] the (state) trial court upheld the commission orders as valid physical waste prevention measures; but in the second, the Macmillan case,[26] the (federal) trial court struck down the affected orders as designed to prevent "economic waste" and fix prices in violation of the 1929 act. Then, in 1931 the Texas legislature enacted a statute prohibiting physical waste only and specifically denying the railroad commission power to limit production on the basis of market demand. Following a period of virtually uncontrolled produc-

---

[22] The California legislature in 1931 passed an act similar to the Oklahoma statute, but the act was nullified in a statewide referendum.

[23] States ultimately represented on the committee were Arkansas, California, Colorado, Kansas, Louisiana, New Mexico, Ohio, Oklahoma, Texas, and Wyoming. The committee was frankly concerned with raising the price of oil from its then depressed level. Murphy's account of the committee's activities is sprinkled with references to its price objectives. Murphy, *Conservation of Oil and Gas*, pp. 545–55.

[24] *Julian Oil and Royalties Co.* v. *Capshaw*, 145 Okla. 237, 292 Pac. 841 (1930); *Champlin Refining Company* v. *Oklahoma Corporation Commission*, 286 U.S. 210, 76 L.Ed. 1062, 52 S.Ct. 559 (1932).

[25] *Danciger Oil & Refining Co.* v. *Railroad Commission of Texas*, 49 S.W.2d 837, 842 (1932).

[26] *Alfred Macmillan* v. *Railroad Commission of Texas*, 51 F.2d 400 (1931).

tion,[27] during which the final decision in the Champlin case was rendered, the legislature late in 1932 reversed itself and enacted a statute that contained no reference to "economic waste" and no prohibition of proration based on market demand, but included as prohibited waste "the production of crude petroleum oil in excess of transportation or market facilities or reasonable market demand."[28] The 1932 act was upheld in the second Danciger case,[29] the original Danciger case and the Macmillan case having been dismissed on appeal as moot. In 1933, Kansas amended its 1931 statute, imitating the language in the Oklahoma statute defining prohibited wastes. Thus, statewide proration programs were established on firm legal ground in Oklahoma, Texas, and Kansas as the experiment in industrial control under the National Industrial Recovery Act began.

The National Recovery Administration (NRA) Petroleum Code, adopted late in 1933, provided for import restrictions, minimum prices, administrative approval of development plans in new reservoirs, limitation of domestic production to total demand less imports, and allocation of allowed domestic production among states, reservoirs, and wells. Recommended state quotas, based on Bureau of Mines demand forecasts, were allocated among reservoirs and wells by established state regulatory agencies, where such existed, in accordance with rules of the agencies' own making. In the two states lacking a regulatory agency under state law but deemed to require production restraint—California and Michigan—a committee of private operators was designated to perform the intrastate allocative function. Production in New Mexico was considered adequately limited by private operator agreements permitted under state law. Interstate and intrastate allocations were backed up by Section 9(c) of the Recovery Act, which prohibited interstate shipment of oil produced or withdrawn from storage in violation of state law or regulation. The brief experience under the code thus strengthened previously established market-demand proration programs and introduced such programs in new areas.

As the demise of the Recovery Act[30] was foreseen, the Congress and

---

[27] The problem of uncontrolled production centered on the great East Texas field, discovered in 1930, where repeated commission orders were disregarded or blocked by injunction.

[28] The language here is almost identical with that in the Oklahoma statute of 1915 upheld in the Champlin case.

[29] *Danciger Oil & Refining Co.* v. *Smith*, 4 F. Supp. 236, 290 U.S. 599, 54 S.Ct. 209, 78 L.Ed. 526 (1933).

[30] Title I of the act, under which industry codes of fair competition were promulgated, was held invalid in *A.L.A. Schechter Poultry Corporation* v. *United States*, 295 U.S. 495 (1935).

the producing states moved to replace some of its features. The Connally "Hot Oil" Act, which replaced Section 9(c) of the Recovery Act, was passed by the Congress early in 1935. In the same year, Louisiana and New Mexico enacted comprehensive conservation statutes containing provision for market-demand proration.[31] To round out the replacement effort, a successor committee to the Oil States Advisory Committee was formed after the 1934 elections to draft an interstate compact. The committee's deliberations were marked by strong disagreement between the respective governors of Oklahoma and Texas on the issue of "economic waste." The governor of Oklahoma held that price stabilization was essential to conservation and urged a compact under which the federal government would limit imports and an interstate agency would allocate total domestic production, adjusted to market demand after allowance for imports, among the producing states. The governor of Texas objected to any federal participation in the compact and opposed any supply-control provisions suggestive of an attempt to fix prices. The "compromise" draft reflected essentially the latter view. The compact as approved by the committee on 16 February, and formally consented to by Congress on 27 August 1935, makes no mention of federal participation or import controls and gives its creature agency, the Interstate Oil Compact Commission, no power to determine and distribute production quotas among the states. Article II (in full) states: "The purpose of this Compact is to conserve oil and gas by the prevention of physical waste thereof from any cause." Article V (in part) states: "It is not the purpose of this Compact to authorize the states joining herein to limit the production of oil and gas for the purpose of stabilizing or fixing the price thereof. . . ." Articles III and IV obligate the compacting states to enact, or to continue in force, effective laws to prevent certain specified physical wastes. Article VI directs the Compact Commission to ascertain and recommend to the states methods of preventing physical waste of oil and gas, and authorizes it "to recommend the coordination of the exercise of the police power of the several states within their several jurisdictions to promote the maximum ultimate recovery from the petroleum reserves of said states, and to recommend measures for the maximum ultimate recovery of oil and gas."[32] With these limited purposes, the Interstate Compact to Conserve Oil and Gas has served chiefly to facilitate the dissemination of technical and legal information

[31] A bill containing provision for market-demand proration was introduced in the Michigan legislature in 1935, but it did not pass. A similar bill did pass in 1939.

[32] Compact drafts submitted by Governor Allred of Texas and Governor Marland of Oklahoma are reproduced together with the draft as finally approved, in Murphy, *Conservation of Oil and Gas*, appendix C, pp. 734–40.

relating to conservation, and to promote the enactment of comprehensive conservation statutes in all the producing states.[33]

When the compact was approved, only Oklahoma, Texas, Kansas, New Mexico, and Louisiana had statutes of the general type contemplated by its authors. From 1935 to 1941, efforts were made to enact similar statutes (containing provision for market-demand proration) in a number of additional states. These efforts were entirely successful only in Michigan (1939) and North Dakota (1941). In California (1939) a bill of the type was passed by the legislature but was nullified in a popular referendum.[34] Arkansas (1939) enacted a comprehensive statute without provision for statewide market-demand proration, and Illinois (1941) enacted a statute of still more limited scope. Meanwhile, the regulatory commissions in Oklahoma, Texas, Kansas, New Mexico, and Louisiana proved their ability to cope with destabilizing influences without direct federal participation. While responding independently to contraction or restricted growth of demand in each state, in total they restrained production sufficiently to absorb most of the market impact of both the recession of 1937-38 and the sharp expansion of Illinois oil production from 1937 to 1940.[35] They also broke new regulatory ground in requiring wider well spacing in new reservoirs, encouraging unitization for pressure maintenance and secondary recovery,[36] and

[33] The Compact Commission has at intervals since 1940 published the form of a suggested conservation statute (containing provision for market-demand proration) for the guidance of bill drafters. The most recent version is given in IOCC, Legal Committee, *A Form for an Oil and Gas Conservation Statute, 1959* (Oklahoma City: IOCC, 1959).

[34] Upon the demise of the NRA Petroleum Code, a voluntary proration program, initiated in 1929, was resumed under the administration of the Conservation Committee of California Oil Producers. The program is still in effect.

[35] The average price of crude oil rose from $0.67 per barrel in 1933 to $1.18 per barrel in 1937, then fell to $1.02 per barrel in 1940. The impact of the unrestrained Illinois oil boom on production in the market-demand prorated states is indicated in the following tabulation of changes in oil production.

	Thousands of barrels per day	
	1933–37	*1937–40*
Texas	+295	−50
Louisiana	+180	+34
Oklahoma	+128	−200
Kansas	+79	−13
New Mexico	+67	+1
Subtotal	+749	−228
Illinois	+9	+382
Total US.	+1,024	+192

[36] In a major 1940 revision of the Louisiana law, the commissioner of conservation was empowered to require unitization of retrograde condensate gas reservoirs for the purpose of pressure maintenance.

using proration of gas to prevent inequities among producers even where no problem of waste was involved.[37]

World War II brought federal controls again, this time not to restrain production and raise depressed prices, but to assure economical use of scarce materials and maximum output consistent with efficient recovery of reservoir fluids. To these ends, the Petroleum Administration for War (PAW) adopted a basic requirement of 40-acre spacing for oil wells and 640-acre spacing for gas wells—far wider spacing than had been typical, even in the regulating states;[38] shaped its materials allocation policy to encourage unitized pressure maintenance and secondary recovery operations; and ascertained maximum efficient rates of production by state, which it then certified to state regulatory agencies for implementation. Three years of experience under PAW regulation helped prepare the industry and state agencies for several postwar advances in conservation regulation, especially wider spacing, compulsory unitization, and more general use of MERs as the basis of production restraint.[39]

Since 1945, most of the older regulating states have adopted major amendments to their statutes, notably to facilitate unitization agreements, and twenty-two other states have enacted comprehensive conservation laws.[40] The regulatory commissions have displayed increasing vigor in enforcing old laws to prevent flaring of casinghead and residue gas[41] and to control disposal of salt water. Several of the commissions

---

[37] Although the Texas Railroad Commission made repeated attempts to prorate gas production for this purpose during the thirties, its power to do so (under a 1935 act) was not upheld until 1945 in *Corzelius* v. *Harrell*, 179 S.W.2d 419, 143 Tex. 509, 186 S.W.2d 961 (1945).

[38] During the thirties, typical spacing in the regulating states was 10–20 acres for oil wells and 40–160 acres for gas wells.

[39] The PAW experience led directly to the postwar adoption of MERs (maximum efficient rates of production) as the basis of production restraint in California's voluntary program. William L. Holloway, "California, 1931–1948," in Murphy, *Conservation of Oil and Gas*, p. 43.

[40] In addition, South Dakota and Tennessee enacted comprehensive statutes in 1943. All of the comprehensive statutes enacted since 1940 show the influence of the IOCC suggested statute, although only five of them—those of North Dakota (1941); Alabama, Florida, North Carolina (all in 1945); and Washington (1951)—contain provision for market-demand proration. The original Arizona statute (1951) contained such a provision, but a 1962 amendment deleted it. At present, the only producing states whose statutes are not comprehensive—i.e., are limited largely to regulating well casing and plugging—are Maryland, Virginia, and West Virginia. The scope of California's statute is relatively limited with respect to oil, but not with respect to gas.

[1] Casinghead gas is gas produced with oil by oil wells. Residue gas is the dry gas remaining after wet gas has been stripped of its liquids.

administering market-demand proration have modified their allocation formulas to make them more equitable and more conducive to wide spacing of wells. This record of legislative and administrative activity reflects in part the spread of petroleum production to new states and the application of accumulated experience; but it also reflects the mounting economic problems of the industry, already noted, which put a premium on any method of reducing costs. In any case, the cumulative results in terms of current regulatory practice are outlined in the next section. Postwar developments in conservation regulation will be analyzed in part III of this study.

Principal forms of regulation and their use by the states[42]

The typical conservation statute defines and prohibits certain wastes, then authorizes an administrative body to make and enforce "rules and regulations" to prevent the prohibited wastes. Some statutes prohibit or require specific acts by operators and list in detail the kinds of regulation the administrative body may impose; others allow the administrative body broad discretion in designing regulations to carry out the statutory intent. Occasionally some authorized form of regulation is not put into effect. The discussion in this section pertains to authorized regulations, whether currently (1970) in effect or not, and currently (1970) effective regulations, whether specifically authorized or not. With a few noted exceptions, the states covered in the discussion are those listed in the body of table 1.

The following enumerations of states that impose particular forms of regulation must be interpreted with care. In terms of their direct impact on utilization of the nation's petroleum resources, the conservation regulations of a few major producing states are far more significant than those of all the other states put together. An indication of relative significance is given by table 1, which shows the relative shares of the producing states in total national reserves and production of liquid hydrocarbons in a recent and an early post–World War II period. The states are ranked in the order of their relative shares of reserves in 1961-63 and, in cases of ties, in the order of growth of relative shares since 1949-51. The first seven states—Texas, Louisiana, California,

---

[42] This section is based on IOCC, Governors' Special Study Committee, *A Study of Conservation of Oil and Gas in the United States, 1964* (Oklahoma City: IOCC, 1965), pp. 174–93, 210–28, and the statutes and regulations of the producing states.

Table 1. Relative Shares of Producing States in U.S. Liquid Hydrocarbon Reserves and Production, 1961–63 and 1949–51

| State | Average percentage of U.S. total liquid hydrocarbons | | | |
| | 1961–63 | | 1949–51 | |
	Reserves	Production	Reserves	Production
Texas	47.8%	37.8%	54.8%	43.2%
Louisiana	16.8	17.1	9.1	10.9
California[a]	10.2	10.7	14.6	16.7
Oklahoma	5.5	7.7	5.5	8.2
New Mexico	4.1	4.5	2.4	2.4
Wyoming	3.8	4.8	2.8	2.7
Kansas	2.7	3.9	3.0	5.0
North Dakota	1.3	0.9	0.2	<0.1
Illinois	1.3	2.6	1.8	3.0
Colorado	1.1	1.5	1.3	1.2
Mississippi	1.1	1.9	1.6	1.7
Arkansas	0.8	1.0	1.3	1.5
Montana	0.7	1.1	0.4	0.4
Utah	0.7	1.2	<0.1	<0.1
Kentucky	0.5	0.8	0.3	0.5
Nebraska	0.3	0.9	<0.1	0.1
West Virginia	0.3	0.4	0.2	0.3
Pennsylvania	0.3	0.2	0.4	0.6
Ohio	0.2	0.2	0.1	0.2
Indiana	0.2	0.4	0.2	0.5
Michigan	0.2	0.6	0.3	0.7
Alaska	na	0.3	np	np
Alabama	0.1	0.3	<0.1	<0.1
New York	0.1	<0.1	0.2	0.2
All others in total[b]	na	<0.1	na	<0.1
Totals[c]	100.0	100.0	100.0	100.0

Source: IOCC, Governors' Special Study Committee, *A Study of Conservation of Oil and Gas in the United States, 1964* (Oklahoma City: IOCC, 1965), pp. 107–40.

<—Less than.
na—Not available.
np—No production.

[a] California is the only state with a significant amount of production that is not a member of the Interstate Compact to Conserve Oil and Gas. The other two nonmember producing states are Missouri and Virginia.

[b] Arizona, Florida, Maryland (gas only), Missouri, Nevada, South Dakota, Tennessee, and Virginia.

[c] May not add due to rounding.

Oklahoma, New Mexico, Wyoming, and Kansas—accounted for over 90 percent of the reserves in 1961-63. Although some marked changes in relative shares between 1949-51 and 1961-63 caution against projecting a fixed pattern into the future, it seems certain enough that for some time to come the presently leading states will continue to produce the great bulk of the nation's total petroleum output. Consequently, particular weight must be assigned to the conservation regulations of these states.

Casing and plugging of wells

Well casing and plugging regulations typically prescribe the quantity and quality of materials and the techniques to be used in lining the well bore and, upon abandonment, closing the hole. The regulations are enforced by some combination of permits, bonds, reports, and inspections. As already indicated, the purpose of such regulations is to prevent damage to petroleum deposits, fresh ground water, surface soil and water, humans, livestock, and other property by confining possible contaminants, such as salt water, to their natural underground strata and by closing the well bore to either exit or entry at the surface. All of the subject states have regulations of this type. Kentucky is unique in that its casing standards do not explicitly include sufficient pipe to protect all fresh water strata.

Salt water disposal

Regulations governing disposal of salt water or other mineral brines brought to the surface with petroleum typically specify acceptable, and prohibit unacceptable, methods of disposal. The purpose of such regulations is, of course, to protect surface soil and water. Consequently, acceptable methods usually include (a) injection underground in such a manner and at such a stratum as not to harm petroleum or fresh ground water, (b) discharge into already saline bodies of surface water, and (c) evaporation in surface pits lined with an impervious material. Reinjection for the combined purposes of disposal and reservoir pressure maintenance is especially encouraged. Unacceptable methods of disposal usually include discharge into fresh surface waters and evaporation in unlined pits. Enforcement is by means of permits, reports, and inspections. All of the subject states impose regulations of this type. In several states, responsibility for enforcement lies with a regulatory body other than the petroleum conservation commission (such as the Water Resources Commission in New York), or is shared by the petroleum conservation commission with one or more other bodies (such as the Water Commission and the Water Pollution Control Board in Texas).

Well spacing

The usual well spacing regulation specifies minimum distances between adjacent wells and between a well and the nearest property line or structure. It may also, or alternatively, specify the minimum acreage assignable to each well and the minimum distance from the well to the nearest border of its assigned acreage. With the few exceptions to be noted, the regulatory bodies are empowered to require the pooling of smaller tracts of land to form "drilling units" of the minimum size if such pooling is not first accomplished by voluntary agreement among property owners. Well spacing regulations are enforced by permits to drill, setting out exact locations of proposed wells, and inspections.

Spacing regulations serve several conservation purposes. By limiting the number of wells in a reservoir, they limit both development costs and the feasible rate of production. By limiting the feasible rate of production, they tend to increase ultimate recovery from the reservoir, reduce price-destabilizing effects, and lessen the volume of surface storage while pipeline facilities are being installed. By limiting development costs, they increase the number of exploratory prospects worth pursuing under any given set of other relevant conditions. By arranging wells in a regular pattern, each some distance from property lines, they help protect the correlative rights of owners of mineral interests; that is, they help protect each owner from adverse drainage and afford him an economical opportunity to recover the petroleum originally in place beneath his land. They also reduce fire hazards and limit interference with ordinary surface land uses.

For these purposes, all of the states under discussion regulate spacing to some degree. The regulations vary widely from state to state, but in the typical case they provide for minimums (subject to exceptions) of 40-acre spacing for oil wells and 160-acre spacing for gas wells. The California regulations apply only to oil wells and require a minimum of only 1 acre per well. In Kansas, direct regulation of spacing is confined to gas wells, but indirect regulation of oil well spacing is accomplished by relating allowable production per well to the number of acres per well. The statutes of all of the states under discussion except Kansas, Ohio, and West Virginia expressly authorize compulsory pooling of small tracts to implement spacing regulations. Administrative regulations in Ohio provide for compulsory pooling under an implied statutory grant of authority.

Gas-oil ratio

Gas-oil ratio regulations limit the amount of gas per barrel of oil that an oil well may produce without penalty. They usually provide for reduction of allowable oil production in proportion to the excess of the actual ratio over some specified maximum.[43] For enforcement purposes, operators are required to make periodic measurements (which may be witnessed occasionally by regulatory personnel) and to report the results to the conservation commission. Standing regulations or special field rules frequently allow the measurements to be made on a net basis, credit being given for gas returned to the reservoir or used for some other approved purpose.

Gas-oil ratio regulations serve two major conservation purposes. First, they serve to avert or limit the loss of ultimate oil recovery which results from uncontrolled production of associated gas. They reduce the drop in reservoir pressure accompanying a given amount of oil production; they limit channeling of gas through the oil zone; and they help create or maintain a gas cap which may contribute to the efficiency of recovery of both oil and gas. Second, gas-oil ratio regulations incidentally yield valuable insights into reservoir behavior. The information contained in required reports allows operators and regulators to trace the migration of fluids in the reservoir and helps them ascertain the nature of the dominant drive or expulsive mechanism. It therefore facilitates determination of the reservoir MER, the most equitable or the most effective allocation of total production among wells, and the desirability of some cooperative approach to reservoir management.

All of the states under discussion except Illinois, Indiana, Kentucky, Ohio, and Pennsylvania limit gas-oil ratios, either in special rules applying to individual reservoirs or in statewide standing regulations. Those states limiting ratios in individual reservoirs are Colorado, Michigan, Montana, Nebraska, and Wyoming. In the remaining states, the typical maximum ratio allowed without penalty under statewide regulations is 2,000 cu.ft. of gas for each barrel of oil.

Gas flaring (or venting)

Regulations restricting gas flaring (or venting) ordinarily pertain to casinghead or residue gas.[44] Their basic purpose is to prevent wasteful

---

[43] To illustrate, suppose the maximum permissible gas-oil ratio is 2,000 cu.ft. to 1 barrel of oil and the regular oil allowable is 50 barrels per day per well. A well with an actual gas-oil ratio of 4,000:1 would be permitted to produce only 25 barrels of oil per day $(2,000/4,000 \times 50)$.

[44] A separate regulation usually prohibits operators from allowing a gas well to burn or to blow into the open air. This type of regulation is aimed at forcing operators to extinguish fires and to close wells producing unused gas, regardless of the profitability of such action to the affected operators.

disposition of gaseous hydrocarbons incidentally produced with oil or natural gas liquids. They are usually so phrased as to allow flaring (or venting) when the affected operators have no economical alternative. But since no individual operator would knowingly destroy a product of economic value to him, such regulations contribute to conservation chiefly by providing an indirect means of forcing operations that are economical only if undertaken jointly by several operators. For example, a commission may determine in a hearing on gas flaring that gas injection for reservoir pressure maintenance would be economically feasible with unitization, but that a few operators with structural advantage under individual exploitation block the necessary agreement. The commission may then order cessation of the affected oil production until such time as the by-product gas can be disposed of in an acceptable way, thus creating incentive for all operators to enter into a unitization agreement.

The regulatory commissions of all the states under discussion, except Kentucky, restrict or are authorized to restrict gas flaring (or venting).

Direct production restrictions

Regulations directly limiting oil and gas production are of two separate types. Those of the first type, which may be labeled *MER restrictions*, are applied to individual oil reservoirs and are intended to prevent rates of production that are so high that they significantly reduce ultimate oil recovery. They may incidentally contribute to price stabilization, of course. Such restrictions serve no physical waste-prevention purpose in ordinary gas reservoirs. As a means of preventing loss of reservoir liquids in retrograde condensate reservoirs, similar restrictions —based in each case on the fluid injection rate—are useful only if they are integral parts of unitized pressure maintenance programs. To be effective, MER restrictions must be accompanied by allocation of total allowed production among wells in the affected reservoirs. Equitable allocation implies protection of correlative rights, another incidental but desired effect. Although other factors may be used in MER allocation formulas, the dominant factors in new formulas today are acreage and recoverable reserves per well.

Direct production restrictions of the second type, *market-demand restrictions*, may be applied to individual reservoirs, to selected areas within states, or to entire states; and they may contribute to desired ends in both oil and gas reservoirs. Under market-demand restrictions, total production per period in the affected area is limited by commission order to the quantity expected to be purchased per period in that area.[45]

The typical administrative procedure in the states practicing statewide restriction based on market-demand for oil is as follows.[46] Once a month in a public hearing, with Bureau of Mines demand forecasts and data on inventories before it, the regulatory commission receives "nominations" (statements of intentions to buy) from the principal oil purchasers in the state. Using these data and any other information considered relevant, including its own demand forecast, the commission then determines the probable market demand for the calendar month shortly to begin. The quantity determined is next related to the "basic" state allowable, which is the sum of: (a) maximum production of fields or wells assigned special allowables or permitted to produce at capacity, such as water-flood fields and stripper wells,[47] (b) the MERs in fields subject to MER restriction, and (c) the maximum production permitted in other fields under a statewide depth-acreage schedule of allowable production per well.[48] If the

---

[45] The enabling statutes define as a prohibited waste either waste incidental to the production of oil and gas, or the actual production of oil or gas in excess of [the capacity of] transportation or marketing facilities, or in excess of "reasonable market demand." The term "reasonable market demand" is rarely defined in either the statutes or the administrative regulations. The current *Rules and Regulations* of the New Mexico Oil Conservation Commission, referring to oil, defines the term as "the demand for such crude petroleum oil for reasonable current requirements for current consumption and use within or outside of the state, together with the demand for such amounts as are reasonably necessary for building up or maintaining reasonable storage reserves [of oil or products]." State of New Mexico, Oil Conservation Commission, *Rules and Regulations* (Santa Fe, 1965), p. 7. The current IOCC-suggested statute, referring to oil, defines the term as "the amount of oil reasonably needed for current consumption, use, storage, or working stocks, within and without the State. . . ." IOCC, *A Form for an Oil and Gas Conservation Statute, 1959*, p. 2.

[46] The states currently practicing statewide market-demand proration are Kansas, Louisiana, New Mexico, Oklahoma, and Texas. In New Mexico, the state is divided for the purpose into two distinct market areas.

[47] A stripper well is usually defined as a well on artificial lift capable of producing no more than ten barrels per day.

[48] The following excerpt from the Texas basic allowable schedule, known as the 1965 Yardstick, is illustrative of depth-acreage schedules. The figures in the body of the table represent the maximum number of barrels that wells in given depth-acreage categories may produce. For example, a 5,500-foot well on 40 acres would have a maximum allowable of 102 barrels per day.

Depth (feet)	Maximum allowables in barrels per day		
	20 acres per well	40 acres per well	80 acres per well
5,000–6,000	52	102	171
6,000–7,000	57	111	184
7,000–8,000	62	121	198

This and other such schedules will be discussed in detail in chapter 9.

quantity determined to be the market demand exceeds the basic allowable, then the latter—in total and in each of its separate components—limits production in the state. If the quantity determined to be the market demand is less than the basic allowable, then the maximum production of fields and wells exempt for one reason or another from market-demand restriction is subtracted from the estimated market demand, and the remainder is allocated to the nonexempt fields and wells in proportion to their respective basic allowables. The proportionate allocation to nonexempt fields and wells in some states (e.g., Texas) is accomplished by means of a "market-demand factor," a decimal fraction representing the ratio of the total nonexempt share of market demand to the total nonexempt basic allowable, which is multiplied by each well's basic allowable to compute its effective allowable for the month.[49]

Market-demand proration of gas is a quite different matter. No issue of physical waste is involved. Producers with market outlets in a given reservoir usually are tied to one or a few buyers under long-term contracts. The problem is to protect the correlative rights of producers—to prevent buyer discrimination or disparate purchases by different buyers in the same reservoir. Consequently, periodic market demand typically is estimated and allocated among producers on an individual reservoir basis, the allocation formula depending on local circumstances.

In terms of the conservation problems defined earlier, market-demand restrictions have several effects within the area covered. First, they tend to prevent buyer and pipeline discrimination among fields and wells. If the sum of field and well allowables is just equal to the effective demand in a period, then buyers are motivated to purchase the full allowable of each field and well.[50] Given the required pattern of purchases, pipeline companies are motivated to extend facilities to all fields and wells that promise sufficient volume over time to warrant, at permissible tariffs, the necessary investment. Second, market-demand restrictions tend to prevent the wastes—such as loss of ultimate recovery or evaporation from makeshift surface storage—that may indirectly result from discrimination or disproportionate purchases by several buyers in oil reservoirs. Third, they tend to stabilize oil prices. They tend to support the going price, whatever it may be, by withholding from the market any potential excess of supply over demand at that price. By the same token,

---

[49] For example, if the market-demand factor were .30, the well referred to in footnote 48 would have an actual allowable of 31 barrels per day (102 × .30).

[50] The corollary is that a market tends to be assured for the allowable of each operator who succeeds in drilling a producing well. Needless to say, small independent operators in areas dominated by integrated companies attach great value to this effect of market-demand proration.

the adjustment of allowed output to demand over the range of outputs
short of the basic allowable tends to preclude a price increase caused by
excess demand at the going price.[51]

All of the states under discussion except California, Illinois, Kentucky, Ohio, Pennsylvania, and West Virginia have statutes that appear
to prohibit waste in terms broad enough to permit production restrictions of the MER type. MER restrictions are at least occasionally
imposed in Alabama, Arkansas, Colorado, Kansas, Louisiana, Michigan, Mississippi, Montana, Nebraska, New Mexico, North Dakota,
Oklahoma, Texas, and Wyoming. In California, MERs are determined
under the auspices of the Conservation Committee of California Oil
Producers for all reservoirs in which they are applicable and are recommended to operators for voluntary use as the basis of production restraint. Recognized and approved in principle by California law,[52] the
recommendations are generally followed.

The statutes of only eight of our subject states—Alabama, Kansas,
Louisiana, Michigan (with respect to oil only), New Mexico, North
Dakota, Oklahoma, and Texas—expressly authorize the regulatory
commissions to impose market-demand restrictions.[53] At present the
commissions of Alabama, Michigan, and North Dakota find it unnecessary to impose such restrictions. In nine of the states under discussion
—Colorado, Illinois, Indiana, Kentucky, Mississippi, Montana, Pennsylvania, Utah, and Wyoming—the statutes explicitly or implicitly prohibit production restrictions of the market-demand type.[54] Of the subject
states whose statutes neither expressly authorize nor prohibit market-
demand restrictions, Alaska, Arkansas, Nebraska, New York, and
Michigan (with respect to gas) have statutes which define and prohibit

---

[51] None of this is to say that the regulatory bodies determine, or manipulate allowables so as to determine, what the going price will be. This and related issues
will receive thorough discussion in chapter 9.

[52] To receive formal approval under California law, the recommended MERs
must be recorded with the State Oil and Gas Supervisor. West's Ann. Calif.
Codes, Public Resources (1956) 1970 Supp., art. 8, §3450.

[53] The statutes of Florida, Iowa, North Carolina, and Washington, of which only
Florida is at present a (minor) producer, also expressly authorize market-
demand production restrictions. As noted earlier, the original (1951) statute of
Arizona authorized such restrictions; but the pertinent waste-prevention clause
in the statute as amended in 1962 forbids only production in excess of trans-
portion or marketing facilities. Although the amendment may seem not to
change the effect of the statute very much, it caused the State Oil and Gas Conservation Commission to abandon an elaborate formula for determining allowables and to revise its *General Rules and Regulations* so as to delete all sections pertinent to market-demand or similarly based proration.

[54] The statute of Idaho, at present a nonproducing state, also prohibits restrictions
of the market-demand type.

waste so broadly that the courts might uphold efforts under them to prevent waste by means of market-demand restrictions of production.[55] No commission in this group of states has ever attempted to test its possible power to impose production restrictions of the market-demand type.

Unitization of reservoirs

Regulations pertaining to unitization of reservoirs (or parts of reservoirs) prescribe either (a) the conditions under which voluntary agreements for the purpose may be approved by the conservation commission, if necessary to remove any possible taint of conspiracy under state anti-trust laws;[56] or (b) the conditions under which the commission may exercise a degree of compulsion to effect reservoir unitization. In general, all states encourage reservoir unitization, recognizing that it is in principle the ideal way to accomplish the major aims of conservation regulation, especially limitation of development costs, production at rates no higher than MERs, full exploitation of pressure maintenance and secondary recovery opportunities, and equitable division of benefits among participating operators; and no state prohibits reservoir unitization.

The statutes of every state under discussion except Kansas, Kentucky, Michigan, Ohio, and West Virginia expressly sanction voluntary unitization. None of the statutes of the excepted states poses any impediment to voluntary unitization. Fourteen of the subject states—Alabama, Alaska, Arkansas, California, Colorado, Indiana, Kansas, Louisiana, Michigan, Mississippi, Nebraska, New York, North Dakota, and Oklahoma—have statutes which authorize a degree of compulsion by the regulatory commission.[57] In these states, the commission may order unitization of a particular reservoir when the owners of some specified percentage of the property interests, ranging from 60 to 85 percent, have agreed upon a plan acceptable to the commission.[58] The authorization in California applies only to pressure maintenance projects for the primary

---

[55] This is the opinion of the committee of conservation lawyers which analyzed the various state statutes for the recent IOCC study. (IOCC, *Conservation of Oil and Gas*, p. 180.) Other states covered by this opinion are Georgia and Oregon (nonproducers) and Nevada, South Dakota, and Tennessee.

[56] Commission approval is not considered necessary or desirable in all states; many agreements are made and put into effect without official recognition.

[57] Seven other states have such statutory authorization: the producing states of Arizona, Florida, Nevada, and South Dakota, and the nonproducing states of Georgia (with respect to gas condensate), Oregon, and Washington.

[58] Except in California, the required agreeing percentages apply equally and separately to the royalty interests and the operating interests. In California, the required percentage (65 percent) applies only to operating interests, their ownership being measured gross of royalty obligations. The Washington statute requires no specified percentage agreement by the ownership interests.

purpose of preventing surface subsidence. Under the statutes of Alabama and Louisiana, the commission may require unitization for the purpose of gas cycling in condensate reservoirs without consent of any of the ownership interests.

Purchaser and pipeline practices

It is generally recognized in the regulating states that in principle petroleum in place belongs to the overlying surface owners, and that the ownership interests should be afforded a reasonable opportunity to recover and market what is theirs. The statutes of all of the subject states except Indiana, Kentucky, Montana, Ohio, and West Virginia formally express this recognition by obligating the regulatory commissions, in varying degrees of explicitness, to protect the correlative rights of operators and royalty owners.[59] To protect correlative rights more directly (and to prevent some wastes that otherwise might indirectly result), Colorado, Louisiana, Michigan, Nebraska, New Mexico, Oklahoma, and Texas, among the subject states, have enacted statutes which, with various qualifications, declare each buyer in a reservoir to be a "common purchaser" in that reservoir and require him as such to purchase ratably and without discrimination from all producers in the reservoir making reasonable offers to sell to him.[60] The public utility statutes of the various states generally designate transporters for hire as common carriers forbidden to discriminate among shippers; but, in addition, the petroleum conservation statutes of Colorado, Kansas, Nebraska, Oklahoma, and Texas declare oil or gas transporters common carriers and require them as such to accept and transport reasonable tenders of oil or gas ratably and without discrimination.

Underground gas storage

A recent development in gas conservation is the employment of the power of eminent domain to enable private firms, usually transmission

[59] The IOCC suggested statute defines "protection of correlative rights" to mean "that the action or regulation by the Commission should afford a reasonable opportunity to each Person entitled thereto to recover or receive the Oil and Gas in his tract or tracts or the equivalent thereof, without being required to drill unnecessary wells or to incur other unnecessary expense to recover or receive such Oil or Gas or its equivalent." IOCC, *A Form for an Oil and Gas Conservation Statute, 1959*, p. 2.

[60] The term "ratably" applies when a buyer cannot or will not purchase the sum total of the petroleum offered to him, including that produced by himself or an affiliate. In addition to the subject states mentioned, Arizona and Nevada have common purchaser statutes.

companies, to acquire partially or wholly depleted underground reservoirs for gas storage purposes. Such storage contributes to conservation in at least two ways. First, it opens additional markets to casinghead gas —the production of which depends on the market for oil—and reduces flaring. By means of storage, transmission companies can regularize supplies to consumers. Second, it enlarges the number of gas prospects worth exploring and the number of discoveries worth developing, and in this way increases the amount of gas effectively recoverable from available natural deposits. With adequate storage facilities, a transmission company can honor long-term contractual obligations even though it secures its supplies from a number of different gas reservoirs, each of different size and producing life. In addition, gas storage may help protect correlative rights in reservoirs that supply two or more transmission companies, each with its own distinctive seasonal or other time-related pattern of deliveries. While collectively taking steadily and ratably from a common reservoir, separate companies can adjust deliverable supplies as required by adding to or withdrawing from storage. All of the subject states except Alabama, Alaska, North Dakota, Texas, Utah, and Wyoming have laws to facilitate acquisition of gas storage reservoirs.

Miscellaneous

Many other forms of regulation are employed in the producing states. Some of them, such as those pertaining to measurements, tests, and records, are designed to supply the information essential to effective administration and need not be discussed here. I shall briefly note only a few more forms of substantive regulation. The regulations of all of the states under discussion except Indiana, Kansas, Kentucky, and West Virginia require the use of a "blow-out preventer" in drilling or servicing a well to prevent the loss of petroleum and the surface damage associated with "gushers." The statutes of all of the subject states except Kentucky, Ohio, Pennsylvania, and West Virginia authorize regulation of underground fluid injection so as to prevent damage to petroleum, fresh water, and individual property rights. The statutes of nine of the subject states—Alabama, Alaska, Arkansas, Kansas, Louisiana, Mississippi, Oklahoma, Texas, and Wyoming—either prohibit or restrict the use of natural gas to manufacture carbon black, the premise being that such use is wasteful of the fuel value of natural gas.

The principal forms of regulation and the various states employing them are summarized in table 2. The direct and indirect relations of the principal forms of regulations to the problems they are intended to cope with are summarized in table 3.

Table 2. Checklist of States Employing Various Forms of Regulation

State	Casing and plugging	Salt water disposal	Spacing — General	Spacing — Compulsory pooling	Gas-oil ratio	Gas flaring	Production restriction — MER	Production restriction — Market demand	Unitization — Voluntary[a]	Unitization — Compulsory	Common purchaser	Common carrier[b]	Gas storage
Alabama	X	X	X	X	X	X	X	X	X	X			
Alaska	X	X	X	X	X	X	X		X	X			
Arkansas	X	X	X	X	X	X	X		X	X			X
California	X	X	O	X	X	X	V		X	L			X
Colorado	X	X	X	X	F	X	X	P	X	X	X	X	X
Illinois	X	X	X	X		X		P	X				X
Indiana	X	X	X	X		X		P	X				X
Kansas	X	X	X		X	X	X	X		X	X	X	X
Kentucky	X	X	X	X				P					X
Louisiana	X	X	X	X	X	X	X	X	X	X	X		X
Michigan	X	X	X	X	F	X	X	O		X	X		X
Mississippi	X	X	X	X	X	X	X	P	X	X			X
Montana	X	X	X	X	F	X	X	P	X				X
Nebraska	X	X	X	X	F	X	X		X	X	X	X	X
New Mexico	X	X	X	X	X	X	X	X	X		X		X
New York	X	X	X	X	X	X	X		X	X			X
North Dakota	X	X	X	X	X	X	X	X	X	X			
Ohio	X	X	X	X		X							X
Oklahoma	X	X	X	X	X	X	X	X	X	X	X	X	X
Pennsylvania	X	X	X	X		X		P	X				X
Texas	X	X	X	X	X	X	X	X	X		X	X	
Utah	X	X	X	X	X	X	X	P	X				
West Virginia	X	X	X		X	X	X		X				
Wyoming	X	X	X	X	F	X	X	P	X				X

X—state employs
O—oil only
L—limited

F—individual fields
P—prohibited by statute
V—voluntary

a No state prohibits; blank indicates no mention in statutes.
b Refers only to common carrier designation in petroleum conservation laws.

Table 3.   Relations of Principal Forms of Regulation to Four General Conservation Problems

Forms of regulation	Problems affected			
	External damages	Internal wastes	Instability	Inequities among producers
Casing and plugging	D	D		
Salt water disposal	D	I		I
Well spacing	I	D	I	D
Gas-oil ratio		D	I	I
Gas flaring	M	D, I[a]	M	
Production restriction:				
MER		D	I	M
Market-demand		I	D	D
Unitization of reservoirs	I	D	I	D
Purchaser and pipeline practices	M	I	I	D
Gas storage		I[b]		I

D—direct effect

I—indirect effect

M—minor indirect effect

[a] Direct with respect to gas, indirect with respect to oil (induced repressurization).

[b] With respect to natural prospects worth exploring and discoveries worth developing.

PART II

THE ECONOMICS OF PETROLEUM CONSERVATION

4. Conservation in the General Economic Process

Constructive analysis of petroleum conservation regulation requires a definition of conservation that is unambiguous, pertinent, and consistent with common usage. The purposes of this chapter are to supply such a definition and to discuss its implications. I shall begin by showing that the activity ordinarily denoted by the term "conservation" is an integral part of the general economic process.

The general economic process

In the simplest, most aggregative terms, the economic process consists of employing productive resources—labor, capital, and natural resources[1] —to produce goods and services of value and then distributing those goods and services (hereinafter shortened to "goods") to final users. The employment of labor and capital in productive activity requires some effort or other sacrifice of enjoyments by their suppliers.[2] Such sacrifice is the real cost of the goods produced and must be compensated if the resource inputs are to be supplied voluntarily.[3] The value of out-

---

[1] For these purposes, "labor" embraces all the productive powers residing in persons, intellectual and artistic as well as physical. "Capital" consists of man-made instruments of production, such as buildings, machinery, highways, and oil wells. (Financial capital represents mere claims to such real assets.) "Natural resources" are attributes of the natural environment unmodified by man, such as rainfall, native soil, and raw mineral deposits. (Capital as defined includes such modifications of nature as dams on rivers, terraces on farm land, and mine shafts or well bores to mineral deposits.)

[2] The presumed sacrifice of the suppliers of capital is postponement of satisfactions. Natural resources as defined, being nature-made, are supplied without human sacrifice. The cost of the goods and services they yield (e.g., crude oil or hydroelectric power) is the labor and capital cost of extraction or conversion from a natural force.

[3] The owners of natural resources receive an income, called "economic rent," which represents the residual product after the required compensation of the owners of labor and capital is deducted. They receive such income because of the competition of the owners of labor and capital (or of their employers) for access to natural resources.

put, on the other hand, derives from the capacity of the constituent goods to give enjoyments, or satisfactions, to their recipients—satisfactions that range from relief of hunger to the most frivolous entertainment. These satisfactions, rather than the specific things that yield them, are the real income from productive effort. Thus the economic process involves an exchange of sacrifices (real costs) for satisfactions (real income). Production is worthwhile if it creates net satisfactions (net real income). Expansion of output from any initial level increases net satisfactions if the required addition to sacrifice is less than the resultant addition to satisfactions.

The volume of net satisfactions available from given resources depends not only on the technical productivity of those resources and the intensity of their use, but also on their allocation among alternative employments. Many possible combinations of labor, capital, and natural resources may be employed to produce any one type of good; but given the quantity and quality of available resources, the different combinations are neither equally costly nor equally productive of the good. Similarly, there are many possible combinations of goods of different type (product mixes) that any set of resources can produce; but, given the pattern of consumers' preferences, the different product mixes are not equally productive of satisfactions. In pursuit of maximum net satisfactions, we must select from among the possible resource combinations and product mixes. The economic process, therefore, embraces the allocation of productive resources among alternative employments in conformity with selected resource combinations and product mixes. From any initial situation, a reallocation of resources adds to net satisfactions if a change in resource combination in any industry or a shift of resources from one industry to another requires a sacrifice that is smaller than the resultant increment to satisfactions. The additions to net satisfactions achieved through resource reallocation are of exactly the same significance to their recipients as those achieved from increasing the quantity or quality of resources employed.

The allocation of resources among alternative employments has two interrelated dimensions: (a) the distribution of effort among all of the various productive activities constituting the economy, and (b) the division of effort between two functionally distinct groups of activities— all activities designed to yield current satisfactions and all activities designed to yield future satisfactions. Current satisfactions are provided for simply by using available resources to produce currently consumable goods.[4] Future satisfactions, in contrast, are provided for in two different

[4] Here and elsewhere in the pertinent discussion, we ignore changes in the inventories of man-made goods in process of production and distribution.

ways. The first way is by using available resources to produce durable goods designed not to yield satisfactions directly, but to facilitate the production of other goods, which presumably will yield satisfactions, over some future period. This process is "real investment" or "capital formation"; and the durable goods currently produced are "capital goods," such as factory buildings, machinery, and oil wells. The second way of providing for future satisfactions is by restraining the current rate of consumption of depletable natural resources so that more of the existing stock may be utilized at some future time. This second way is ordinarily called conservation.

Real investment and conservation (as thus far loosely defined) require similar sacrifices, or costs, and play similar roles in the general economic process. Both require the sacrifice of satisfactions that would have been currently obtainable from the existing supply of labor, capital, and natural resources. Both look to the provision of future satisfactions that would not be obtainable without some present sacrifice. Both involve a transfer of consumption from present to future; therefore both, as rational activities, require a comparison of present sacrifice with expected future satisfactions. Either investment or conservation increases net satisfactions if the transfer of some consumption from present to future necessitates a present sacrifice which is smaller than the present equivalent of the expected increase in future satisfactions.

To derive the present equivalent of expected future satisfactions, and thus to permit a comparison with present sacrifice, it is necessary to allow for the sacrifice involved in postponing satisfactions. It is necessary to discount future satisfactions at a rate reflecting consumers' "marginal time preference," that is, their preference at a given time for a small increment to current satisfactions over an alternative increment to future satisfactions. For example, if consumers view with indifference an increment of X amount of current satisfactions or, alternatively, an increment of $1.05X$ amount of satisfactions one year from now, X being very small, their marginal rate of time preference is 5 percent per annum. Forgoing X amount of current satisfactions would therefore increase consumers' net satisfactions only if they could with certainty expect to receive in exchange more than $1.05X$ amount of satisfactions one year from now.[5] This generalization holds equally for sacrifices of

---

[5] If expectations of future satisfactions are held with less than certainty, and consumers have an aversion to uncertainty, then those sacrificing current satisfactions would demand a still higher price in terms of future satisfactions. They might insist, for example, that the most probable increase in future satisfactions be $1.10X$, the difference between 1.10 and 1.05 being the "premium" for risk or uncertainty.

current satisfactions due to current investment and for sacrifices of current satisfactions due to postponement of use of natural resources.

It is useful to examine the discounting of expected future satisfactions still further. The generalized formula for the present value of an expected stream of satisfactions (income) for n periods is:

$$P = \frac{A_1}{1+r} + \frac{A_2}{(1+r)^2} + \cdots \cdot \frac{A_n}{(1+r)^n} \, ;$$

where P = present value,
    A = satisfactions received at the end of each period,
    r = rate of discount per period.

To illustrate, note that for a one-time receipt of satisfactions at the end of a year the formula reduces to $P = \dfrac{A}{1+r}$. Thus, if $A = 1.06X$ and the marginal rate of time preference is .05 (or 5 percent per annum), then $P = \dfrac{1.06X}{1+.05} = 1.01X$, so that the exchange of X amount of current satisfactions for $1.06X$ amount of satisfactions one year from now results in an increase in present net satisfactions by $.01X$. The gain may be stated in another way. The rate of return on the "investment" of postponed satisfactions in this sample is 6 percent per annum, while the sacrifice experienced from postponing satisfactions is only 5 percent per annum. Thus there is a net gain of 1 percent per annum on the investment. If additional investments of this kind were made, driving down the return and forcing up the sacrifice on each successive investment until the rate of return was just equal to the rate of sacrifice on the last one, then the flow of satisfactions over time would have the maximum possible present value consistent with the (then) marginal rate of time preference.

In summary, conservation (still loosely defined as some postponement of natural resource use) is one of the interrelated means by which we seek to gain satisfactions (real income) from the use of labor, capital, and natural resources. It is, thus, an integral part of the general economic process. It shares with investment the role of making provision for future satisfactions out of currently available resources—of shifting consumption from present to future so as to increase the total net satisfactions obtainable from currently available resources. It also shares with investment the cost of postponing satisfactions.

Economic efficiency

Economic efficiency is defined in terms of the "optimum" allocation of resources among alternative employments, which results in the largest

possible total of net satisfactions being obtained from available resources.[6] More specifically, with an optimum allocation of resources no
increase in net satisfactions could be obtained by increasing or decreasing the employment of any resource, by increasing the output of one
good at the expense of another, or by shifting some consumption in
either direction between present and future. These conditions, in turn,
mean that the marginal sacrifice of employing more or less of any resource is exactly equal to the marginal gain of satisfactions,[7] that marginal net satisfactions per dollar of expenditure are the same for all
goods, and that the marginal rate of return on both investment and postponement of natural resource use is equal to the marginal rate of time
preference. The last condition further means that the present worth,
expressed in terms of net satisfactions, of both capital assets and natural
resources is maximized, given the marginal rate of time preference.

Any deviation from the optimum allocation of resources among alternative employments implies economic inefficiency; and economic inefficiency implies waste. Waste results when some unit of a resource
that could be employed at a sacrifice smaller than the satisfactions its
product would yield lies unemployed, or when the product of some unit
of an employed resource yields satisfactions smaller than the sacrifice
incurred in employment. Waste results when some unit of product yields
satisfactions smaller than the satisfactions a unit of an alternative product, producible by the same resources, would yield. Waste results when
either investment in capital assets or postponement of natural resource
use fails to be pushed to the point at which the marginal rate of return
is equal to the marginal rate of time preference, or when either is pushed
beyond that point. Measures to achieve and maintain the optimum allocation of resources are, therefore, measures to eliminate and prevent
waste.

From some nonoptimal situation, the optimum allocation of resources
is approached by comparing sacrifice with gain of satisfactions at the
margin. If employing an additional unit of a resource, or transferring a
unit of a resource from one use to another, or shifting a unit of consumption between present and future adds less to sacrifice than to satisfactions, then something is added to net satisfactions and the optimum
allocation of resources is more closely approached. When all oppor-

[6] "Optimum" means "best" or "best for the purpose." Here the presumed purpose
is to obtain the maximum possible amount of net satisfactions.

[7] In the present context, "marginal" denotes small increments to some initial total.
For example, the marginal sacrifice of employing more of a resource is the addition to total sacrifice resulting from a small increase in the employment of that
resource.

tunities for marginal gain are exhausted, the optimum allocation of resources is achieved.

However, the optimum allocation of resources is not some fixed pattern of resource use which can be specified and achieved once and for all. Its specifications change with every advance in technology, every alteration of consumer preferences or expectations, and every change in the quantity or quality of productive resources. In short, its specifications change continuously in a growing, dynamically developing economy. It must be continuously sought. Consequently, the efficient economy is one which has built into its structure a flexible, positive mechanism for continuously seeking the optimum allocation of resources.

The price system and economic efficiency

In a predominantly private-enterprise economy, the principal mechanism governing the allocation of resources is the price system, functioning in interplay with gain-motivated behavior of individual firms and persons.[8] The system is a flexible, positive mechanism for continuously seeking the optimum allocation of resources if three essential conditions are satisfied: (a) participants in the economy are knowledgeable about their opportunities and actively exploit them; (b) markets are "competitive"—that is, in each market there are so many buyers and sellers that the actions of no one of them can significantly affect the going price, and each buyer and seller makes decisions independently of the others; and (c) sellers initially bear and incorporate into the selling price all of the costs to society of preparing each good for sale, and consumers pay for and appropriate in each good purchased all of the benefits to society derived from that good. The allocation of resources under the price system will now be examined briefly, at first assuming that the above three conditions are satisfied.

In a free price system, the price in each market tends to find and come to rest at that level at which the quantity of the pertinent good supplied is equal to the quantity demanded. This is the correct meaning of the commonplace observation that prices are determined by "supply" and "demand." The significance of such determination lies in what supply and demand respectively represent, hence in what conditions obtain when quantity supplied equals quantity demanded in a given market.

When the owner of a resource engages it in productive activities he

---

[8] "Gain-motivated behavior" means simply that firms and persons seek to maximize the real incomes obtainable from the resources at their disposal.

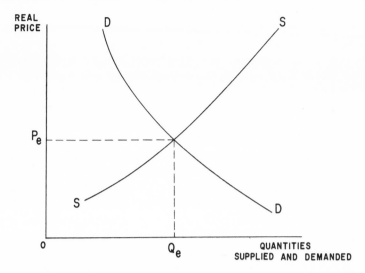

Figure 3. Supply and demand schedules.

incurs a personal sacrifice and receives in exchange a real price (e.g., real wage) which measures his acquisition of command over sources of satisfactions.[9] If he may freely choose the resource input supplied within the limits imposed by his total command over resources, each resource owner's desire to maximize net satisfactions leads him to supply such a quantity that the addition to total sacrifice caused by the last unit of input is just equal to the command over satisfactions acquired in the form of resource price, or unit compensation. Short of that quantity, additional net satisfactions could be obtained by supplying still more units. As a resource owner increases resource inputs, given the total resources at his disposal, the addition to total sacrifice caused by each successive unit tends to increase. Consequently, the quantities supplied at which marginal sacrifice equals real price vary directly with real price. At a relatively low real price, a relatively small quantity supplied equates marginal sacrifice with price; at a relatively high real price, the required quantity is larger. It follows from summing individual resource owners' behavior that the supply of a particular resource at a given time is a schedule of quantities owners stand ready to offer at various real prices, the quantities being directly related to prices as in the positively sloping curve *SS* in figure 3.

The demand for resource inputs by firms reflects the worth to firms of such inputs. It pays a firm to employ a given resource in such quantity

---

[9] A given real price may represent any amount of money, of course, depending on the general purchasing power of the monetary unit.

that the last unit adds to total output an amount just equal to the real price of the resource. Short of that quantity, additional real profits could be obtained by employing still more units. Given the inputs of other resources, the additions to output made by successive units of a given resource (the marginal products of that resource) tend to decline. Consequently, the quantities employed at which marginal product equals real price vary indirectly with real price. Summing individual firms' demands for a resource yields a total demand for that resource which is a schedule of quantities firms stand ready to employ at various real prices, the quantities being inversely related to prices as in the negatively sloping curve DD in figure 3.

Given the supply and demand schedules indicated, the market price tends to the level labeled P_e in figure 3. At a higher price, the quantity supplied exceeds the quantity demanded, and some suppliers offer lower prices in order to sell the excess supply. At a lower price, the quantity demanded exceeds the quantity supplied, and some demanders offer higher prices in order to acquire the excess demanded. As the price is lowered or raised toward P_e, both quantity supplied and quantity demanded adjust until they are equal at P_e. The equality of quantity supplied with quantity demanded at the "equilibrium" price P_e is significant for our purposes because it represents equality of marginal sacrifice with marginal gain of satisfactions from resource use, which is a condition of the optimum allocation of resources.

Reasoning similar to the foregoing applies to individual product markets. Under the specified market circumstances, it pays a firm to produce a given good in such a quantity that the amount added to total real cost by the last unit (marginal cost) just equals real price.[10] Short of that quantity, additional real profit could be obtained by producing still more units. Marginal costs tend to rise with increasing output over the relevant range. Consequently, as a result of summing individual firms' behavior, the supply of a particular good at a given time becomes a schedule of quantities firms stand ready to offer at various real prices, the quantities varying directly with prices as in the positively sloping curve SS in figure 3.

The demand for a good derives from the satisfactions the consumer receives from its use. If he may freely choose the quantity of a good he will buy within the limits imposed by his total command over goods, each consumer's desire to maximize net satisfactions leads him to purchase that good in such a quantity that the last unit acquired adds to

[10] Real cost to the firm measures the sacrifice of those supplying resources to the firm.

total satisfactions an amount just equal to the sacrifice incurred in the form of real price.[11] Short of that quantity, additional net satisfactions could be obtained by consuming still more units. As a consumer increases his consumption of a particular good, given his total command over goods, the satisfactions added by each successive unit of the good tend to decline. Consequently, the quantities consumed at which marginal gain of satisfactions equals real price vary inversely with real price. At a relatively high real price, a relatively small quantity consumed equates marginal gain in satisfactions with price; at a relatively low real price, the required quantity is larger. It follows from summing individual consumers' behavior that the total demand for a particular good at a given time is a schedule of quantities consumers stand ready to buy at different real prices, the quantities being inversely related to prices as in the negatively sloping curve DD in figure 3.

As in an individual resource market, the market price of a particular good tends to the level which equates quantity supplied with quantity demanded. And, as with an individual resource, equating the quantity of a good supplied with the quantity demanded is significant for our purposes because it represents equating the marginal sacrifice of producing the good with the marginal gain of satisfaction from consuming it, a condition of optimizing the allocation of resources among alternative employments.

It is scarcely necessary now to detail the characteristics of supply and demand in the remaining type of market, the capital market. Suffice it to say that it is a market in which present command over goods is traded with a view to increasing future command over goods, the price determined being the rate of interest; and that the equilibrium rate of interest equates the marginal sacrifice of current satisfactions with the marginal gain of future satisfactions, a final condition of optimizing the allocation of resources among alternative employments.

When in any market the demand or the supply changes, a new optimum allocation of resources is specified; a reallocation is required to maintain or reestablish the optimum allocation. For example, suppose that the demand for good A increases at the expense of the demand for good B (due, say, to a change in tastes), as indicated by the shifts of the demand schedules in figure 4.[12] Immediately following the increase

---

[11] The real price paid by a consumer may be thought of as sacrifice of command over either goods and services in general or resources capable of producing goods and services.

[12] Note that an increase or a decrease in demand means an increase or decrease in the quantities demanded at given prices. Change in supply is defined in parallel terms.

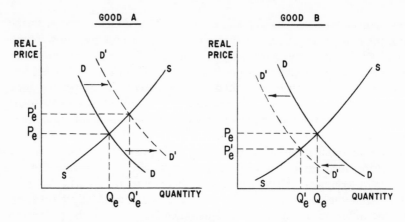

Figure 4.   Illustration of shift in demand.

in demand, there is excess demand at the old equilibrium price of good A. Consequently, the equilibrium price rises to the new level P_e', at which quantity supplied is once again equal to quantity demanded, additional resources having been applied to the production of good A to increase equilibrium output from Q_e to Q_e'. At the old equilibrium price of good B, on the other hand, excess supply immediately follows the decrease in demand for that good. The equilibrium price therefore falls to the new level P_e', at which quantity supplied is once again equal to quantity demanded, the amount of resources employed in producing good B having declined sufficiently to reduce equilibrium output from Q_e to Q_e'. Indirectly, therefore, the shift of demand from good B to good A draws resources from the production of good B to the production of good A, as it should to continue maximizing net satisfactions. An increase in the supply of good A at the expense of good B (due, say, to opposite changes in marginal costs) also involves a shift of resources from the production of good B to the production of good A, the price of good A falling and the price of good B rising so that quantity demanded in each case changes in the same direction as output.[13] Thus a well-functioning price system induces the appropriate reallocations of resources in response to those shifts of demand and supply necessarily associated with change in a dynamically developing economy and therefore tends to maintain the optimum allocation of resources as the specifications of that optimum change over time.

As suggested by the provisos listed at the beginning of this discussion,

[13] This example is not diagrammatically illustrated, but the reader may easily adapt figure 4 for the purpose.

the price system does not adequately function to maintain the optimum allocation of resources if market participants are ill-informed or for some other reason fail to exploit opportunities for gain, if markets are not competitive (as defined), or if producers' costs and consumers' benefits fail to coincide with total costs and benefits to society. The effect on resource allocation of market participants' failure to exploit opportunities for gain is obvious: net satisfactions can scarcely be maximized if those immediately involved do not systematically attempt to increase them at every opportunity. But the effects on resource allocation of noncompetitive markets and noncoincidence of direct private and total social net benefits require additional explanation.

Firms maximize profits when they push resource input and goods output to the point at which the addition to total costs from the last increment (marginal cost) just equals the addition to total revenue from the last increment (marginal revenue). If no firm's resource input or goods output is large enough to affect the pertinent price significantly and each firm acts independently, then marginal cost (of resource input) equals resource price and marginal revenue (from output) equals product price. Since resource and product prices measure resource owners' sacrifice and consumers' gain of satisfactions, respectively, maximizing each firm's profits is consistent with equating marginal sacrifice with marginal gain of satisfactions and thus maximizing net satisfactions of all concerned. But if a firm's (or a combination's) resource input and goods output are large enough to affect prices significantly (additional inputs raising resource prices and additional outputs lowering product prices), then marginal cost exceeds resource price and marginal revenue falls short of product price. Maximizing the firms' profit therefore calls for smaller resource input (lower resource prices) and smaller goods output (higher product prices) than those consistent with maximizing the net satisfactions of all concerned. This is why unregulated monopolies and "conspiracies in restraint of trade" are outlawed in the United States as harmful to society as a whole.

If, in addition to being competitive, producing firms initially bear all the costs of preparing a good for sale, and if all the benefits from use are appropriated in the good as bought by consumers, then equating the producing firms' marginal cost with their marginal revenue is the same as equating the aggregate marginal sacrifice of producing the good with the resulting aggregate marginal gain of satisfactions. But if some costs (e.g., water pollution from oil wells) are not borne by producing firms, or if some benefits (e.g., regularization of water supplies below timbered watersheds) accrue to others than purchasers of the salable good (in the latter example, wood) then equating firms' marginal costs with their marginal revenue is not the same as equating the aggregate marginal sacrifice of producing the good with the resulting aggregate marginal gain of satisfactions. In such cases, maximizing the net satisfactions of those persons directly involved does not maximize the net satisfactions of all concerned. This sort of discrepancy often accounts for various penalties or regulations imposed by society on otherwise privately profitable actions of business enterprises.

Thus, although the price system in combination with gain-motivated private behavior is a pervasive and powerful instrument of economic efficiency, its free working alone cannot always be relied on to induce the optimum allocation of resources among alternative employments. The price system's performance often may be improved, from the point of view of society as a whole, by means of supplementary regulation designed to assure reasonably competitive markets or to equate business marginal costs and prices with aggregate marginal sacrifice and gain of satisfactions. As will be shown in later chapters, ideal conservation regulation supplements the price system for the latter type of purpose.

Definition of conservation

Thus far we have seen (a) that conservation as ordinarily conceived is an aspect of the allocation of productive resources among alternative employments, specifically an aspect of making provision out of currently available resources for future satisfactions; (b) that efficiency in resource allocation is conceived in terms of an "optimum," an allocation among alternative uses which maximizes net satisfactions; and (c) that the free working of the price system assures efficiency in resource allocation only if market participants fully exploit opportunities for gain, if markets are competitive, and if direct private net benefits from the use of resources coincide with total social net benefits. In this light, the term "conservation" can be given a precise, operational definition for purposes of the remainder of this study. For maximum clarity, the definition, which contemplates depletable natural resources, will be stated in several ways.

Conservation is action designed to achieve or to maintain, from the point of view of society as a whole, the optimum distribution of natural resource use over time. A given stock of depletable natural resources (or of a particular depletable natural resource) may be consumed over shorter or longer periods of time; the portions of the total consumed in different subdivisions of the period may be relatively small or relatively large. Thus the distribution of use over time may fall into any one of an infinity of possible patterns. But, given expectations at a particular time, there is in principle only one time-distribution of use which promises to maximize the net satisfactions of all persons concerned. Conservation consists of selecting and implementing that time-distribution of use.

Conservation is action designed to avoid, from the point of view of society as a whole, the wastes resulting from a faulty distribution of natural resource use over time. A time-distribution of use of natural resources (or of a particular natural resource) other than the optimum time-distribution results in wastes of one or more kinds. The possible wastes include loss without beneficial use[14] of some resource units that would have yielded net satisfactions at some time, beneficial use at any time of resource units capable of yielding only negative net satisfactions, and beneficial use of some resource units at a time when the net satisfactions yielded are smaller than the (discounted) net satisfactions that would have been yielded at another time. Conservation consists of avoiding all such wastes.

Conservation is action designed to achieve or to maintain, from the point of view of society as a whole, the maximum present value of natural resources (or of a natural resource). For this purpose, prospective net satisfactions must be comprehensive of the sacrifices and satisfactions of all concerned, and these, in turn, must be valued at prices determined in competitive markets; furthermore, prospective net satisfactions must be discounted at a rate determined in a competitive capital market, that rate measuring the marginal rate of time preference (adjusted for risk and uncertainty). These conditions satisfied, if shifting some units of planned resource use from one time to another yields some increase in discounted net satisfactions, then the sum of discounted prospective net satisfactions is increased. When all opportunities for increasing discounted net satisfactions by shifting planned resource use in time are exhausted, the present value of the resource in question is maximized. Conservation consists of exhausting all opportunities for increasing discounted net satisfactions by means of rearranging the pattern of prospective resource use in time.

Although the three variations on the definition of conservation mean the same thing, the third and last is the preferred version. It runs in the most familiar, least abstract terms. It also most clearly conveys that conservation is an instrument of improving man's material well-being. To maximize the present value of natural resources at all times (discounting total future net satisfactions at the marginal rate of time pref-

---

[14] Beneficial use means use which yields satisfactions to some person or persons. The *net* satisfactions resulting from beneficial use need not be positive.

erence) is to maximize, in the only unambiguous sense possible, the benefits flowing from natural resource use.

Conservation is defined in terms of intelligent action to achieve a purpose. As a form of human behavior, conservation is always prospective and tentative. The maximum present value of resources can pertain only to one moment of time, only to one specific set of prospects. Conservation is, then, a continuous search for a changing optimum time-distribution of resource use as events continuously unfold and shape new expectations.

The definition of conservation adopted here is not new to the economic literature. Mason, for instance, defines conservation as "the avoidance of wastes associated with a faulty time-distribution of use of resources."[15] Ciriacy-Wantrup defines conservation as a shift "in the inter-temporal use [of a resource] in the direction of the future,"[16] and Scott similarly defines it as "a public policy which seeks to increase future usable supplies of a resource by present actions";[17] but to both Ciriacy-Wantrup and Scott the optimum extent to which use should be postponed is defined by that time-distribution of use that maximizes the present value of resources.[18] Nor is the definition adopted here necessarily inconsistent with such vague (and anonymous) definitions as "wise use of resources" and "avoidance of wastes in the use of resources." The major virtue of the definition adopted here is that it gives a precise, operational meaning to such expressions as "wise use" and "waste."[19]

The definition of conservation given here is unambiguous, significant, and operational. It recognizes that the purpose of conservation—if it is indeed a good thing—is to improve the lot of users of natural resources. Allowance is made for the prospective demands of future users; but the sacrifice involved in postponing the use of natural resources is recognized and a meaningful rule is yielded for dividing the use of resources between the present and future points in time. The definition emphasizes the fact that conservation is an element in the general eco-

---

[15] Edward S. Mason, "The Political Economy of Resource Use," in *Perspectives on Conservation*, ed. Henry Jarrett (Baltimore: Johns Hopkins Press for Resources for the Future, 1958), p. 162.

[16] S. V. Ciriacy-Wantrup, *Resource Conservation: Economics and Policies* (Berkeley: University of California Press, 1952), p. 51.

[17] Anthony Scott, *Natural Resources: The Economics of Conservation* (Toronto: University of Toronto Press, 1955), p. 18.

[18] Ciriacy-Wantrup, *Resource Conservation*, p. 77; Scott, *Natural Resources*, p. 6.

[19] For a thoughtful review of various efforts to define conservation, see Wallace F. Lovejoy and Paul T. Homan, *Economic Aspects of Oil Conservation Regulation* (Baltimore: Johns Hopkins Press for Resources for the Future, 1967), pp. 8–30.

nomic process, sharing criteria of appropriate action with investment. Therefore, in terms familiar both to resource exploiting firms and to their regulators, it suggests a definite form of desired action in response to given economic prospects.

The stock of resources to be conserved

The total stock of a depletable natural resource such as petroleum consists of two substocks. The first is the known stock, consisting of deposits that have been discovered and sufficiently developed to establish their technical characteristics. Some part of the known stock is at any time submarginal—i.e., incapable of supporting economical exploitation at existing and prospective costs and prices. The supramarginal portion of the known stock is, then, the source of current production. Specific deposits in the supramarginal portion of the known stock are the objects of definite plans for the time-distribution of production and use. With continued production over time, such deposits are necessarily exhausted or reduced to submarginal status. The other substock, the unknown stock, consists of the remainder of natural deposits in the crust of the earth. Its quantitative dimensions are unknown, and its qualitative characteristics can only be inferred from those of the known stock. The unknown stock is, of course, the source of new discoveries to augment or replace exhausted deposits in the known stock. Continued exploration and development must eventually exhaust the unknown stock or reduce the remaining discoverable deposits in it to (probable) submarginal status.

Thus for any depletable resource the conservation problem as a whole may be viewed on two interrelated levels. On the first level, the problem is the optimum time-distribution of use of supramarginal deposits in the known stock. On the second level, the problem is the optimum rate of transfer of deposits from the unknown to the known stock—the optimum allocation of productive resources to exploration for and development of new deposits eligible for inclusion in the supramarginal portion of the known stock. The two problems together constitute the general problem of the optimum time-distribution of use of the total natural stock of the resource in question.

Neither level of the general conservation problem can be treated in isolation. The size of the known stock depends in part on the line of demarcation between supramarginal and submarginal deposits. That line depends in part on present and prospective prices, which depend in part on the quantity and quality of deposits being transferred from the unknown to the known stock by current exploration and development. Similarly, the optimum time-distribution of use of any supramarginal deposit depends in part on the relation of present to expected prices, which depends in part on the volume and success of current exploration and development activities. Conversely, the basic determinants of the chosen time-distribution of use of supramarginal deposits, including trends in the size and quality of the known stock, are also determinants of the prospective profitability of investment in exploration and development. Thus the conceptually separate processes of using up known deposits and preparing new ones for use are essentially one integrated process of using up the total natural stock.

For these reasons, I take the view that conservation pertains to the total natural stock, known and unknown, of the resource under discussion. The optimum time-distribution of use of the total natural stock embraces the optimum allocation of resources to exploration and development. Maximizing the present value of petroleum resources requires that both postponement of use of supramarginal deposits and investment in exploration and development be pushed continuously to the point where the marginal rate of return is equal to the marginal rate of time preference (adjusted for risk and uncertainty).

5. The Optimum Time-Distribution of Use

The optimum time-distribution of use of petroleum resources requires (a) an optimum time-distribution of production from each reservoir and (b) an optimum allocation of labor, capital, and other natural resources to the exploration for and development of new reservoirs. For the latter requirement to be satisfied, those engaged in exploration and development must expect that the former requirement will be satisfied in all new discoveries. Consequently, I shall begin my examination of the optimum time-distribution of use by discussing the nature and determinants of the optimum time-distribution of production from a given reservoir in terms of the optimum rate of production from the reservoir at any time. The purpose is to clarify the fundamental basis of petroleum conservation regulation.

For convenience and clarity of exposition, it is at first assumed that each reservoir is found, developed, and depleted as a unit by a single operator and that each operator initially bears all the social costs incurred as a result of his activities. These assumptions will be relaxed at appropriate points in the discussion. For simplicity with no essential loss of realism, it is assumed throughout that each operator assiduously exploits opportunities for private gain and that all relevant markets are reasonably competitive. Finally, to limit the analysis to fundamentals pertinent to regulation, the discussion disregards taxes of all kinds.[1]

---

[1] The procedure is justified on two grounds. First, the taxes paid by a particular firm or industry are not necessarily related to the social costs incurred by that industry. They are a matter of tax policy rather than the essential requirements of productive activity in that industry. Second, tax policy in relation to conservation is a subject separate from conservation regulation per se, a subject requiring a different, much enlarged framework of analysis. For some exploratory and limited analyses of tax policy in relation to petroleum conservation see two articles by Stephen L. McDonald: "Percentage Depletion, Expensing of Intangibles and Petroleum Conservation," in *Extractive Resources and Taxation*, ed. Mason Gaffney (Madison: University of Wisconsin Press, 1967), pp. 269–88, and "The Effects of Severance vs. Property Taxes on Petroleum Conservation," *Proceedings of the 58th Annual Meeting of the National Tax Association, 1965* (1966), pp. 320–27.

The optimum rate of production—unit operation

Suppose that a petroleum reservoir has been found and developed sufficiently to establish its volume and basic operating characteristics. The
operator's problem is to determine and implement the time-distribution
of production that will maximize the present value of the reservoir,
given the minimum acceptable rate of return.[2] Put another way, the
operator's problem is to determine and implement the most profitable
rate of production at each point of time in the reservoir's life.

The operator must consider the following factors: the alternative
drives that may be employed to deplete the reservoir, the maximum
volume of recoverable reserves under each drive, the feasible rates of
production under each drive using different numbers of wells, the costs
of drilling and equipping additional wells (which may be used to speed
up depletion), the loss of potentially recoverable reserves under each
drive at different rates of production, expected operating costs under
each drive at different rates of production, and expected prices of oil and
gas over the life of the reservoir. The operator must weigh speed of
depletion and consequent reduction of time discount against additional
well costs and loss of potentially recoverable reserves; he must weigh
potential discounted net revenue in early periods against potential discounted net revenue in later periods of reservoir life.

Although the problem is in principle amenable to straightforward
solution, the operator may choose to select a tentative drive and production rate within the capabilities of his existing wells and then work
toward an optimum by making small changes in either production rate
or the number of wells when such changes promise to add something to
present value. He may choose to exhaust the possibilities for gain first
by adjusting production within the limits imposed by existing wells, then
by adjusting the number of wells and repeating the process. Thus, as a
first step, he would compare the discounted gains and losses of shifting
some production between present and future periods. He would achieve
a maximum present value (within the limits imposed by existing wells)
by pushing present-value-increasing shifts between periods to the point
at which the gain (or loss) of present net revenue on the last small shift
is just equal to the loss (or gain) of discounted future net revenue. The
net revenue in each period is inclusive of associated gas revenue and the
cost of injecting fluids to maintain or increase reservoir preserve.

---

[2] The minimum acceptable rate of return is assumed to be equal to the rate of
interest (adjusted for risk and uncertainty) which, in turn, is assumed to be
equal to the marginal rate of time preference (adjusted for risk and uncertainty).

The present-value-maximizing condition is expressed mathematically in the following equation:

$$MNR_0 = (1 + b_t) \frac{(MNR_t)}{(1 + r)^t}; \tag{5.1}$$

where MNR = marginal net revenue, or increment to net revenue resulting from a unit shift in production between periods (subscript 0 indicates the present; subscript t indicates any point in future time);

b = fraction of a unit of production lost from ultimate recovery in the period indicated as the result of producing the last unit at present;

r = rate of discount (i.e., rate of interest adjusted for risk and uncertainty).

To illustrate the present-value-maximizing condition, assume that $MNR_0 = 2.20$, $MNR_t = 2.31$, $b = .048$, $r = .10$ and $t = 1$. Then

$$2.20 = (1.048) \frac{(2.31)}{(1.10)} = 2.20.$$

To shift a barrel of production between the present and one year from now (in either direction) would add nothing to net present value: the gain of present value would be 2.20 and the sacrifice of present value would be 2.20. But if MNR_0 were greater than 2.20 (the other values given), it would pay to shift some production from a year from now to the present; or if MNR_1 were greater than 2.31 (the other values given), it would pay to shift some production from the present to one year from now.

Of course, b may assume a value of zero, signifying no loss of recovery a year from now as a result of the last unit presently produced.[3] If so, and if $MNR_0 = 2.20$, then the present-value-maximizing condition requires that $MNR_1 = 2.42$. Thus

$$2.20 = \frac{2.42}{1.10} = 2.20.$$

This result may be interpreted as saying that if (expected) marginal net revenue a year from now is 2.42 (given the present marginal net revenue of 2.20 and the discount rate of 10 percent), then present value may be maximized without shifting so much production to the present as to reduce feasible recovery a year from now.

For simplicity, the examples suppose a one-year span of time. Note, however, that equation (5.1) is perfectly general with respect to all

---

[3] In a nonassociated gas reservoir, b is always zero since ultimate recovery from such a reservoir does not depend on the rate of production.

spans of time between present and future points in time. Thus, in more detailed form with respect to time,

$$MNR_0 = (1 + b_1) \frac{(MNR_1)}{(1 + r)^1}$$

$$= (1 + b_2) \frac{(MNR_2)}{(1 + r)^2}$$

$$= (1 + b_3) \frac{(MNR_3)}{(1 + r)^3}$$

$$\vdots$$

$$= (1 + b_n) \frac{(MNR_n)}{(1 + r)^n}.$$

If discounted marginal net revenue of any future time equals present marginal net revenue, then the discounted marginal net revenues of any pair of points in time are equal. Thus, for example,

$$MNR_0 = (1 + b_1) \frac{(MNR_1)}{(1 + r)^1}$$

$$MNR_0 = (1 + b_3) \frac{(MNR_3)}{(1 + r)^3}$$

$$(1 + b_1) \frac{(MNR_1)}{(1 + r)^1} = (1 + b_3) \frac{(MNR_3)}{(1 + r)^3}.$$

Therefore, the present-value-maximizing equation states that no gain in net present value may be had from shifting production from one to any other point in time.

The question arises: What assurance is there that some feasible time-distribution of production exists at which discounted marginal net revenues are equal at all points in time? There are two possible assurances, one of which always can be made effective. The explanation is facilitated if we rewrite equation (5.1) in the form

$$(MR - MC)_0 = (1 + b_t) \frac{(MR - MC)_t}{(1 + r)^t} \; ;$$

where MR = marginal revenue, or increment to total revenue resulting from a unit shift in production between periods;

MC = marginal cost, or increment to total cost resulting from a unit shift in production between periods.

The first assurance arises from the fact that marginal cost in some range of the rate of output (at least near capacity) is a positive function of the rate of output, as illustrated in figure 5. Thus, as production in

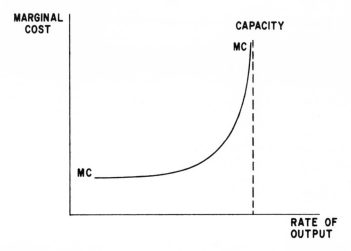

Figure 5. Illustrative marginal cost function.

that range is shifted from one period to another, marginal net revenue tends to fall in the period to which production is shifted and to rise in the period from which production is shifted. To illustrate, suppose that initially

$$MNR_0 < (1 + b_1) \frac{(MNR_1)}{(1 + r)^1}$$

$$2.18 < (1.048) \frac{(2.33)}{(1.10)}.$$

It therefore pays to shift production from the present to time 1. As production is so shifted, MNR_0 tends to rise (as MC_0 falls) and MNR_1 tends to fall (as MC_1 rises). Eventually the changes become large enough that

$$MNR_0 = (1 + b_1) \frac{(MNR_1)}{(1 + r)^1}$$

$$2.20 = (1.048) \frac{(2.31)}{(1.10)}.$$

The second assurance arises from the fact that ultimate recovery in some range of the rate of output is a negative function of the rate of output.[4] The more production is shifted from future to present, the more likely it is that total recovery will be reduced. Thus, as production is shifted from future to present, b_t tends to rise; and as production is

---

[4] See figure 2, ch. 2, for graphic illustration.

shifted from present to future, b_t tends to fall. To illustrate, suppose that initially

$$MNR_0 < (1 + b_1) \frac{(MNR_1)}{(1 + r)^1}$$

$$2.20 < (1.06) \frac{(2.31)}{(1.10)}.$$

It therefore pays to shift production from the present to time 1. As production is so shifted, b_1 tends to fall until

$$MNR_0 = (1 + b_1) \frac{(MNR_1)}{(1 + r)^1}$$

$$2.20 = (1.048) \frac{(2.31)}{(1.10)}.$$

Having achieved the maximum present value of expected income within the limits imposed by existing wells, the operator faces the second step in the process of determining and implementing the optimum time-distribution of production. He must now consider whether increasing the number of wells and reachieving the maximum present value of expected income with each number will result in a higher net present value for the reservoir. He must compare the increments to maximum present value made possible by additional wells with the necessary increments to well cost.

If the operator adds more wells he increases present capacity and lowers current marginal operating costs (at least in the range between old and new capacity), as illustrated in figure 6. Consequently, the time-distribution which now maximizes the present value of expected income is different from that which maximized the present value of expected income using the original number of wells. (Production is more heavily concentrated in early periods.) The new maximum present value is different from the original. If it is larger, then the additional wells are worth drilling if they add less to total well cost than the increment to maximum present value. The operator achieves a *top* maximum net present value for the reservoir by pushing the addition to wells to the point where incremental well cost is just equal to incremental maximum present value of expected income.

The principle involved in the second step of the process of determining the optimum time-distribution of production is schematically illustrated in figure 7. The axes of the top panel of the chart measure net present value and current rate of production, respectively, the latter serving as proxy for time-distribution of production. (The higher the

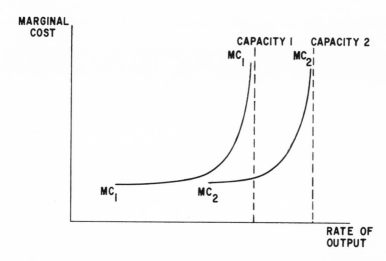

Figure 6.   Shift in marginal cost function resulting from increased capacity.

current rate of production, the more concentrated is production in early periods.) Each of the several curves labeled W_1, W_2, etc., represents net present values obtainable from a given number of wells, the number increasing from W_1 to W_2, etc. Each curve has a maximum (M_1, M_2, etc.), but the third curve (W_3) has the highest, or top maximum. Thus the operator would drill the number of wells corresponding to W_3 and would produce at a current rate indicated by point C on the horizontal axis. The lower panel of figure 7 shows the curve MWC, representing incremental well cost (assumed to be a constant amount), intersecting the curve MPV, representing incremental maximum present value, at the same current rate of production C.

The foregoing discussion shows that the optimum time-distribution of production necessarily has as its companion the optimum number of wells.[5] The two optimums are codetermined by well costs, income expectations, and reservoir operating characteristics. Neither can be determined independently of the other.

We may now consider the significance of the optimum time-distribution of production achieved by the operator. Recall that under our assumptions the operator's costs correspond to sacrifice by society at large and his gross income corresponds to satisfactions received by society at

[5] For a graphic explanation of the codetermination of optimum time-distribution of production and optimum number of wells, see James W. McKie and Stephen L. McDonald, "Petroleum Conservation in Theory and Practice," *Quarterly Journal of Economics*, vol. 76 (February 1962), pp. 101–10.

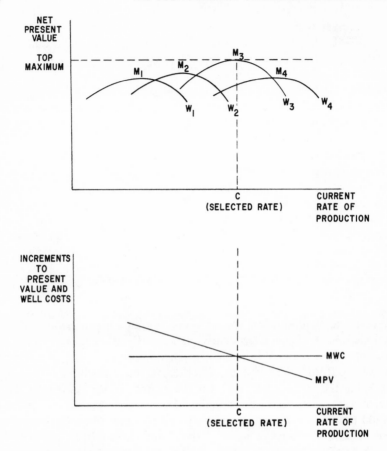

Figure 7. Determination of optimum rate of production and number of wells.

large. Furthermore, the operator's minimum acceptable rate of return is equal to the rate of interest (adjusted for risk and uncertainty), which, in turn, is equal to society's marginal rate of time preference (adjusted for risk and uncertainty). Now the operator has pushed investment in wells to the point where the last increment to investment yields a rate of return just equal to the adjusted rate of interest. He has also postponed production to the point at which the last unit postponed yields a rate of return just equal to the same adjusted rate of interest. Further well investment or further postponement of production might yield some return, but the rate of return would be lower than the adusted rate of interest. Consequently, the gain in satisfactions to society would be less than the sacrifice (including the sacrifice of postponing satisfactions) incurred by society. Thus the result of the operator's action to maximize his own income over time (reduced to present value) is the maximization of society's net satisfactions over time (reduced to present value). His pursuit of private gain results in conservation from the social point of view. This is achieved because of the (assumed) identity of the operator's costs and income with society's sacrifices and satisfactions.[6]

The time-distribution of production selected as most profitable to the operator may involve some loss of ultimate recovery. If so, is this conservation? Is this in society's interest? It is both when the operator's costs and income truly reflect society's sacrifices and satisfactions, as in the present case. The loss of ultimate recovery could be eliminated by sufficiently postponing production, but the sacrifice of satisfactions in the postponement would outweigh the gain of satisfactions from additional (later) recovery. Thus conservation may be consistent with some loss of ultimate recovery.

As emphasized earlier, the optimum time-distribution of production is defined for one point in time only. It changes as its determinants change from point to point in time. In particular, it changes with every change in current and expected costs and prices. A decline in present well costs, for instance, tends to encourage the drilling of additional

---

[6] For some students of conservation (and investment) the critical assumption here is that the private rate of discount is socially appropriate. It is often contended that the socially appropriate rate is lower than the private rate because investments (or postponements of use) are less risky to society than to private firms or individuals due to the insurance principle. If, however, uncertainty rather than risk is viewed as the relevant condition facing investors, this argument loses force. It is also possible to imagine plausible utility functions such that private individuals would be willing to save more if they knew that others were saving more also, so that with some sort of social saving program the rate of discount would be driven below that prevailing when all saving is independently done by private individuals. But plausible counterexamples can be constructed. For discussions of these and other issues see: William J. Baumol, "On the Social Rate of Discount," *American Economic Review*, vol. 58 (September 1968), pp. 788–802; R. C. Lind, "Further Comment," *Quarterly Journal of Economics*, vol. 78 (May 1964), pp. 336–44; Stephen A. Marglin, "The Social Rate of Discount and the Optimal Rate of Investment," *Quarterly Journal of Economics*, vol. 77 (February 1963), pp. 95–112; Paul A. Samuelson, "Principles of Efficiency: Discussion," *American Economic Review*, vol. 54 (May 1964), pp. 93–96; A. K. Sen, "On Optimizing the Rate of Saving," *Economic Journal*, vol. 71 (September 1961), pp. 479–96; Gordon Tullock, "The Social Rate of Discount and the Optimal Rate of Investment: Comment," *Quarterly Journal of Economics*, vol. 78 (May 1964), pp. 331–36; Dan Usher, "The Social Rate of Discount and the Optimal Rate of Investment: Comment," *Quarterly Journal of Economics*, vol. 78 (November 1964), pp. 641–44; William Vickery, "Principles of Efficiency: Discussion," *American Economic Review*, vol. 54 (May 1964), pp. 88–92.

wells and the acceleration of reservoir depletion. In terms of the lower panel of figure 7, the curve representing incremental well costs (*MWC*) shifts downward, intersecting the curve representing incremental maximum present value (*MPV*) at a point corresponding to a larger number of wells and a higher current rate of output. A rise in expected future prices relative to current prices, for another instance, encourages further postponement of production. In terms of equation (5.1), expected marginal net revenue (MNR_t) rises relative to current marginal net revenue (MNR_0), making it profitable to shift some production toward the future. Thus continuously maximizing net present value (continuously conserving) requires flexible adjustments in the time-distribution of production as the economic values reflecting sacrifice and gain of satisfactions (costs and prices) change over time.

The optimum rate of production—unrestrained operation

The assumption that each reservoir is developed and depleted as a unit by a single operator will now be temporarily dropped. Instead it will be assumed that each reservoir is developed and depleted by numerous operators in competition with each other for the available petroleum in the reservoir (unrestrained operation). I shall continue to assume that (otherwise) operators initially bear the full social costs of their activities.

As before, the individual operator wishes to determine and implement the time-distribution of production that maximizes the present value of his portion of the reservoir. He must consider the same factors as if he were the sole operator, plus one other: the possibility of drainage across property lines. He must consider that to the degree he postpones production he exposes himself to drainage by his neighbors; that to the degree he accelerates production he enhances the possibility of draining petroleum from his neighbors' properties to his own. This consideration enters, then, as a negative component in the sacrifice of future income required to secure present income from production.

As before, the individual operator achieves a maximum present value of his property (within the limits imposed by existing wells) by pushing present-value-increasing shifts of production between periods to the point at which the gain (or loss) of present net revenue on the last small shift is just equal to the loss (or gain) of discounted future net revenue. With the new negative element in it, the present-value-maximizing condition is expressed mathematically in the following equation:

$$MNR_0 = (1 - x_t)(1 + b_t)\frac{(MNR_t)}{(1 + r)^t}; \qquad (5.2)$$

where x = fraction of a unit of production drained by neighbors in the period indicated as the result of the last unit of production postponed.

The size of x_t is inversely related to the speed with which the given operator develops and produces from his portion of the reservoir.

To illustrate the present-value-maximizing condition numerically, assume that $MNR_0 = 2.16$, $MNR_t = 2.40$, $x_t = .12$, $b_t = .12$, $r = .10$, and $t = 1$:

$$2.16 = (.88)(1.12)\frac{(2.40)}{(1.10)} = 2.16$$

Shifting a barrel of production between the present and one year from now (in either direction) would add nothing to present value: the gain of present value would be 2.16 and the sacrifice of present value would be 2.16.

Compare equation (5.1), which reflects unit operation of a reservoir, with equation (5.2), which reflects unrestrained operation of a reservoir. The equations are identical except for the negative element (x_t) in the latter. It is evident that for any set of other values in the equations, the right-hand side of the unrestrained operation equation is smaller than that of the unit-operation equation. Unrestrained operation, therefore, provides more incentive for accelerating production than unit operation, other factors given. For example, suppose that initially $MNR_0 = 2.18$, $MNR_t = 2.32$, $x_t = .14$, $b_t = .05$, $r = .10$, and $t = 1$. In the unit-operated reservoir

$$MNR_0 < (1 + b_1)\frac{(MNR_1)}{(1 + r)^1}$$

$$2.18 < (1.05)\frac{(2.32)}{(1.10)} = 2.21.$$

Consequently, it pays initially to shift some production from the present to a year from now, raising MNR_0 and lowering both b_1 and MNR_1. In the present-value-maximizing situation, where no further shift would pay, the equation might appear as

$$2.20 = (1.048)\frac{(2.31)}{(1.10)} = 2.20.$$

In the reservoir operated without restraints, with the same data except for the introduction of x_1,

$$MNR_0 > (1 - x_1)(1 + b_1)\frac{(MNR_1)}{(1 + r)^1}$$

$$2.18 > (.86)(1.05)\frac{(2.32)}{(1.10)} = 1.91.$$

In this case, in contrast, it pays initially to shift some production from a year from now to the present, in the process lowering MNR_0 and x_1 and raising b_1 and MNR_1. In the present-value-maximizing situation, where no further shift would pay, the equation might appear as:

$$2.16 = (.88)(1.12)\frac{(2.40)}{(1.10)} = 2.16.$$

Thus the same initial circumstances lead to slower current production from the unit-operated reservoir but faster current production from the reservoir operated without restraints. They also lead to greater loss of ultimate recovery in the latter reservoir.

The incentive to accelerate production under unrestrained operation carries over into the decision on how many wells to drill into a given portion of the reservoir. The unrestrained operator can reduce the size of x_t at any given number of wells if he can sink new producing wells faster than his neighbors. There is, then, a bonus increment to maximum present value as the number of wells is increased. Consequently, the curve of incremental maximum present value intersects the curve of incremental well costs at a point corresponding to more wells and higher current output than under unit operation (see figure 7, lower panel). Hence the familiar conclusion that unrestrained development of petroleum reservoirs results in excessively dense drilling, excessively high initial production, and excessively large loss of ultimate recovery.

The significance of x_t for conservation is that it represents a purely private cost (of postponing production) to individual operators. It has no social counterpart. For the operators as a whole (or for society) x_t is nonexistent. It therefore creates an incentive for individual private operators to take action that is not in the interest of the operators as a whole (or of society). It breaks down the identity of private costs and incomes with social sacrifice and satisfactions; it therefore destroys the consistency between private pursuit of gain and conservation from the social point of view. The consistency can be restored only by so organizing the operators that they may develop and deplete the reservoir as a unit.

The optimum rate of exploration—unit operation

I shall now return to the assumption of unit operation of reservoirs, and continue for a time to assume that operators initially bear as private costs the full social costs of their activities.

Petroleum operators, whose working deposits are subject to depletion with production, confront an array of exploratory prospects from which replacement deposits may be derived. The prospects differ from one another in respect to (a) probability of yielding productive deposits of given quality, (b) cost of exploration, and (c) cost of development and operation should productive discovery occur. The evaluation of this array yields a set of prospects of differing degrees of prospective profitability, such as that represented by the curve PR in figure 8. Some of the prospects (*OB*) offer a positive prospective rate of return; a smaller number (*OA*) offer an acceptable prospective rate of return, that is, a prospective rate of return equal to or greater than the rate of interest (adjusted for risk and uncertainty).

With unit operation, for reasons already explained, development and production can occur on the most profitable terms from the point of view of both operators and society. Therefore, given the probability of discovery and the cost of exploration, the volume of exploration corresponding to *OA* in figure 8 is optimal from the point of view of society. It represents the optimum allocation of labor, capital, and other natural resources to the exploration for petroleum deposits; it results in the optimum rate of transferring deposits from the unknown to the known stock. Together with the optimum time-distribution of production from supramarginal portions of the known stock, it constitutes conservation of the total natural stock of petroleum deposits.

Now drop the assumption that operators initially bear the full social

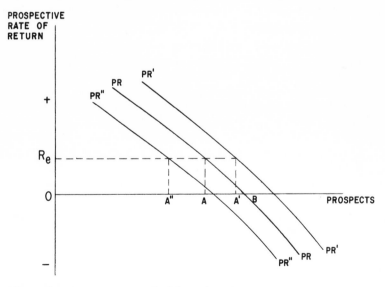

Figure 8.   Prospective profitability of exploration.

costs of their activities. Suppose, for instance, that operators are not required to avoid or to compensate for the water pollution they may cause. The result is that to private operators (but not to society) both exploration and production are cheaper than before. Each exploratory prospect is now prospectively more profitable than before. Consequently, the curve of prospective profitability is to the right of PR in figure 8, in the position, say, of PR'. The optimum rate of exploration from society's point of view remains at OA, but the optimum rate from operators' point of view is the larger rate OA'. Pursuit of private gain therefore results in an excessive application of labor, capital, and other natural resources to the exploration for petroleum deposits. Deposits are transferred too rapidly from the unknown to the known stock; and some deposits that from society's point of view are submarginal are developed and utilized as supramarginal from the operators' point of view. Conservation is violated, and society as a whole is worse off because the resources employed in excessive exploration, development, and production could have been employed more effectively (for society) elsewhere in the economy.

Even with unit operation of reservoirs, therefore, conservation requires that operators initially bear the full social costs of their activities. If they do not, the total natural stock of petroleum deposits tends to be depleted too rapidly and some deposits that are submarginal from society's point of view tend to be utilized. Waste results from using some deposits too soon and from using some deposits which really do not pay for themselves.

The optimum rate of exploration—unrestrained operation

I shall now restore the assumption that operators initially bear the full social costs of their activities and drop the assumption of unit operation.

With unrestrained operation, private operators tend to drill an excessive number of wells and to produce at rates that result in an excessive loss of ultimate recovery. Both to the operators as a whole and to society, reservoirs of given characteristics prove less profitable to utilize in these circumstances than if unit operation were the rule. Consequently, each exploratory prospect is prospectively less profitable than it would be with unit operation. The curve of prospective profitability is to the left of PR in figure 8, in the position, say, of PR''. The optimum rate of exploration from society's point of view remains at OA, but the optimum rate from the operators' point of view is the smaller rate OA''. Pursuit of private gain in the absence of unit operation therefore results in a deficient application of labor, capital, and other natural resources to the exploration for petroleum deposits. Deposits are transferred too slowly from the unknown to the known stock; and some deposits that are supramarginal from society's point of view are rejected as submarginal by private operators. Conservation is violated, and society as a whole is worse off because resources that might have been profitably employed in petroleum exploration, development, and production must be employed less productively to society elsewhere in the economy.

Therefore, consistency of private pursuit of gain with conservation requires both assumption of full social costs by operators and unit operation of reservoirs. If the latter essential is lacking, the total natural stock of petroleum deposits tends to be depleted too slowly and some socially supramarginal deposits tend to go unutilized. Waste results from not using some deposits soon enough and from not using at all some deposits that really would pay for themselves.

Interactions between optimum rate of production and optimum rate of exploration

As noted in chapter 4, the two levels of the conservation problem—optimum time-distribution of use of known deposits and optimum allocation of resources to exploratory effort—are closely interrelated. The nature of the interrelationship can be better understood with the aid of some hypothetical illustrative cases. The conclusions drawn from the cases hold whether reservoirs are operated without restraint or as units, whether operators bear full social costs or not.

1. Assume initial optimality at both levels, disturbed by the expectation that future demand will grow at a faster rate than previously supposed. The new expectation means that, other things constant, future prices will be higher (perhaps increase at a faster rate) than previously supposed. At the current production level, expected future marginal net revenue rises relative to current marginal net revenue, and operators are induced to shift some production from present to future. Their action, a proper response to an increase in future demand relative to present demand, tends to raise current prices somewhat and to moderate somewhat the expected increase in future prices. Thus present consumers are made to bear some of the burden of increased expected future demand. At the exploratory level, the increase in expected future prices (modified by action at the current production level) makes exploration prospectively more profitable. All prospects now promise higher re-

turns, and some previously submarginal prospects become supramarginal. Consequently, more labor, capital, and other natural resources are devoted to exploration, and deposits are transferred more rapidly from the unknown to the known stock. The faster growth of the known stock, in turn, further moderates the expected future increase in prices, with feedback effects on action at the current production level. In the new equilibrium (new state of conservation), present and future prices are somewhat higher, production is less concentrated in the present, and the known stock is somewhat larger relative to current production. The additional exploratory effort has diverted resources from other industries, presumably those industries from which expected future demand was diverted (at least relatively) in the initial assumption.

2. Assume initial optimality at both levels, disturbed by a significant improvement in the technology of drilling. Current and expected well drilling costs are reduced. Other things constant, petroleum becomes cheaper to find and produce; some previously submarginal known deposits and exploratory prospects become supramarginal. At the current production level, two stimuli are felt: present development well costs are lower and, on the assumption that exploration will respond appropriately, expected future prices are lower than previously. Both stimuli encourage the drilling of additional wells and the acceleration of production in known reservoirs. Operators' response to these stimuli has the effect of depressing current prices somewhat (allowing present consumers to benefit immediately) and moderating the expected decline in future prices. Two stimuli are also felt at the exploratory level: reduced cost of current exploratory drilling and reduced prospective development cost. Both stimuli encourage exploration and, through the prospect of faster growth of the known stock, tend to depress the level of expected future prices. In the new equilibrium (new state of conservation) current and expected prices are somewhat lower, current output is greater, and the known stock is larger. A material has become economically more plentiful and therefore cheaper, and productive resources have been attracted to the industry so that a new mix of total output is achieved that takes advantage of the relatively less expensive means of getting satisfactions.

3. Assume initial optimality at both levels, disturbed by the prospective introduction of a competitive source of energy. Expected future prices of petroleum are depressed. At the current production level, the effect is to encourage a shift of production from future to present. Such a shift by many operators results in depressed current prices, so that consumers immediately benefit from the prospective substitute. At the

exploratory level, the effect of lower expected future prices is to discourage exploration, so that the known stock tends to be used up faster. In the new equilibrium (new state of conservation), current and expected prices are lower, current output is greater, and the known stock is smaller relative to current output. In this case, because a resource has become less rare—has become potentially obsolescent—the existing stock is consumed more rapidly and fewer resources are devoted to replacement. The resources freed from exploration and development are now available to a new industry which is expected to produce a substitute material.

These cases not only illustrate operators' coordinated responses on two levels to common economic stimuli, they also emphasize the role of free adjustments of output and prices in continuously conserving a depletable natural resource such as petroleum. Enforced rigidity of either output or prices poses an impediment to the adjustments required for conservation in a dynamically developing economy.

On "running out"

Conservation is sometimes viewed as an effort to delay the inevitable day when we must "run out" of given depletable natural resources. There is a sense in which this view of conservation is valid, but in a more significant sense it is invalid and misleading. It diverts attention from the real process of resource extinction and leaves us with no criterion as to the appropriate period of time over which to delay the "inevitable."

Natural resources such as petroleum occur in deposits which vary almost infinitely as to accessibility and quality and tend to be discovered and developed in the order of their accessibility and quality.[7] As replacement of depleted deposits proceeds, exploration and development must be extended to less accessible, lower quality deposits. Relative prices tend to rise with increasing cost of replacement. Technological advance may delay or moderate the increase in relative prices, but it

---

[7] The term "quality" is used here to embrace reservoir operating characteristics and volume as well as the chemical properties of the petroleum contained. Because of uncertainty about the characteristics of possible discoveries, the tendency alleged here is weak with regard to quality. Prospects can be crudely appraised as to quality, however, and the better ones—given the degree of accessibility—have prior claim on the available exploratory capital. Of course, high quality may offset poor accessibility, and vice versa.

cannot prevent it entirely at extreme degrees of depletion of the total natural stock.[8]

Natural resources such as petroleum yield goods which in turn yield satisfactions of particular kinds. Although petroleum (or iron ore or sulfur) is unique, it is not necessarily the sole possible source of the satisfactions it yields. It is chosen as the source (or as one of the sources) of those satisfactions because, and only because, it is cheaper than alternative sources at the margin. As it becomes less cheap relatively, other sources tend to be substituted for it; if it becomes sufficiently expensive, it will cease altogether to be a resource.

Thus natural resources such as petroleum do not abruptly "run out" as we exhaust the total natural stock. Rather, they become progressively more expensive, at least at some phase of their resource-life. As they become progressively more expensive, they yield to other resources which then provide the satisfactions demanded. The issue in conservation, then, is not to postpone inevitable exhaustion as such, but to assure that the process of substitution is neither accelerated nor delayed by socially unnecessary costs or impediments. Conservation cannot save us from the problem of increasing replacement costs, but it can assure that those costs do not unnecessarily increase, and do not unnecessarily accelerate substitution of higher cost materials for petroleum and thereby unnecessarily restrain the growth of human welfare.

[8] This is based on the assumption that relative price must rise to bring substitutes into use. If a substitute becomes cheap enough, the price of oil may only remain equal to the substitute price until oil ceases to be produced.

6. Demand, Supply, and Price of Crude Oil

As noted in chapter 3, one of the problems with which regulation historically has sought to cope is short-run instability of the price of crude oil. However, as indicated in chapter 5, price fluctuations play a useful role in conservation. In order to clarify the relation of price to conservation, I shall now examine the relevant characteristics of petroleum demand and supply. The major emphasis is on supply, because it is a peculiarity of unregulated supply that causes the price of petroleum to behave in a manner inconsistent with conservation.

For convenience, the discussion is confined largely to crude oil (and associated gas). The general conclusions, however, apply equally to nonassociated gas. Throughout it is assumed that markets are reasonably competitive and that, except in relation to unrestrained extraction, private operators bear the full social costs of their activities.

The demand for crude oil

As explained earlier, the demand for a good is derived from the satisfactions that good yields to consumers. Consumers maximize satisfactions by purchasing each good in such quantity that the sacrifice represented by the real (or relative) price paid is just equal to the incremental (or marginal) gain of satisfactions. The marginal satisfactions from consuming a good tend to decline as consumers increase their consumption of that good relative to their consumption of other goods. Therefore, the quantity demanded varies inversely with relative price.

The demand for a good can be defined as the schedule of quantities consumers stand ready to buy, in a given period, at different relative prices. An increase (or decrease) in demand means an increase (or decrease) in the quantity demanded at each relative price. Demand changes (the schedule shifts) with a change in tastes, a change in real income, or a change in alternative goods available.

Of particular relevance to our inquiry is the elasticity of demand with respect to relative price. Price-elasticity of demand is a measure of the response of quantity demanded to a difference in relative price. More formally, it is the ratio of the percentage change in quantity demanded to the causative percentage change in relative price. If, for example, a 1 percent change in relative price should cause a 0.75 percent change in quantity demanded, the price-elasticity of demand (in the pertinent range of the schedule) would be 0.75/1, or 0.75. By convention, a demand is said to be price-elastic if elasticity so measured is greater than unity, and price-inelastic if elasticity so measured is less than unity.

The demand for crude oil in the short run is believed to be quite inelastic with respect to price. It is doubtful that its price-elasticity exceeds 0.25 over the usually relevant range of the schedule.[1] The reason is not hard to find.

The short-run price-elasticity of demand for a good depends on the closeness of available substitutes. If B is a close substitute for A, a small increase in the relative price of A (which is the same as a small decrease in the relative price of B) would cause a major shift in consumption from A to B. But if there is no close substitute for A, a small rise in its relative price would cause very little, if any, reduction in its consumption. Thus, for example, the demand for pork is price-elastic since beef, lamb, and chicken are close substitutes for pork, but the demand for table salt is price-inelastic since it has no close substitute.

Crude oil is the source of gasoline, jet fuel, kerosene, diesel fuel, burner oils, lubricating oils, asphalt, waxes, and various petrochemical raw materials. Historically, there have been no very close substitute sources of these products. (Shale oil recently has become prospectively a close substitute for crude oil.) Furthermore, none of these products, except burner oils and asphalt, have close substitutes. There are reasonably close substitutes for burner oils in stationary plants (natural gas, coal, and nuclear fuels) and for asphalt in highway construction (concrete), but burner oils and asphalt need not represent a large or fixed

---

[1] I am not aware of any authoritative econometric estimate of the elasticity of demand for crude oil. Since the volume of actual sales at a given price depends on interactions of supply and demand, it is extremely difficult—and sometimes impossible—even by means of the most sophisticated econometric techniques, to measure the price-elasticity of demand for a product. Simple regression of quantity sold on relative price is worse than useless in most cases. Where demand shifts dominate relative price changes, the regression of quantity sold on relative price more nearly describes the supply function than the demand function, because in this case the demand function intersects the supply function (and determines market-clearing prices) at different points along the latter. For a pioneering and classic work on the measurement of demand, see Henry Schultz, *The Theory and Measurement of Demand* (Chicago: University of Chicago Press, 1938).

fraction of the total products from crude oil. Refiners may alter the fraction in response to change in quantity demanded and thus avoid proportionate change in the quantity of crude oil demanded.[2] In addition, as they are produced in a joint-cost process,[3] burner oils and asphalt may be priced flexibly in relation to gasoline and the other products for which there are no close substitutes, so that variations in crude oil prices need not reflect themselves proportionately in variations in burner oil and asphalt prices. In consequence of these several circumstances, the quantity of crude oil demanded in the short run is only slightly responsive to change in its relative price.

(The short-run elasticity of demand for natural gas is probably greater than that for crude oil. In many industrial uses, which account for about one-half of total gas consumption, and in some household and commercial uses, coal, burner oil, and nuclear fuels—or electricity generated with such fuels—are close substitutes for natural gas.)

In the long run, the elasticity of demand for a good depends also on substitute techniques of production and use. A change in relative price expected to persist leads to innovations which permit a change in quantity consumed. For instance, a rise in the relative price of crude oil expected to persist might now lead to the technological innovations required to produce shale oil commercially on a modest scale. Or a rise in the relative price of gasoline expected to persist might lead to significant fuel-saving innovations in automotive design. Thus the long-run price-elasticity of demand for crude oil undoubtedly is greater than its short-run price-elasticity.

The significance of an inelastic demand for our purposes is that shifts in such a demand, or shifts in supply relative to such a demand, produce relatively large changes in price. The principle is illustrated in figure 9. In panel (a) of the figure, an elastic demand is shifted downward (smaller quantities demanded at each price), and a relatively small drop in price (from P_e to P_e') results. In panel (b), an inelastic demand is shifted downward by the same amount (the same reduction in quantity demanded at each price), the resultant price decrease (P_e to P_e'') being relatively large. In panel (c), supply is increased relative to an elastic demand, and a relatively small drop in price (P_e to P_e') results.

---

[2] The fraction of burner oils, in particular, is subject over a wide range to manipulation by refinery management. Additional cracking reduces the fraction of heavier oils and increases the fraction of lighter products, such as gasoline.

[3] Many refinery costs must be incurred regardless of the number and ratio of products in the refinery product mix. These costs are not divisible, then, among different products. Hence it is impossible, except through arbitrary allocation of joint costs, to determine the actual full costs of a joint product.

In panel (d), finally, supply is increased by the same amount relative to an inelastic demand, and the resultant price decrease (P_e to P_e'') is relatively large.

Thus the price of crude oil tends to be unstable as the result of modest shifts in supply and demand, partly because of the price-inelastic demand for crude oil. However, instability from this source cannot be said to be inconsistent with conservation or otherwise socially undesirable. It simply reflects the preferences of consumers and the alternatives available to them. Socially undesirable instability in the crude oil industry arises from the supply side.

The supply of crude oil—short run

The supply of a good depends on the cost of making units of the good available for sale. In competitive markets, it is in the interest of any seller to offer a unit for sale whenever the necessary increment to his total cost is less than the price. It follows that the quantity offered by all sellers together is pushed to the point where the incremental cost resulting from the last unit—marginal cost—for each seller is equal to the price. With a given state of technology and over the usually relevant range of output, marginal cost tends to rise with increasing quantities offered for sale. Consequently, the quantity supplied varies directly with the price.

The supply of a good can be defined as the schedule of quantities producers stand ready to sell, in a given period, at different prices.[4] An increase (or decrease) in supply means an increase (or decrease) in the quantity supplied at each price. Supply changes (the schedule shifts) with a change in technology, a change in the cost of productive resources and, in the case of resources such as petroleum, with a change in the size or quality of new discoveries.

In a manner parallel with the case of demand, the price-elasticity of supply is a measure of the response of quantity offered for sale to difference in relative price. Price-elasticity of supply depends on the rate at which marginal cost increases with increased volume of production.

Since supply is a function of marginal cost, defined as the increment to total cost necessary to add successive units to the quantity available for sale, supply during a period depends on the types of cost that are variable during that period. In relatively short periods, during which productive facilities and related expenses may be regarded as fixed, only

---

[4] To make supply comparable with demand, both marginal cost and price should be measured on a real (relative price) basis.

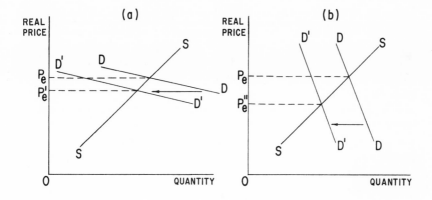

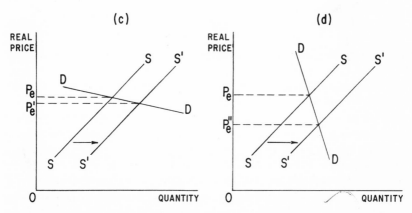

Figure 9. Illustration of effects of price-elasticity of demand.

user costs[5] and such direct operating costs as labor, fuel, and materials are variable. Short of the technical capacity of the installed facilities, therefore, only such user and operating costs limit the different quantities of product made available for sale at different prices. Supply tends to be relatively inelastic; and, if demand is sufficiently depressed, sales may willingly be made at prices below full cost per unit. In the long run, at the other extreme, all costs are variable, including the cost of replacing and adding to facilities. Consequently, it is total cost per unit that

[5] User costs represent capital consumption as the result of use (e.g., wear), as distinguished from capital consumption as the result of mere passage of time (e.g., weathering and obsolescence).

limits the quantities made available for sale at different prices in the long run. At prices above total cost, capacity is expanded; at prices below total cost, worn-out facilities are not replaced and capacity is contracted. Long-run supply thus tends to be substantially more elastic than short-run supply, and the long-run market-clearing price tends to cover full cost per unit.

In order to examine the short-run supply of crude oil in more detail, assume in operation a given number of well-developed reservoirs of specified quality, these being the result of past exploratory and developmental effort. (The costs of such effort are sunk, of course.) At first, assume each reservoir to be operated as a unit by a single operator. The decision before each operator is the rate of extraction for sale from his reservoir at any point in time.

In the interest of maximizing his income, each operator pushes the rate of extraction from his reservoir to the point at which marginal cost equals the going price. The relevant marginal cost is the sum of two components: marginal operating cost and marginal user cost. Marginal user cost, in turn, is the sum of two components: marginal user cost of timing and marginal user cost of nonrecovery.[6]

Marginal user cost of timing is the discounted present value of the net revenue sacrificed in future as the result of extracting a unit now that might have been extracted at a later time.[7] Given the total recoverable oil in a reservoir, a unit produced now is a unit that cannot be produced later; a cost of producing a unit now is, therefore, the present value of the future income consequently sacrificed. Marginal user cost of nonrecovery is the discounted present value of net revenue sacrificed in future because of additional loss of ultimate recovery resulting from a unit extracted now.[8] This type of user cost (which is not present in nonassociated gas reservoirs) stems from the fact that, at least beyond some critical point, ultimate recovery from an oil reservoir is inversely related to the rate of current extraction. It may have a value of zero at moderate rates of current extraction. From the social point of view, the two types of marginal user cost together represent the incremental sacrifice of future satisfactions necessary to acquire incremental current satisfactions from a depletable resource.

---

[6] The user cost terminology is adapted from Paul Davidson, "Public Policy Problems of the Domestic Crude Oil Industry," *American Economic Review*, vol. 53 (March 1963), pp. 91–96.

[7] Marginal user cost of timing corresponds to $\dfrac{MNR_t}{(1+r)^t}$ in the right-hand side of equation (5.1), p. 77.

[8] Marginal user cost of nonrecovery corresponds to $\dfrac{b_t\,(MNR_t)}{(1+r)^t}$ in the right-hand side of equation (5.1).

Marginal user cost obviously depends on expected future prices and extraction costs. The higher the expected future prices and the lower the expected future extraction costs, the larger is the present value of future net revenue sacrificed because of extracting a unit now. Thus, for instance, the expectation of higher future prices raises marginal user cost and reduces the quantity currently supplied, while the expectation of lower future prices lowers marginal user cost and increases the quantity currently supplied.

This latter property of marginal user cost in combination with stable expectations imparts additional elasticity to current supply. If current price rises (discounted expected future prices not rising the same amount) the quantity currently supplied is increased as operators attempt to shift some production from future to present. Similarly, if current price falls (discounted expected future prices not falling the same amount) the quantity currently supplied is decreased as operators attempt to shift some production from present to future. The additional elasticity of supply, in turn, imparts additional short-run stability to crude oil prices.

But now drop the assumption of unit operation and assume instead that each reservoir is exploited by numerous unrestrained operators. Now the possibility of drainage across property lines is introduced, and with it an additional form of marginal user cost—marginal user cost of unrestrained extraction.

Marginal user cost of unrestrained extraction is the discounted present value of the net revenue sacrificed to a neighbor as the result of extracting a unit now from one's own property.[9] The cost (which is present in nonassociated gas reservoirs) is negative, of course. A unit extracted now is a unit that cannot be lost to a neighbor; a unit not extracted now is a unit potentially lost to a neighbor. When this negative element is incorporated, marginal user cost in total is correspondingly reduced and current supply is increased: each unit of current output is marginally less costly than before to the private operator. For any given number and quality of operating reservoirs, therefore, short-run price under unrestrained operation is lower than it would be under unit operation. This effect is the counterpart of the previously discussed tendency of private operators to deplete individual reservoirs more rapidly under unrestrained operation than under unit operation.

Moreover, if the negative marginal user cost of unrestrained extraction is substantial, it so reduces the effect of marginal user cost of tim-

---

[9] Marginal user cost of unrestrained extraction corresponds to $\dfrac{-x_t\,(MNR_t)}{(1+r)^t}$ in the right-hand side of equation (5.2), p. 84.

ing and marginal user cost of nonrecovery that the elasticity those costs impart to supply is significantly reduced or eliminated. Consequently, short-run prices under unrestrained extraction tend to be more unstable than those under unit operation.

The principle underlying greater price instability under unrestrained operation is illustrated in figure 10. Panel (a) shows the effect on price of a reduction in demand when supply is moderately elastic, as when reservoirs are operated as units (price falls from P_e to P_e'). Panel (b) shows the effect on price of the same reduction in demand when supply is less elastic, as when reservoirs are operated unrestrainedly (larger fall in price, from P_e to P_e''). Panel (c) shows the effect on price of an increase in a moderately elastic supply, as when a new reservoir comes into production, all reservoirs being under unit operation (price falls from P_e to P_e'). Finally, panel (d) shows the effect on price of an increase by the same amount in a less elastic supply, as when a new reservoir comes into production, all reservoirs being under unrestrained operation (larger fall in price, from P_e to P_e'').

Thus, relative to a situation of unit operation, short-run crude oil prices under unrestrained operation tend to be both lower for any number and quality of operating reservoirs and less stable for any degree of demand or supply fluctuation. (Hence the sharp depression and later elevation of prices following major discoveries under unrestrained operation.) The significance of this conclusion derives from the fact that the (negative) user cost of unrestrained extraction is a purely private cost with no social counterpart. From the social point of view, it tends to make the short-run crude oil supply artificially large and inelastic, and therefore tends to make short-run crude oil prices artificially low and unstable. It violates conservation in the short run by causing waste in the form of current consumption at prices which do not fully reflect current social costs of production from the reservoirs in use.[10]

The supply of crude oil—intermediate run

It is useful to approach the long-run supply of crude oil in two steps, the first of which corresponds to an intermediate run.

The short run was defined as a period only long enough to permit decisions relating to production from existing developed reservoirs.

[10] In the long run, as will be explained later in this chapter, such waste takes the form of excessively restrained exploration and, therefore, an excessively low ratio of known stock to output. Through restraint on exploration, it manifests itself in excessively high long-run prices.

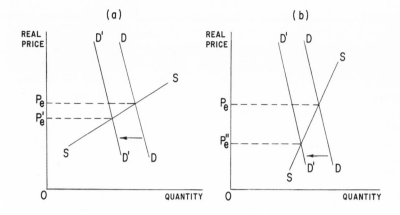

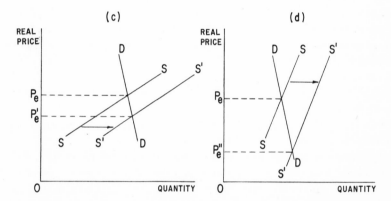

Figure 10. Illustration of effects of price-elasticity of supply.

We may define the intermediate run as a period long enough to permit development of already discovered reservoirs. Assume now a given number of undeveloped oil discoveries of specified variation in quality, these being the result of past exploratory effort. (Exploration costs are sunk, of course.) At first, assume that each reservoir is to be developed and operated as a unit by a single operator. The decision faced by the several operators affected is the rate of investment in development wells and equipment with a view to making new extractive capacity available for use.

For the purpose of maximizing the present value of his expected income, each operator pushes development investment to the point at which the present value of the expected increment to net revenue from

the last well is just equal to the incremental well cost. In forming estimates of incremental net revenue, the unit operator projects a number
of wells and a time-distribution of production which are optimal from
both his and society's point of view. The last reservoir developed—
the marginal reservoir—just promises to pay for itself under these
socially optimal conditions of development and production. Those discoveries not developed are prospectively incapable of paying for themselves under socially optimal conditions of development and production.
Consequently, the number of discoveries developed by gain-motivated
private operators is optimal from society's point of view.

Other factors being the same, the higher the expected level of oil
prices, the lower the quality of discovery it is (privately and socially)
profitable to develop.[11] The elasticity of supply in the intermediate run
therefore reflects the gradations of quality in the collection of available
discoveries. If quality rapidly decreases from best to worst discovery,
supply is relatively inelastic; if quality more gradually declines from best
to worst discovery, supply is relatively elastic.[12] In any case, no discovery is developed unless the expected price covers expected extraction
costs plus development costs, while an already developed reservoir is
operated if the price covers no more than extraction costs. Consequently, the elasticity of supply in the intermediate run is greater than
that in the short run.

Now drop the assumption of unit operation and assume instead that
each discovery is to be developed and operated by numerous unrestrained operators. As under unit operation, each operator pushes investment to the point at which the present value of the expected increment
to net revenue from the last well is just equal to incremental well cost.
For investment planning, each operator projects a number of wells and
a time-distribution of production that are optimal from his point of
view. For reasons explained earlier, both the projected number of wells
and the projected loss of ultimate recovery for any given reservoir are
larger than if unit operation were the rule. Thus each reservoir is more
costly to develop and operate. Consequently, fewer of the available discoveries—less than the optimum number from society's point of view—
are developed at any prospective price. The quantity of new capacity
supplied at each prospective price of oil is therefore smaller, and intermediate-run supply is less than optimal from society's point of view.
The result is that under unrestrained development and operation the
intermediate-run price tends to be above the socially optimum level. The

[11] See chapter 5, footnote 7.
[12] "Rapid" decline in quality means here that the number of barrels per day of
   capacity between quality gradations is small.

excessively high intermediate-run price reflects the waste of not using all the available discoveries that socially would pay for themselves.

Excessively low short-run prices and excessively high intermediate-run prices are reconciled through the number of reservoirs developed and operated. Short-run prices under unrestrained operation tend to be low *for any given number and quality of reservoirs*.[13] But where unrestrained operation is anticipated, the number of reservoirs developed is restricted until the quality of the marginal reservoir is high enough that prospective price covers its artificially high development and operating costs. Hence, the quantity supplied at each price in the intermediate run under unrestrained development is less than under a unitized procedure of development, and the average price is higher.

The supply of crude oil—long run

The "long run" may be defined as a period long enough to permit exploration and development of existing prospects. Assume now a given number of unexplored prospects of specified variation in quality, these being given by nature and hence costless.[14] At first, assume each discovered reservoir is to be developed as a unit by its finder. The decision before explorers (and prospective developers) is the rate of investment in exploration with a view to making new discoveries available for development and eventual production.

For the purpose of maximizing the present value of expected income, each explorer pushes exploratory investment to the point at which the present value of the expected increment to net revenue from the last outlay is just equal to that outlay. In forming estimates of incremental net revenue from each probable discovery, the explorer projects a plan of developing and operating it—a plan involving a number of development wells and a time-distribution of production. With unit operation the rule, he projects a number of wells and a time-distribution of production that are optimal from both his and society's point of view. The last prospect explored—the marginal prospect—just promises (in some probabilistic sense) to pay for itself under these socially optimal conditions of development and production. Those exploratory prospects not pursued (probably) are incapable of paying for themselves under socially optimal conditions of development and production. Consequently, the number of prospects explored by gain-motivated private operators is optimal from society's point of view.

[13] See pp. 84–85.
[14] "Exploration" is taken to embrace the very earliest preliminary surveys and geological mapping.

Other factors being the same, the higher the expected level of oil prices, the lower the quality of prospect it is (privately and socially) profitable to explore. The elasticity of supply in the long run therefore reflects the gradations of quality in the available collection of prospects. If quality rapidly decreases from best to worst prospect, supply is relatively inelastic; if quality more gradually declines from best to worst prospect, supply is relatively elastic. In any case, no prospect is explored unless the expected price covers expected exploration plus development plus extraction costs (total costs), while an already discovered reservoir is developed if the expected price covers no more than expected development plus extraction costs. Consequently, the elasticity of supply in the long run is greater than that in the intermediate run (which, in turn, is greater than that in the short run).

Now drop the assumption of unit operation and assume instead that each discovery is to be developed and operated by numerous unrestrained operators. As under the prospect of unit operation, each explorer pushes investment in exploration to the point at which the present value of the increment to expected net revenue from the last outlay is just equal to that outlay. But under the prospect of unrestrained operation of a probable discovery, both the projected number of wells and the projected loss of ultimate recovery are larger than they would be under the prospect of unit operation. Consequently, each reservoir promises to be more costly to develop and operate under the prospect of unrestrained operation, and each exploratory prospect is economically less attractive. Fewer prospects—less than the optimum number from society's point of view—are explored at any prospective price. The quantity of new discoveries supplied at each prospective price of oil is therefore smaller, so that the long-run supply is smaller than the optimum from society's point of view. The result is that under the prospect of unrestrained development and operation the long-run price tends to be above the socially optimum level. The excessively high long-run price reflects the waste of not exploring all of the available prospects that socially would pay for themselves.[15]

---

[15] It may be noted in passing that the economic rent paid to landowners in the form of lease bonus and royalty tends to be maximized under unit operation. Explorers competitively bidding for exclusive producing rights on tracts of land are willing to pay as much as, but not more than, the discounted present value of prospective income net of prospective exploration and development outlays. (Discounted present value embodies an acceptable prospective return on invested capital, of course.) Because none of the excessive development and production costs of unrestrained operation need be allowed for, the net present value of any given tract of land is maximized under the prospect of unitized development and operation of a discovery.

The long-run case is, thus, an extension of the intermediate-run case. Under the prospect of unitized development and operation of reservoirs, there is no discrepancy between the actual and the socially optimum long-run supply (hence no discrepancy between the actual and the socially optimum long-run price). But under the prospect of unrestrained development and operation of reservoirs, there is such a discrepancy. The discrepancy reflects the cost of the excessive number of wells and the excessive loss of ultimate recovery resulting from unrestrained development and operation.

Interaction between short-run and long-run price

The relation between short-run and long-run supply is illustrated graphically in figure 11. Panels (a) and (b) illustrate short-run and long-run supply under conditions of unrestrained and unitized operation, respectively. In each instance, short-run supply (curve SS_s) is relatively inelastic, reflecting limited capacity in the short run and producers' willingness to sell, if necessary, at a price covering no more than direct operating plus user cost per unit. But short-run supply under competitive operation is less elastic than that under unitized operation because of the (negative) user cost of unrestrained extraction, which offsets in some degree the elasticity-imparting user costs of timing and nonrecovery. In each instance, long-run supply (curve SS_1) is relatively elastic, reflecting the flexibility of capacity in the long run (given a large inventory of prospects) and the willingness of producers

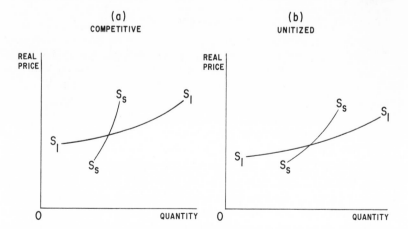

Figure 11. Relation of short-run and long-run supply.

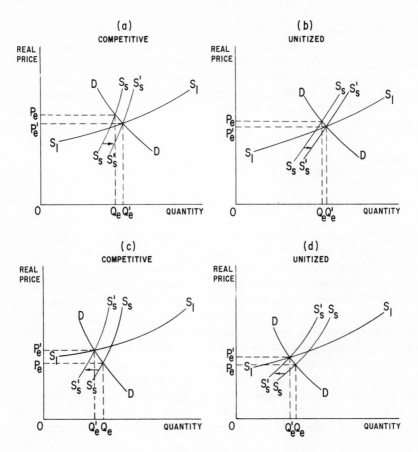

Figure 12.   Interaction of short-run and long-run price.

to maintain or expand capacity only if expected price covers full cost per unit. Long-run supply under unitized operation is greater than that under unrestrained operation (the curve lies farther to the right on the quantity scale or lower on the price scale) because of the lower cost of development and operation: more prospects are explored, developed, and operated at any given unexpected price.

Now let us introduce a demand which, for convenience, will be taken to prevail for both the short and the long run. In panels (a) and (b) of figure 12, the demand curve intersects the short-run supply curve at a point (P_e) which lies above the long-run supply curve. (The distance above the long-run supply curve is greater under competitive operation than under unitized operation because short-run supply is less elastic under competitive operation.) The short-run price determined by the intersection is above the level required merely to maintain existing capacity; it is high enough to support a larger capacity involving some higher-cost reservoirs. Consequently, if demand is expected to remain stable, exploration and development are stimulated and, as results are obtained, short-run supply is increased (the curve shifts rightward to SS_s') until it intersects the demand curve at a point (P_e') on the long-run supply curve. At this point, the short-run price provides just sufficient inducement to maintain existing capacity, and no further intended expansion of short-run supply occurs.[16]

In panels (c) and (d) of figure 12, the demand curve intersects the short-run supply curve at a point (P_e) which lies below the long-run supply curve. The short-run price determined by the intersection is below the level required to maintain existing capacity; it is only high enough to support a smaller capacity involving lower-cost reservoirs at the margin. Consequently, if demand is expected to remain stable, exploration and development are restrained and, as old reservoirs are depleted, short-run supply is decreased (the curve shifts leftward to SS_s') until it intersects the demand curve at a point (P_e') on the long-run supply curve. At this point, the short-run price provides just sufficient inducement to maintain existing capacity, and no further intended contraction of capacity occurs.

As demand grows, the demand curve tends to intersect the short-run supply curve at points lying above the long-run supply curve, thus stimulating growth of capacity. If operators could precisely predict the growth of demand and as precisely adjust capacity by the desired amount, short-run supply would grow in step with demand and short-run price would always lie on the long-run supply curve. But because neither the growth of demand nor the results of exploration and development are exactly predictable, short-run price rarely lies on the long-run supply curve. Instead, short-run price tends to fluctuate around a trend corresponding to the long-run supply curve, each deviation setting in motion the corrective adjustment in exploration and development just outlined. Because of the greater elasticity of short-run supply under unitized operation, the degree of fluctuation is less in this case than in the case of unrestrained operation. The lower costs of development and production under unitized operation make the trend line around which short-run price fluctuates lower in this case than in the case of unrestrained operation.

It is readily apparent that if the inventory of prospects were not re-

---

[16] Erratic, unplanned changes in capacity may occur, of course, as a result of variation in the success of exploration and development effort.

plenished in some way, the long-run trend in (relative) oil prices would be upward: replacement and expansion of capacity would require utilization of more and more costly reservoirs. In reality, of course, both areal extension of geological knowledge and technological progress tend to replenish (and perhaps enlarge) the inventory of prospects, the latter by reducing exploration, development, and production costs and thus bringing previously submarginal prospects into the inventory. With either extension of geological knowledge or technological progress (or both), long-run supply increases. As the long-run supply curve shifts rightward on the quantity scale (downward on the price scale) in the neighborhood of the intersection of the short-run supply and demand curves, the short-run price is left above it (perhaps farther above or not as far below), exploration and development are stimulated, and short-run price tends to fall toward a new lower trend line. So long as long-run supply is increased by extension of geological knowledge and technological progress as rapidly as demand grows, the trend in (relative) oil prices does not turn upward. A horizontal price trend produced by matched growth of long-run supply and demand is illustrated in figure 13.

But extension of geological knowledge and technological progress cannot forever offset the depletion of the total natural stock of oil deposits. At some point the inventory of prospects must shrink and further growth of short-run supply must be effected by means of utilizing reservoirs of increasing cost. At this point the trend in (relative) oil prices must turn upward. If the relative price of some substitute, such as shale oil, is constant (or perhaps declining because of technological progress in mining or retorting), it must eventually be approached by the relative price of crude oil. At a common price, at which crude oil and shale oil

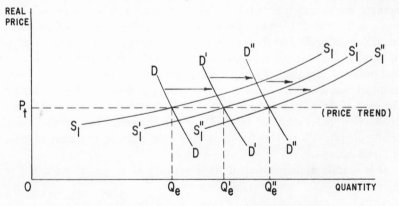

Figure 13. Matched growth of long-run supply and demand.

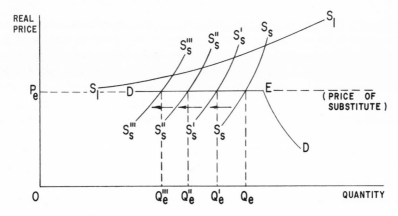

Figure 14.   Phase of decline caused by low-priced substitute.

become near-perfect substitutes for each other, the demand for crude oil becomes highly elastic and growth of crude oil production is checked. An effective ceiling on crude oil prices is imposed; and as the long-run crude oil supply curve rises above that ceiling, exploration for and development of new reservoirs declines. Short-run supply then declines continuously with depletion of oil reservoirs, and the industry's output shrinks accordingly.

The phase of decline caused by the rise of the long-run supply curve above the price of a substitute is illustrated in figure 14. The demand curve *DED* represents both short-run and long-run demand. Demand is assumed to be perfectly elastic to the left of *E*, lying at the level of the substitute's price, since no one would pay more for crude oil than for its perfect substitute. Since the demand curve lies below the long-run supply curve, all of the short-run prices determined by intersections of demand and short-run supply curves are below the long-run supply curve: all short-run prices are below the level required to induce operators to maintain capacity. With exploration and development so discouraged, short-run supply is continuously reduced (the curves shift leftward from SS_s to SS_s', etc.) and crude oil output continuously falls (from Q to Q', etc.).[17]

Under unitized operation of reservoirs, the long-run supply curve lies lower (on the price scale) than it would under unrestrained operation of reservoirs. Consequently, the trend of oil prices under unitized operation does not as soon approach the level of substitute prices. Growth continues longer and depletion of the total natural stock of oil deposits

---

[17] The diagram may also be used to illustrate the effect of long-run supply rising above the price of imports.

proceeds further before the industry begins to decline. Moreover, growth continues for the optimum period from society's point of view, since substitution of a new product does not begin until that product becomes cheaper, in terms of real social sacrifice, than crude oil. Under unrestrained operation of reservoirs, in contrast, growth ceases and substitution begins too soon because of the socially unnecessary costs imposed by an excessive number of wells and excessive loss of ultimate recovery.

Thus conservation, which coincides with the time-distribution of use of total natural deposits that would occur under universal unitized operation of reservoirs, implies the optimum resource-life of crude oil. The wastes, which are the opposite of conservation, unnecessarily shorten the resource-life of crude oil, to the harm of both producers as a whole and society at large. (This conclusion holds no less true for natural gas.)

PART III

EVALUATION OF CONSERVATION REGULATION

7. The Concept of Prohibited Waste

Conservation regulation in practice can scarcely be better than the concept on which it is based. In recognition of this, I shall begin my evaluation of conservation regulation by examining the concept of conservation that underlies the states' statutes and regulations.

The basic legal approach to conservation is to prohibit certain defined "wastes." No existing statute or regulation defines conservation as such. The underlying concept of conservation must be deduced from the various statutory definitions of waste and the administrative interpretation of such definitions. For this purpose, I shall first sample a sufficient number of statutory definitions to illustrate the range of prohibited wastes and then discuss the practical meaning given them by those responsible for day-to-day regulation.

Illustrative definitions of prohibited waste

The Interstate Oil Compact Commission (IOCC) "model statute" is a distillation of views and experience from many states, especially those which pioneered in conservation regulation. Moreover, it has been such an influential guide in the drafting of statutes adopted since 1940 that most present statutes reflect its language to a major degree.[1] The model statute therefore provides a largely representative illustration and a useful point of reference.

Following a declaration that the prevention of waste of oil and gas and the protection of correlative rights are in the public interest, the statute begins with a definition of prohibited waste.

"Waste" means and includes:
(1) physical waste, as that term is generally understood in the oil and gas industry;
(2) the inefficient, excessive, or improper use, or the unnecessary dissipation of, reservoir energy;

---

[1] The first version of the IOCC model statute was published in 1940. It has since been revised several times, most recently in 1959.

113

(3) the inefficient storing of Oil and Gas;

(4) the locating, drilling, equipping, operating, or producing of any Oil or Gas well in a manner that causes, or tends to cause, reduction in the quantity of Oil or Gas ultimately recoverable from a Pool under prudent and proper operations, or that causes or tends to cause unnecessary or excessive surface loss or destruction of Oil or Gas;

(5) the production of Oil or Gas in excess of (a) transportation or marketing facilities; (b) Reasonable Market Demand; (c) the amount reasonably required to be produced in the proper drilling, completing, or testing of the well from which it is produced; or (d) Oil or Gas otherwise usefully utilized; except Gas produced from an Oil well or Condensate well pending the time when with reasonable diligence the Gas can be sold or otherwise usefully utilized on terms and conditions that are just and reasonable; and

(6) underground or above ground waste in the production of storage of Oil, Gas, or Condensate, however caused, and whether or not defined in other subdivisions hereof.[2]

Note that the statute does not define "waste" in the abstract. Neither does the statute of any state.

The definition of waste in the Texas statute, which was written before the IOCC model was prepared, is somewhat more detailed and specific. It is noteworthy also for a couple of important qualifications, and for its unusual attention to the use of gas. Especially in view of the relative importance of Texas as a producer, these characteristics of the state's statutory definition of waste justify its quotation almost in full. With respect to oil,

[t]he term "waste" among other things shall specifically include:

(a) The operation of any oil well or wells with an inefficient gas-oil ratio, and the Commission is hereby given authority to fix and determine by order such ratio; provided that the utilization for manufacture of natural gasoline of gas produced from an oil well within the permitted gas-oil ratio shall not be included within the definition of waste.

(b) The drowning with water of any stratum or part thereof capable of producing oil or gas, or both oil and gas, in paying quantities.

[2] IOCC, Legal Committee, *A Form for an Oil and Gas Conservation Statute, 1959* (Oklahoma City: IOCC, 1959), §1. The capitalized terms (reproduced from the original) are terms also defined in the statute. "Reasonable Market Demand" is defined as "the amount of Oil reasonably needed for current consumption, use, storage, or working stocks, within and without the State, or the amount of Gas of any type reasonably needed for current consumption, use, or storage, within and without the State."

(c) Underground waste or loss however caused and whether or not defined in other subdivisions hereof.
(d) Permitting any natural gas well to burn wastefully.
(e) The creation of unnecessary fire hazards.
(f) Physical waste or loss incident to, or resulting from, so drilling, equipping, locating, spacing or operating a well or wells as to reduce or tend to reduce the total ultimate recovery of crude oil or natural gas from any pool.
(g) Waste or loss incident to, or resulting from, the unnecessary, inefficient, excessive or improper use of the reservoir energy, including the gas energy or water drive, in any well or pool; *however, it is not the intent of the Act to require repressuring of an oil pool or that the separately owned properties in any pool be unitized under one management, control or ownership.*
(h) Surface waste or surface loss, including the storage either permanent or temporary of crude petroleum oil, or the placing of any product thereof, in open pits or earthen storage, and all other forms of surface waste or surface loss, including unnecessary or excessive surface losses, or destruction without beneficial use, either of crude petroleum oil or of natural gas.
(i) The escape into the open air, from a well producing both oil and gas, of natural gas in excess of the amount which is necessary in the efficient drilling and operation of the well.
(j) The production of crude petroleum oil in excess of transportation or market facilities or reasonable market demand. The Commission may determine when such excess production exists or is imminent and ascertain the reasonable market demand.

Nothing in this Section shall be construed to authorize limitation of production of marginal wells, as such marginal wells are defined by Statute, below the amount fixed by Statute for such wells.[3]

Elsewhere in the statute,[4] a "marginal well" is defined as an oil well capable, using artificial lift, of producing daily no more than 10 barrels from a depth of 2,000 feet or less, 20 barrels from a depth of 2,001 to 4,000 feet, 25 barrels from a depth of 4,001 to 6,000 feet, 30 barrels from a depth of 6,001 to 8,000 feet, or 35 barrels from a depth of 8,001 feet or more. The statute continues:

To artificially curtail the production of any "Marginal Well" below the marginal limit as set out above prior to its ultimate plugging and abandon-

[3] Vernon's Rev. Civ. Stat. of Texas (1962) title 102, art. 6014. Italics added.
[4] Ibid., art. 6049b, §1.

ment is hereby declared to be waste, and no rule or order of the Railroad Commission of Texas, or other constituted legal authority, shall be entered requiring restriction of the production of any "Marginal Well" as herein defined.[5]

In the article of the Texas statute defining waste of gas, paragraphs (a) through (g) are essentially the same as paragraphs (a) through (f) and (i) in the article defining waste of oil. The definition of waste with respect to gas continues as follows.

(h) The production of natural gas in excess of transportation or market facilities, or reasonable market demand for the type of gas produced.

(i) The use of natural gas for the manufacture of carbon black without first having extracted the natural gasoline content from such gas, except where it is utilized in a plant producing an average recovery of not less than five (5) pounds of carbon black to each one thousand (1,000) cubic feet of gas it shall not be necessary to first extract the natural gasoline content from such gas.

(j) The use of sweet gas produced from a gas well for the manufacture of carbon black unless it is utilized in a plant producing an average recovery of not less than five (5) pounds of carbon black to each one thousand (1,000) cubic feet and unless such sweet gas is produced from a well located in a common reservoir producing both sweet and sour gas.[6]

(k) Permitting any natural gas produced from a gas well to escape into the air before or after such gas has been processed for its gasoline content.

(l) The production of natural gas from a well producing oil from a stratum other than that in which the oil is found, unless such gas is produced in a separate string of casing from that in which the oil is produced.

(m) The production of more than one hundred thousand (100,000) cubic feet of gas to each barrel of crude petroleum oil unless such gas is put to one or more of the uses authorized for the type of such gas so produced under allocations made by the Commission.[7]

In comparison with that in the Texas statute, the definition of waste in the Kansas statute is a model of brevity. It is noteworthy also for its inclusion of "economic waste."[8] Thus, with respect to oil, it states

[5] Ibid., art. 6049b. §2.

[6] Sour gas is natural gas containing more than 1½ grains of hydrogen sulphide or 30 grains of sulphur per hundred cubic feet. (Ibid., art. 6008, §2.)

[7] Ibid., art. 6008, §3.

[8] Oklahoma is the only other state to include "economic waste" in its definition of prohibited waste. Except with respect to gas in Kansas, the statute of neither state defines economic waste.

[t]hat the term "waste" as used herein, in addition to its ordinary meaning, shall include economic waste, underground waste, surface waste, waste of reservoir energy, and the production of crude oil or petroleum in excess of transportation or marketing facilities or reasonable market demands.[9]

With respect to gas, it states

[t]hat the term "waste" as herein used, in addition to its ordinary meaning, shall include economic waste, underground waste and surface waste. Economic waste as used in this act shall mean the use of natural gas in any manner or process except for efficient light, fuel, carbon black manufacturing and repressuring, or for chemical or other processes by which such gas is efficiently converted into a solid or a liquid substance.[10]

Although it is somewhat lengthy, the definition of waste in the New Mexico statute is worth quoting in full. It is unusual for a couple of explanatory sentences, as well as for its reference to potash deposits.

As used in this act, the term "waste," in addition to its ordinary meaning, shall include:

(a) "Underground waste" as those words are generally understood in the oil and gas business, and in any event to embrace the inefficient, excessive, or improper use or dissipation of the reservoir energy, including gas energy and water drive, of any pool, and the locating, spacing, drilling, equipping, operating, or producing of any well or wells in a manner, to reduce or tend to reduce the total quantity of crude petroleum oil or natural gas ultimately recovered from any pool, and the use of inefficient underground storage of natural gas.

(b) "Surface waste" as those words are generally understood in the oil and gas business, and in any event to embrace the unnecessary or excessive surface loss or destruction without beneficial use, however caused, of natural gas of any type or in any form or crude petroleum oil, or any product thereof, but including the loss or destruction, without beneficial use, resulting from evaporation, seepage, leakage or fire, especially such loss or destruction incidental to or resulting from the manner of spacing, equipping, operating, or producing a well or wells, or incident to or resulting from the use of inefficient storage or from the production of crude petroleum oil or natural gas in excess of the reasonable market demand.

(c) The production of crude petroleum oil in this state in excess of the reasonable market demand for such crude petroleum oil. *Such excess production causes or results in waste which is prohibited by this act.*

[9] Kan. Stat. Ann. (1964) §55-602.
[10] Ibid., §55-702.

[A definition of "reasonable market demand" similar to that in the IOCC model statute follows.]

(d) The non-ratable purchase or taking of crude petroleum oil in the state. *Such non-ratable taking and purchasing causes or results in waste, as defined in the sub-sections (a), (b), and (c) of this section and causes waste by violating Section 12 (a) of this act.*[11]

(e) The production in this state of natural gas from any gas well or wells, or from any gas pool, in excess of the reasonable market demand from such source of natural gas of the type produced or in excess of the capacity of gas transportation facilities for such type of natural gas. [A definition of "reasonable market demand" similar to that in the IOCC model statute follows.]

(f) Drilling or producing operations for oil or gas within any area containing commercial deposits of potash where such operations would have the effect unduly to reduce the total quantity of such commercial deposits of potash which may reasonably be recovered in commercial quantities or where such operations would interfere unduly with the orderly commercial development of such potash deposits.[12]

The statutory definition of waste in Illinois includes damage not only to mineral resources other than oil and gas, but to nonmineral resources as well. Paragraphs (4) and (7) define waste as

(4) the unreasonable damage to underground fresh or mineral water supply, workable coal seams, or other mineral deposits in the operations for the discovery, development, production, or handling of oil and gas;

(7) permitting unnecessary damage to or destruction of the surface, soil, animal, fish or aquatic life or property from oil or gas operations.[13]

The Michigan definition, otherwise quite similar to that in the IOCC model statute, also includes damage to resources other than oil and gas; but it goes further and embraces waste in the form of unnecessary wells. Under the category "underground waste," the definition includes

(2) unreasonable damage to underground fresh or mineral waters, natural brines, or other mineral deposits from the operations for the discovery, development, and production and handling of oil and casinghead gas.[14]

Under the category "surface waste," the definition includes

[11] Section 12 of the act provides for the allocation, on a reasonable basis, of the total state crude oil allowable among fields of the state and the granting of allowables to pools with low-capacity wells in such size as to prevent general premature abandonment of the wells in the affected fields.

[12] N.M. Stat. Ann. (1953) §65-3-3.

[13] Smith-Hurd, Ill. Ann. Stat. (1935) 1970 Supp., ch. 104, §62.

[14] Mich. Stat. Ann. (1967) §13.139(2).

(2) the unnecessary damage to or destruction of the surface, soils, animal, fish or aquatic life or property from or by oil and gas operations; and (3) the drilling of unnecessary wells.[15]

Pennsylvania provides another significant instance of statutory definition of waste to include the drilling of an excessive number of wells. The definition embraces "physical waste" and, in addition,

(ii) The drilling of more wells than are reasonably required to recover, efficiently and economically, the maximum amount of oil and gas from a pool.[16]

The definition of waste in the Colorado statute differs from that in the IOCC model statute in two important respects: it excludes any reference to production in excess of market demand, but it includes the "abuse" of correlative rights. With respect to correlative rights, paragraphs (12.c) and (13) of the definition read:

(12.c) abuse of the correlative rights of any owner in a pool due to non-uniform, disproportionate, unratable, or excessive withdrawals of oil or gas therefrom, causing reasonably avoidable drainage between tracts of land or resulting in one or more producers or owners in such pool producing more than his just and equitable share of the oil and gas from such pool.

(13) The term "correlative rights" shall mean that each owner and producer in a common pool or source of supply of oil and gas shall have an equal opportunity to obtain and produce his just and equitable share of the oil and gas underlying such pool or source of supply.[17]

Mississippi's statutory definition of waste includes language with respect to correlative rights almost identical to that in Colorado's definition. In addition, like that of Texas, Mississippi's definition includes— with significant qualification—the use of gas to manufacture carbon black. Thus, the final paragraph of the definition reads:

(10) The use of gas from gas wells, except sour gas, for the manufacture of carbon black, except and unless the board shall find that there are no adequate pipe line connections to otherwise market the gas.[18]

To summarize, each of the following appears in at least one instance in the states' various definitions of waste:

[15] Ibid.
[16] Purdon's Pa. Stat. Ann. (1964) tit. 58, ch. 7, §402.
[17] Colo. Rev. Stat. (1963) §100-6-3.
[18] Miss. Code Ann. (1942) 1952 Recomp., tit. 23, §6132-08.

A. Physical waste, as the term is generally understood in the oil and gas industry.
B. Underground waste of oil or gas.
    1. Inefficient use or unnecessary dissipation of reservoir energy.
    2. Operations tending to cause loss of ultimate recovery of oil or gas.
    3. Drowning of a stratum capable of producing oil or gas commercially.
    4. Inefficient underground storage of gas.
C. Surface waste of oil or gas.
    1. Inefficient surface storage of oil.
    2. Unnecessary venting or flaring of natural gas.
    3. Creation of unnecessary fire hazards.
D. Waste incident to production in excess of transportation or market facilities, or of market demand.
E. Waste in the use of gas (e.g., carbon black manufacture).
F. Waste of resources other than oil or gas.
    1. Damage from petroleum operations to fresh water, soil, wildlife, and other mineral deposits.
    2. Drilling of unnecessary wells.
G. Economic waste.
H. Violation or abuse of correlative rights.
I. Causing, by production restriction, the "premature" abandonment of "marginal" wells.

The categories "physical waste," "underground waste," and "surface waste," which together constitute the heart of the definition in the IOCC model statute, appear in some form in the statutory definitions of all the states with comprehensive conservation laws. "Waste incident to production in excess of transportation or market facilities, or of market demand," also in the IOCC model statute, appears in a dozen state definitions, including, most significantly, those of Texas, Louisiana, New Mexico, Oklahoma, and Kansas. The remaining categories appear only in isolated instances in the various state definitions of waste.

Practical meaning of prohibited wastes[19]

The concept of conservation underlying the states' statutes and regulations is revealed in part by administrators' practical interpretation of

---

[19] This section is based on analysis of the general rules and regulations of the various state commissions and personal interviews with regulatory officials of the principal producing states.

prohibited wastes. Their interpretation, in turn, is revealed in part by the preventive measures employed. Without implying perfect uniformity of interpretation among the states employing similar definitions of waste, we offer the following generalizations as reasonably representative.

Physical waste, as generally understood in the industry

"Physical waste" is meant to be a blanket term covering the forms of waste itemized under "underground waste" and "surface waste," plus any other losses of the *substances* oil and gas. Its significance as a separate category of waste reflects two legislative intents: (a) to prohibit (or at least to limit) all losses of the substances oil and gas, regardless of the form such losses might take, and (b) emphatically to distinguish the wastes prohibited from "economic waste," which is generally associated with "unduly" depressed prices and/or "inferior" uses. The latter intent, therefore—except in Oklahoma and Kansas, where economic waste is prohibited—reflects a desire to avoid any implication of purpose to stabilize or fix prices through regulation. The emphasis in the IOCC model statute on prevention of physical waste—an emphasis repeated in most of the state statutes—stems from the limited authorized objectives of the Interstate Compact to Conserve Oil and Gas. As noted in chapter 3, under "Brief Historical Background," article II of the compact states that the authorized purpose is "to conserve oil and gas by the prevention of physical waste thereof from any cause," while article V denies any intent "to authorize the states joining herein to limit the production of oil and gas for the purpose of stabilizing or fixing the price thereof. . . ."

The effort to distinguish "physical waste" from "economic waste" does not mean that economic considerations may not enter the implementation of regulations designed to prevent physical losses of oil and gas. Such considerations often do enter the regulatory process, if only out of legal necessity. All regulations must satisfy the rule of reasonableness under the law, and economic feasibility—at least, the avoidance of confiscation—is a major criterion of reasonableness.[20]

Underground waste of oil and gas

Inefficient use or unnecessary dissipation of reservoir energy. The natural pressure present in a reservoir, which, together with gravita-

---

[20] IOCC, Governors' Special Study Committee, *A Study of Conservation of Oil and Gas in the United States, 1964* (Oklahoma City: IOCC, 1965), p. 188.

tional force, is the primary means of expelling petroleum from saturated rock, is commonly referred to as the "reservoir energy." The inefficient use or dissipation of such energy reduces the amount of petroleum recoverable by primary methods. Full potential recovery by secondary methods may then be technically infeasible or prohibitively—at least, unnecessarily—expensive. Since regulators ordinarily use the term "efficient" in an engineering rather than in an economic sense, prevention of inefficient use or dissipation of reservoir energy is designed to assure maximum recovery of petroleum by primary means.

The inefficient use of reservoir energy includes both failure to utilize the most productive available natural drive and withdrawal of petroleum at such a rate that water or gas channels through and bypasses otherwise recoverable oil. The chief means of preventing such inefficient use is limitation of the production rate to the MER corresponding to the most productive natural drive. Dissipation of reservoir energy may result from leakage through improperly cased wells, venting of gas wells, or excessive production of water or gas with oil. It can be prevented by regulation of casing methods, prohibition of gas well venting, and limitation of produced water-oil and gas-oil ratios. Control of well density helps prevent both inefficient use and dissipation of reservoir energy.

Operations tending to cause loss of ultimate recovery. Operations tending to cause loss of ultimate recovery coincide with practices resulting in inefficient use or dissipation of reservoir energy, and they are prevented in the same ways. Only two additional observations need be made. First, despite the economic consideration implied in the definition of the MER referred to in figure 2 and associated text, regulators almost universally treat the MER as a purely engineering concept: the rate of production from a reservoir which if exceeded would result in (technically) avoidable loss of ultimate recovery. Second, the prevention of operations tending to cause loss of ultimate recovery does not in practice extend to positive requirement that all feasible means be employed to maximize recovery. For example, regulators encourage but do not require pressure maintenance, repressuring, or secondary recovery as means of maximizing recovery.[21] Nor, except with respect to retrograde condensate reservoirs in Louisiana and Alabama, may regulators require unitization to facilitate maximum recovery without the prior consent of

[21] In significant exception to this generalization, the Texas Railroad Commission has issued some orders requiring pressure maintenance and thus indirectly compelling unitization. B. M. Murphy, *Conservation of Oil and Gas: A Legal History, 1948* (Chicago: American Bar Association, 1949), p. 472; and Robert E. Sullivan, *Conservation of Oil and Gas: A Legal History, 1958* (Chicago: American Bar Association, 1960), p. 230.

a large majority of the affected property interests. The main force of regulation is directed toward maximum recovery by natural, primary means.

Drowning of a stratum capable of producing oil or gas commercially. The uncontrolled encroachment of water on an oil or gas deposit may cause such migration, fragmentation, or dispersal of the deposit as to render it unproducible, or producible only at prohibitive or unnecessary expense. Prevention of such encroachment, which is accomplished by means of casing, production, and injection regulations, thus tends to maximize the number and quality of active or discoverable commercial deposits.

Inefficient underground storage of gas. Underground storage of gas is inefficient if the storage reservoir leaks through improperly cased or plugged wells or permits gas to escape in consequence of underground migration. Prevention thus requires supervision of well casing and plugging, location of injection and recovery wells, total storage volume, and reservoir pressure. The need for regulation is minimized by the fact that the owner of the stored gas, typically a single transmission or distributing company, normally has adequate incentive and control to avoid loss of his property.

Surface waste of oil or gas

Inefficient surface storage of oil. The lighter fractions of crude oil readily evaporate or burn. If oil is stored in leaky tanks or open pits, therefore, it is subject to substantial physical loss. The need for regulation arises out of the incentive an individual producer has to drain his neighbor's property, or to avoid drainage of his own, by producing as rapidly as possible and storing any produced oil not readily marketable. Under competitive exploitation of a reservoir, partial loss through evaporation and the risk of fire may be less costly to the individual producer than restrained production. Prevention of inefficient surface storage is accomplished by means of direct prohibition of unsatisfactory containers (e.g., earthen pits) or restriction of production from a reservoir and pro rata allocation of total allowed production among individual producers.

Unnecessary venting or flaring of natural gas. When a market or processing and transportation facilities are not readily available, it is often less expensive for an individual producer to vent or flare natural gas than to close his well(s) or return produced gas to its native formation. This is true particularly in the case of casinghead gas, since a shutdown of production would involve loss of current oil revenues and, if competitive operators did not also cease production, adverse drainage as well. It may be true also in the case either of nonassociated gas discovered in the search for oil or of residue gas at liquids plants in areas remote from gas pipeline facilities and markets. In any case, of course, gas vented or flared represents a complete physical loss.[22]

Such physical loss is prevented by means of direct prohibition—sometimes so qualified, however, as to be almost meaningless. The venting or flaring of gas from gas or condensate wells is generally prohibited without qualification. The operator has nothing to lose from compliance except the expense of plugging or otherwise closing the affected wells. But the venting or flaring of casinghead or residue gas is generally prohibited only if it is "unnecessary" or "unreasonable." Regulators generally view it as necessary or reasonable if the operator has no economically feasible alternative. In some states—e.g., Illinois and Indiana —flaring of casinghead or residue gas is prohibited only if there is no market for the gas at the well or liquids plant. The usefulness of prohibition with such broad qualification is unclear, since it is difficult to imagine why an operator would willingly destroy gas that is marketable at the point of production. In most states, no specific exception to the general prohibition is made; actual prohibition or exception in individual reservoirs is based on the immediate circumstances. Prohibition usually is based on the feasibility of some project to be undertaken jointly by the affected operators—construction of a liquids plant or transmission line, for instance. Often it is based on the feasibility of reinjecting casinghead or residue gas for pressure maintenance under a unitized plan of reservoir operation. Where joint action is required, an aggressive commission may provide initiative and moral encouragement for the required negotiations; and, if necessary, it may in effect force some recalcitrant operators to join a cooperative project or reservoir unit under reasonable terms by flatly prohibiting gas flaring in the affected reservoir and, as the means of enforcement, suspending oil production until provision is made for some beneficial use of casinghead gas.[23]

Creation of unnecessary fire hazards. Fire is an obvious cause of

---

[22] It may also create an air pollution or fire hazard.

[23] Compulsion of joint action appears to have been the intent and effect of a number of no-flare orders issued by the Texas Railroad Commission beginning in 1947. (Sullivan, *Conservation of Oil and Gas*, pp. 230–35.) Although the courts upheld the commission orders as valid waste prevention measures (*Railroad Commission* v. *Sterling Oil and Refining Company*, 147 Tex. 547, 218 S.W.2d 415, 1949), indirect compulsion of joint action per se is of questionable legality. The Colorado Supreme Court has held that a no-flare order is an illegitimate means of compelling unitization, lacking specific statutory grant of authority to the Conservation Commission. (*Union Pacific Railroad Company* v. *Oil and Gas Conservation Commission*, 131 Colo. 528, 284 P.2d 242, 1955.)

large physical loss of oil and gas, particularly if gas becomes ignited in
a flowing well. Fire hazards in petroleum operations are created by uncontrolled flow of oil and gas from wells; leakage from well fittings,
pipelines, and storage tanks; open pit storage of oil; gas flaring; the
burning of wastes; and the operation of machinery producing sparks or
flames near wells and storage facilities. Especially during completion of
new wells, some fire hazards are inescapable. Unnecessary hazards are
prevented by means of various technical requirements (e.g., use of
blow-out preventers in well drilling), prohibitions (e.g., open pit storage of oil), and specification of minimum distances (e.g., between a
well and a source of flame). Control of well density also helps minimize
fire hazards. The various preventive regulations typically are absolute
and not conditioned on economic feasibility to the affected operators.

Waste incident to production in excess of transportation or market facilities, or of market demand

As explained earlier, individual operators in a competitively operated
reservoir often have an incentive to produce oil or gas so rapidly that
the total produced cannot immediately be transported or marketed. The
situation has three effects that possibly lead to physical loss of some
sort: (a) it invites discriminatory purchases by buyer-producers, (b) it
permits disparate rates of withdrawal by various buyers in different sectors of the reservoir, and (c) it tends to depress prices. In oil reservoirs,
the first two effects may result in a pattern of withdrawal that utilizes the
reservoir drive inefficiently and therefore causes loss of ultimate recovery. Moreover, those operators who experience adverse drainage are
induced to produce for makeshift storage, where fire or evaporation may
cause physical loss. The depression of prices may cause the premature
abandonment of some marginal oil or gas wells which it would be economically infeasible to reclaim at a later date, and consequently the loss
of some otherwise recoverable reserves. In the interpretation of regulatory officials, all such losses constitute (physical) waste incident to production in excess of (the capacity of) transportation or market facilities,
or of market demand.

The practical meaning of "(the capacity of) transportation or market facilities" is clear enough. The practical meaning of "market demand," in contrast, requires some explanation. Regulators interpret
market demand as the quantity buyers stand ready to take during a
period, not as a schedule of different quantities they would stand ready
to take at different prices. Those regulators familiar with the concept of
demand as a schedule functionally related to price take the view that
demand is so inelastic with respect to price that a single quantity ade-

quately describes the schedule over the relevant price range. In this view, regulators may abstract from price in estimating "market demand."

The primary means of preventing the type of waste under discussion is the restriction of production (from a district or an entire state) to the smaller of (a) the capacity of transportation or market facilities or (b) market demand as estimated for the relevant area. Supplementary regulatory devices include control of well density and prohibition of discrimination, unratable purchases, and makeshift surface storage. In ways to be detailed later, the implementation of production restriction is heavily affected by economic considerations.

Waste in the use of gas

Occasionally state conservation legislation reflects the view that gas is wasted, at least in part, if it is not used in ways that fully exploit its chemical properties. In one version, the view seems to arise from a notion of intrinsic value apart from value determined in the marketplace.[24] Waste so conceived is prevented by specifying acceptable uses and prohibiting (or limiting) uses deemed unacceptable or inferior. As indicated by earlier quoted definitions of waste, the use of gas to manufacture carbon black, a process which allows the heat of combustion to be lost from beneficial use, is widely regarded as an inferior use to be permitted only conditionally.

Waste of resources other than oil and gas

Damage from petroleum operations to fresh water, soil, wildlife, and other mineral deposits. In general, petroleum conservation statutes define waste with respect to oil and gas only. The regulatory commissions ordinarily are charged with protecting the environment from damage by petroleum operations, but typically in statutory provisions separate from the definition and prohibition of waste. In isolated instances, however, damage to the environment is included in the definition of waste, implying that the conservation of oil and gas is conditional on, or no more than equal partner with, conservation of other natural resources.

Petroleum operations may damage the environment in several ways. They may cause pollution of underground fresh water, surface fresh water, and soil; they may cause grass and forest fires; they may weaken existing mine structures and expose mines to flooding and gas infiltra-

---

[24] See the definition of economic waste with respect to gas in Kansas quoted on pp. 116–17.

tion; and they may interfere with the new development or extension of mines. Regulators attempt to prevent "unreasonable" damage of such kinds by means of controls over well-casing methods, well spacing, waste disposal, creation of fire hazards, and drilling in areas known to be underlain with mineral deposits other than oil and gas. Economic considerations—e.g., the assessment of potential damage in relation to the cost of avoidance—necessarily enter the determination of what is "unreasonable."

Drilling of unnecessary wells. The drilling of unnecessary wells, identified as prohibited waste in a few isolated instances, arises from competitive operators' now-familiar incentive to avoid adverse drainage and, if possible, to induce beneficial drainage across property lines. From the point of view of all operators taken together (and of society), such drilling represents unnecessary expenditure of labor and capital to secure given amounts of oil and gas. It may be interpreted as leading to waste of oil and gas by making development and exploration artificially expensive and thereby rendering some discoveries and prospects artificially submarginal.

Regulators typically define an "unnecessary well" as one not required for (technically) efficient drainage of a reservoir. They seek to prevent the drilling of such wells primarily by means of control over well spacing. To the extent that they follow an announced policy of restricting the production rate from any reservoir to the MER or less, they discourage application for a spacing pattern in a new reservoir that would raise aggregate capacity above the probable MER.

Economic waste

Despite its apparent breadth, the term "economic waste" is usually employed narrowly to mean the sale of oil or gas at a price below its full cost or actual value and/or the use of oil or gas in ways which fail fully to exploit its intrinsic value.[25] In the two states which prohibit economic waste, Oklahoma and Kansas, the concept is of little practical use. There is, of course, no way to determine "actual" or "intrinsic" value as distinct from market value; no way to determine full cost without reference to some arbitrary group of producers, state of technology, and rate of output. To the extent that economic waste as conceived can have any practical meaning, it is prevented by restricting production to

[25] Occasionally the term "economic waste" is used in the industry to mean the incurring of unnecessary expense, as for the drilling of unnecessary wells. However, this latter meaning does not appear to have been the legislative intent where economic waste is included in the statutory definition of prohibited waste.

market demand and prohibiting uses of natural gas other than those specified as approved.

Violation or abuse of correlative rights

For reasons explained earlier, a production pattern in an oil reservoir that permits competitive drainage across the property lines may reduce the efficiency of recovery and induce makeshift surface storage, both resulting in physical loss of oil. Such loss is prevented by attempting to assure to each competitive producer an equal opportunity to recover the oil beneath his land—by prohibiting discrimination and unratable purchases, and by restricting production in a reservoir to the MER or less and allocating total allowed production equitably among producers.

Causing, by production restriction, the "premature" abandonment of "marginal" wells

Since regulatory production restriction reduces the current income and present value of the affected wells, it is capable of causing early abandonment. The reserves underlying abandoned wells may be lost forever, particularly if whole reservoirs are involved, because reopening plugged wells and preparing them for production again may be prohibitively expensive. To avoid causing loss of reserves in this way, regulators typically refrain from restricting production per well below some minimum figure, or schedule of figures related to depth, taken to be essential for economic survival.

An evaluation of the concept of prohibited waste

As practiced by the regulating states, petroleum conservation means the prevention of specified wastes in oil and gas production. In nearly all cases, the specified wastes represent physical losses of oil and gas that tend to occur under competitive exploitation of petroleum deposits by individual operators using primary means of recovery. The losses considered preventable by *regulation* (as distinguished from inducement or voluntary cooperation) ordinarily do not include those which result from failure to use supplementary or secondary means of recovery. Otherwise, the typical list of prohibited wastes is essentially exhaustive of the ways in which recoverable oil and gas may be lost or destroyed without beneficial use in the processes of drilling, extraction, and storage; and, in general, the prohibitions imposed are conditioned by economic considerations only to the extent necessary to avoid "unreasonable" or confiscatory deprivation of property or income. Thus, subject to the constraints imposed by economic feasibility under individual operation, the conservation aim of regulation in practice is to maximize the physical recovery and beneficial use of discovered oil and gas.

Particularly in comparison with none at all, the effective concept of conservation in the regulating states is a constructive and useful one. Most of the physical losses associated with unregulated petroleum operations undoubtedly represent wastes from society's point of view; their prevention contributes to the general welfare. Moreover, the definition of waste in physical terms facilitates objective detection and measurement of both the occurrences to be prevented and the results of regulatory action, so that the definition facilitates administration. Nonetheless, the concept of conservation as the prevention of specified physical losses is, for several reasons, seriously inadequate.

At the root of the inadequacy is the lack of an abstract definition of waste in any of the statutes, including the IOCC model statute. The statutory definitions of waste may fairly be characterized as mixed lists of (a) general classifications of waste and (b) categories of occurrences constituting waste if "unnecessary," "excessive," "unreasonable," or even "wasteful." For example, waste in Kansas includes such broad classifications as "underground waste," "surface waste," and "waste of reservoir energy" (which are not further defined), while waste in Texas includes such indefinite occurrences as "unnecessary or excessive surface losses" and "permitting any natural gas well to burn wastefully." Nowhere are we told what waste itself is; nowhere are we given any guidance as to what might be "unnecessary" or "excessive." A proper abstract definition of waste would enlighten us in both respects.

An abstract definition of any term imparts generality by conveying the essential implications of the term as ordinarily used. Waste implies a preventable loss which reduces human welfare. Surely that is the central implication of waste which is to be prohibited by a public body in the name of conservation. The implication is clearly conveyed in such a definition as: *Waste is a preventable loss the value of which exceeds the cost of avoidance.* A preventable loss reduces human welfare and therefore is waste if, and only if, it deprives humans of more satisfactions than they would have to sacrifice to avoid it. Being perfectly general and implying a decision rule, an abstract waste definition of the sort suggested would simultaneously give specific content to such broad classifications as "underground waste" and indicate a meaningful way in which to determine whether a questionable occurrence is "unnecessary," "excessive," or "wasteful."

A proper abstract definition of waste would make it clear that mere physical loss is no indication of waste, that maximizing physical recovery and beneficial use is not an adequate conservation objective. A loss has a value representing the human satisfactions the thing lost might have given. Its prevention has a cost representing the necessary sacrifice of human satisfactions. If the value that would be lost is greater than the cost of prevention, then human welfare is increased by prevention. But if the value that would be lost is less than the cost of prevention, then human welfare is reduced by prevention. The valid conservation objective is not to save *things* for use but to increase the *welfare* of those using the things, not to maximize physical recovery and beneficial use but to maximize the net value to society of the resource in question.

This last observation points to another serious weakness of the concept of prohibited waste that defines conservation as practiced. The concept does not incorporate the waste of value (satisfactions) that may arise from the manner of distributing use over time. Postponement of use involves a sacrifice of current satisfactions and a prospective gain of future satisfactions. If in a given postponement the sacrifice of current satisfactions is less than the discounted prospective gain of future satisfactions, then the postponement adds to human welfare. If, instead, the current sacrifice is greater than the discounted future gain, then the postponement subtracts from human welfare. The net addition to or subtraction from satisfactions resulting from redistribution of use over time has the same significance for human welfare as the net addition to or subtraction from satisfactions resulting from physical gain or loss of the substance in use. Redistribution of use over time and change in physical recovery are twin means, sometimes competitive and sometimes complementary, of achieving a single objective—maximizing the net value to society of the resource in question. Neglect of the time-distribution of use leads to loss of net satisfactions and reduction of human welfare in any of three ways: (a) pursuit of additional physical recovery to be realized in future, the current cost being greater than the discounted gain in value; (b) approval of current use involving no present or future physical loss, the current value being less than the discounted future value; and (c) disapproval of a current use (e.g., carbon black manufacture), the discounted future value of the best alternative use being less than the value of the disapproved use.

Neglect of the time-distribution of use is linked to another weakness of the concept of prohibited waste. Except in the rare states that define waste to include excessive well drilling and damage to other resources, the concept pertains only to the use of the known portion of the total natural stock of petroleum resources. It contains no reference to the manner of exploiting the unknown portion. It reveals no recognition that the prospective conditions under which new discoveries may be developed and produced in part determine (a) the rate at which resources are transferred from the unknown to the known stock, (b) the lowest quality of usable deposits and, therefore, (c) the net value of satisfactions to be derived from the total natural stock of petroleum resources before oil and gas are displaced by other materials. The manner of using supramarginal known deposits may be dictated by regulators; but discovery and development are voluntary investment activities undertaken only when prospective additions to income, discounted at an acceptable rate of return, have a present value equal to or in excess of the necessary current outlays. If that present value is depressed by pursuit of maximum physical recovery to the neglect of time-distribution of use, or if current outlays are inflated by excessive drilling, then the net benefits to be derived from the total natural stock over time are reduced. Surely reduction of net benefits, from whatever source, is the waste that conservation regulation should prevent.

In further reference to benefit maximization, a final criticism of the prevailing concept of prohibited waste is that it lacks an explicit social frame of reference. The purpose of conservation presumably is to benefit society at large. If no other consideration intervenes, it follows that the costs and benefits pertinent to determining what specific regulations are desirable, feasible, or reasonable are those of society at large. But the various definitions of waste, in their total statutory contexts, are based on the assumption that oil and gas will be produced competitively by individual operators unless at least a large majority in a given reservoir voluntarily associate themselves. Given this premise, feasibility and reasonableness usually must be based, as a practical matter, on the costs and benefits of individual competitive operators. Since these often differ from society's costs and benefits, acceptable regulations often must differ from those which would maximize net benefits to society (or to associations of operators in common reservoirs). Thus, for example, despite all its emphasis on maximizing physical recovery, in practice regulation does not generally require the use of supplementary or secondary means of recovery, which normally require cooperative action by operators in a common reservoir, regardless of whether such means would yield net benefits to society and to the affected operators as a whole. Nor does it uniformly and unqualifiedly prohibit the flaring of gas that, under a cooperative plan, might with profit to society and cooperating producers be returned to a common reservoir for pressure maintenance. The concept of conservation in practice is limited by the premise of exploitation by individual competitive operators who may be forcibly restrained, but not forcibly organized, by regulation.

8. Control of External Damages

Although the conservation statutes of only a few states define waste to include damage to resources other than oil and gas, all of the regulating states undertake incidentally to avert or to limit such damage. All of them vest at least partial responsibility for protecting other resources in petroleum conservation commissions. The objective and the administrative approach stand on their own merits, of course. Society has the same interest in conserving its other mineral, water, soil, wildlife, human, and capital resources as it has in conserving oil and gas; and established petroleum conservation commissions can most directly and cheaply control those activities of the petroleum industry conducive to external damages. For our purposes, however, the control of external damages through petroleum conservation commissions has additional significance. It tends to assure that oil and gas production bears its full social costs, and thus tends to satisfy one of the conditions of optimizing, from society's point of view, the rate of exploiting the total natural stock of petroleum resources. It is for this reason that the control of external damages merits detailed examination here. Such examination will both indicate the extent of regulatory effort and convey some sense of the general magnitude of the industry's compliance costs.

Acting under general or specific statutory directives, state petroleum conservation commissions control external damages through the promulgation and enforcement of operating regulations. The general tenor of these regulations will be indicated by quotations from the IOCC 1959 model regulations,[1] supplemented by quotations from or other references to illustrative regulations of individual states. The discussion

[1] IOCC, Regulatory Practices Committee, *A Suggested Form of General Rules and Regulations for the Conservation of Oil and Gas* (Oklahoma City: IOCC, 1959). This document was superseded in 1969 by IOCC, Regulatory Practices Committee, *General Rules and Regulations for the Conservation of Oil and Gas* (Oklahoma City: IOCC, 1969). However, since the 1959 model regulations appear to be more representative of current regulatory practices in the states, they are the source of the following quotations. Differences between the suggested regulations in the 1969 version and those quoted are indicated in footnotes.

of regulations relating to external damages will be presented under the headings of well drilling and completing, well plugging, waste disposal, and control of surface subsidence. This discussion will be followed by a review of the more important pertinent legislative and regulatory developments since 1948 and an evaluation of commissions' control of external damages.

Operating regulations in control of external damages

Well drilling and completing

The control of external damages begins with the application for a permit to drill, required by all states. This application enables the regulatory commission to prohibit drilling in a location or under circumstances conducive to external damages or, if a permit is granted, to identify each new well for purposes of further regulation over its lifetime. Rule IV of the IOCC 1959 model regulations is illustrative of the requirement of a permit to drill.

Prior to the commencement of operations to drill, deepen or plug back to any source of supply other than the existing producing horizon, application[2] shall be delivered to the Commission of intention to drill any well for oil or gas, and approval obtained upon Form P-1.[3]

Compliance with regulations over the lifetime of a proposed well ordinarily is assured by means of a bonding requirement. Thus Rule VI of the IOCC 1959 model regulations[4] provides for a bond

... in the sum of not less than five thousand dollars ($5,000) in favor of the _____ Commission, conditioned that the well upon abandonment shall be plugged in accordance with the rules and regulations of the Commission, and that the well be operated and repaired in compliance with the rules and regulations of the Commission. Such bond shall remain in force and effect until the plugging of said well is approved by the Commission, or the bond is released by the Commission. . . .[5]

[2] In the 1969 version of suggested regulations the quoted language ("application . . . of intention to drill") is changed to "application shall be filed with the agency indicating such intention. . . ." Otherwise, no significant change is made. IOCC, _General Rules and Regulations_, p. 28.

[3] IOCC, _A Suggested Form_, Rule IV, p. 4. Form P-1 provides space for identifying the well with respect to ownership, location, and purpose.

[4] IOCC, _A Suggested Form_, Rule VI, p. 4.

[5] The rule also provides for a blanket bond covering all wells drilled in the state in lieu of a separate bond for each well. Ibid., Rule VI, p. 5. The 1969 version of the suggested rules makes no mention of a bond.

The regulations of the Oklahoma commission, for instance, require somewhat broader assurances under the bond, providing that the bond be "conditioned that said well be drilled, produced, plugged and all forms filed in compliance with the rules and regulations of the Commission."[6]

In states where coal, metal, or other mining is significant, the oil and gas regulations commonly require that wells be located some minimum distance from mine openings and surface installations. Thus Colorado's regulations provide that

. . . no well drilled for oil or gas shall be located within 200 feet of a shaft or entrance to a coal mine not definitely abandoned or sealed, nor shall such well be located within 100 feet of any mine shaft house, mine boiler house, mine engine house, or mine fan; and the location of any proposed well must insure that when drilled it will be at least fifteen (15) feet from any mine haulage or airway.[7]

Such regulations are designed to assure that well drilling and operation neither interfere with mining activities nor create fire, asphyxiation, explosion, or flooding hazards in operable mines.

Where mines are unaffected, the primary concern of drilling regulations is with the protection of fresh-water-bearing underground strata. To avoid pollution of fresh water, such strata must be sealed off from the well bore so that they cannot be invaded by oil or brines entering the bore from deeper strata under differentially high pressure. The prescribed method is to line the well bore with steel casing from the surface to a point below the deepest fresh water stratum, fixing the casing in place and sealing off fresh water strata by filling the space between casing and well wall with cement. Thus the drilling rule of the IOCC 1959 model regulations provides in part:

Suitable and safe surface casing shall be used in all wells. In all wells drilled in areas where pressure and formation are unknown, sufficient surface casing shall be run to reach a depth below all potable fresh water levels, and shall be of sufficient size to permit the use of an intermediate string of casing. Surface casing shall be cemented by the pump and plug or displacement method with sufficient cement to circulate to the top of the hole.

In wells drilled in areas where subsurface conditions have been established by drilling experience, surface casing size at the operator's option shall be

---

[6] Corporation Commission of Oklahoma, *General Rules and Regulations* (Oklahoma City, 1961), Rule 201, p. 14.

[7] Oil and Gas Conservation Commission of the State of Colorado, *Rules and Regulations* (Denver, 1964), Rule 316, pp. 16–17.

set and cemented to the surface by the pump and plug or displacement method at a depth sufficient to protect all potable fresh water. . . .

Where cable tools are used, sufficient surface casing shall be set to protect all potable fresh water levels, and such surface casing shall be tested by bailing to insure a shut-off before drilling below the casing point proceeds.[8]

Some states require surface casing to be set at a minimum depth varying directly with the proposed depth of the well. In Mississippi, for instance, the minimum casing depth ranges from 200 feet for wells intended to be less than 2,500 feet in depth to 930 feet plus 25 percent of proposed depth in excess of 9,000 feet for wells intended to be 9,000 feet or more in depth. The casing must be cemented with the lesser of 500 sacks of cement or the amount required to circulate from the bottom of the casing to the surface; and the casing must be tested with a pressure of the lesser of 1,000 pounds per square inch or the equivalent of one pound per square inch for each foot of casing set.[9] Other states have only general regulations requiring adequate measures to protect fresh waters. See, for instance, the regulations of Alaska.

All fresh waters and waters of present or probable value for domestic, commercial or stock purposes shall be confined to their respective strata and shall be adequately protected by methods approved by the Committee. Special precautions by methods satisfactory to the Committee shall be taken in drilling and abandoning wells to guard against any loss of any fresh water from the strata in which it occurs, and the contamination of any fresh water by objectionable water, oil or gas.[10]

In coal producing states, special casing requirements typically are imposed to protect mines through which oil or gas wells are drilled. See, for instance, the oil and gas regulations of Illinois.

All wells drilled through an active coal mine or through an abandoned portion of an active mine shall be located if possible in order to pass through an adequate pillar.

Whether drilled through a pillar or not, a mine string of casing of good

---

[8] IOCC, *A Suggested Form*, Rule VII, p. 5. The comparable rule in the 1969 version of suggested regulations is somewhat more explicit, requiring surface casing "to a depth not less than fifty (50) feet below all fresh water strata. . . ." IOCC, *General Rules and Regulations*, p. 29.

[9] Mississippi State Oil and Gas Board, *Statewide Rules and Regulations* (Jackson, n.d.), Rule 11, p. 39.

[10] Alaska, Department of Natural Resources, Division of Mines and Minerals, *Oil and Gas Conservation Regulations and Statute* (Juneau, 1964), Rule 2059, p. 12.

quality shall be set to protect the mine. The mine string shall be treated with a heavy impervious coating of asphalt, plastic, or other acid-resisting material from fifty (50) feet above the mine roof to a point fifty (50) feet below the mine floor or base of coal seam.

The outside diameter of the mine string shall be at least four (4) inches smaller than the diameter of the well bore and equipped with centralizers or similar mechanical device above and below the coal seam. The mine string shall be set at an approximate depth of fifty (50) feet below the base of the coal seam and cemented from the casing seat to the surface.[11]

Similar measures are prescribed in potash producing states to protect potash mines.[12]

Well plugging

When a well is abandoned, because it is "dry" or has ceased to be commercially productive, it must be properly plugged to prevent three kinds of external damages: invasion of underground fresh water strata by oil and brines; flooding of the surface—and pollution of soil and surface waters—by oil or brines; and injury to humans, livestock, and agricultural machinery falling into or striking the cased walls of the hole. All states prescribe plugging methods designed generally to preclude such damages, and the IOCC 1959 model requirements that follow are representative.

The operator or owner shall not permit any well drilled for oil, gas, salt water disposal or any other purpose in connection with the production of oil and gas to remain unplugged after such well is no longer used for the purpose for which it was drilled or converted.

1. *Notice of intention to abandon; supervision*

Before any work is commenced to abandon any well drilled for the discovery of oil or gas, including any well drilled below the fresh water level, except such holes as are described in Rule XXXVI-4,[13] the owner or operator thereof shall give written notice to the Commission of his intention to abandon such well, which notice shall contain, among other things, the location

---

[11] Illinois, Department of Mines and Minerals, Division of Oil and Gas, *Rules and Regulations* (Springfield, 1961), Rule VIII, pp. 61–62.

[12] Utah, Oil and Gas Conservation Commission, *General Rules and Regulations* (Salt Lake City, 1965), Rule C-23, p. 35.

[13] The holes referred to are seismic, core, and other such exploratory holes. They must be plugged simply "in such manner as to properly protect all water bearing formations." IOCC, *A Suggested Form*, Rule XXXVI, p. 14.

of the well and when the abandonment will commence. The notice shall be upon forms prescribed by the Commission, and shall contain all of the information requested thereon. Upon receipt of such notice the director shall send a duly authorized representative of the Commission to the location specified, to be present at the time indicated in such notice, to supervise the plugging of such well. . . .

2. *Plugging methods and procedure*

The methods and procedure for plugging a well shall be as follows:

(a) The bottom of the hole shall be filled to the top of each producing formation, or a bridge shall be placed at the top of each producing formation, and in either event a cement plug not less than 15 feet in length shall be placed immediately above each producing formation whenever possible.

(b) A cement plug not less than 15 feet in length shall be placed at approximately 50 feet below all fresh water bearing strata.

(c) A plug shall be placed at the surface of the ground in each hole plugged in such a manner as not to interfere with soil cultivation.

(d) The interval between plugs shall be filled with an approved heavy mud-laden fluid. . . .

3. *Report on completion*

Within thirty (30) days after the plugging of any well has been accomplished, the owner or operator thereof shall file a plugging report with the Commission setting forth in detail the method used in plugging the well. Such report shall be made on a form prescribed by the Commission.[14]

The required bond, noted earlier, helps assure proper plugging of abandoned wells. Additional assurance is provided in the IOCC 1959 model regulations by the licensing of individuals or firms engaged in plugging wells for hire.

No person, firm, or corporation shall engage in the business of pulling casing and plugging oil or gas wells, or contracting to salvage casing therefrom, until a license has been secured from the Commission. . . . Upon notice given as required by the procedural rules of the Commission and hearing, the Commission will issue a license if it deems applicant possesses sufficient technical and scientific information and is financially responsible. Such license may at any time be cancelled by the Commission upon a complaint filed (a) on motion of the Commission; (b) by the Conservation

[14] Ibid., Rule XXXVI, pp. 13–14. The 1969 version of this rule is quite similar, the principal difference being the requirements of 50-foot plugs below fresh water bearing strata and of a 30-foot plug at the surface. IOCC, *General Rules and Regulations*, pp. 32–33.

Officer; (c) by the Conservation Attorney; or by any person interested in oil and gas production in this state.[15]

The plugging requirements of some states, while quite definite as to purpose, are indefinite as to methods. North Dakota's regulations provide that

. . . before any well is abandoned, it shall be plugged in a manner which will confine permanently all oil, gas and water in the separate strata originally containing them. This operation shall be accomplished by the use of mud-laden fluid, cement and plugs, used singly or in combination as may be approved by the Commission. Casing shall be cut off below plow depth.[16]

In other states, the prescribed plugging methods are not only explicit in detail but often go beyond those of the IOCC model regulations. Some states, such as Texas, Oklahoma, and Colorado, prohibit the removal of surface casing. The pertinent Texas rule, for instance, states that "fresh water sands are to be protected with casing which has been cemented, and such casing shall not be removed from the well at abandonment."[17] The coal producing states prescribe plugging techniques especially designed to protect commercial seams. Thus Indiana requires that in plugging,

. . . each commercially workable coal seam of thirty (30) inches or more of thickness lying above the depth of five hundred (500) feet shall be protected by a cement plug extending one hundred (100) feet above said coal seam to a distance of fifty (50) feet below the same or to the bottom of the hole whichever is less.[18]

The Indiana regulations further require a general clean-up and restoration of the surface around a well upon abandonment.

In plugging and permanently abandoning a well, an owner or operator shall clear the area around the location of all refuse material, burn waste oil and drain and fill all excavations, remove concrete bases, discarded machinery and material and restore the surface as nearly as possible to the condi-

---

[15] IOCC, *A Suggested Form*, Rule XXXVI, p. 14. The comparable rule in the 1969 version of suggested regulations is not significantly different. IOCC, *General Rules and Regulations*, p. 33.

[16] Industrial Commission of North Dakota, *General Rules and Regulations for the Conservation of Crude Oil and Natural Gas* (Bismarck, 1963), Rule 202, p. 39.

[17] Railroad Commission of Texas, *Rules Having Statewide General Application to Oil and Gas Operations* (Austin, 1964), Rule 15, p. 39.

[18] Indiana Division of Oil and Gas, Department of Natural Resources, *Rules and Regulations* (Indianapolis, 1964), Rule 33, p. 22.

tion it was in prior to the drilling of the well within one (1) year from date of completion and/or plugging.[19]

Waste disposal

As explained in chapter 2, petroleum deposits usually are found in association with salt water. Often the expansion or migration of free (nonconnate) salt water under pressure is the principal force displacing oil and driving it toward producing wells. Even where gas expansion is the principal driving force, free water underlying oil tends to expand or migrate toward wells, perhaps channeling through the more viscous oil, as pressure in the reservoir declines. Consequently, as oil and gas are withdrawn from the reservoir and the water-oil contact advances, salt water progressively enters producing well bores and is lifted with oil to the surface. There it must be separated from oil and disposed of in some way.

In some states and areas the volume of salt water to be disposed of is very great. In Kansas, for instance, the ratio of brine production to oil production is 16 to 1; in Texas the ratio is 2.5 to 1.[20] Moreover, the brines produced with oil typically are highly concentrated. On average, their sodium chloride content is over 40,000 parts per million (ppm), as compared with sea water's content of 20,000 ppm.[21] (Water containing sodium chloride in a ratio greater than 300 ppm is considered unfit for drinking.) Brines of such concentration, if dumped indiscriminately in relatively large volume, may quickly pollute soil and fresh water, destroying vegetation and wildlife, ruining irrigation waters, and imposing high desalination costs on municipal water systems.

Oilfield brines may be disposed of in three general ways. First, they may be discharged into surface drainage systems or bodies of water. Except in offshore or tidewater areas, some degree of damage to soil, fresh water, and wildlife must result from this method of disposal. Second, they may be discharged into specially excavated holding pits. There the water tends to evaporate, leaving a residue of solid minerals. If the pits are lined with impervious material, if their walls are never allowed to break or otherwise leak, if rainstorms never overflow them, and if the evaporation rate generally exceeds the rainfall rate, no pollution need result from this method of disposal. Finally, oilfield brines may be disposed of by injecting them into underground formations. If

[19] Ibid., Rule 33, p. 20.
[20] "Oilfield Pollution and What's Being Done About It," *Oil and Gas Journal*, vol. 61 (June 24, 1963), pp. 76–77.
[21] Ibid., p. 77.

the receiving formations do not contain fresh water and are not in com-munication with fresh water strata or the surface, no pollution can result from this method. If the receiving formation is the same as the produc-ing formation, then disposal may be combined with pressure mainte-nance or secondary recovery.

As the governing rule in the IOCC 1959 model regulations indicates, the regulating states generally accept disposal by discharge into tight surface pits or by underground injection into salt water bearing formations.

No person shall dispose of brine or salt water liquids except in the follow-ing manner. Any other method of disposal is hereby prohibited.

1. *Disposal in earthen pits*

Brine or salt water may be disposed of by evaporation when impounded in excavated earthen pits, which may only be used for such purpose when the pit is underlaid [*sic*] by tight soil such as heavy clay or hardpan.

Where the soil under the pit is porous and closely underlaid [*sic*] by a gravel or sand stratum, impounding of brine or salt water in such earthen pits is hereby prohibited. When such water is impounded in an earthen pit, it shall be so constructed and maintained to prevent escape of such water therefrom.

The Commission shall have authority to condemn any pit which does not properly impound such water and order the disposal of such water into an underground formation, as herein provided.

The level of brine or salt water in earthen pits shall at no time be per-mitted to rise above the lowest point of the ground surface level. All pits shall have a continuous embankment surrounding them sufficiently above the level of the surface to prevent surface water from running into the pit. Such embankment shall not be used to impound brine or salt water.

At no time shall brine or salt water impounded in earthen pits be allowed to escape over adjacent lands or into streams.

2. *Disposal by injection*

Salt water may also be disposed of by injection into the strata from which produced or other proven salt water bearing strata, after application for such injection has been approved by the Commission.[22]

---

[22] IOCC, *A Suggested Form*, Rule XXXIV, p. 12. The comparable rule in the 1969 version of suggested regulations is quite different. It reads in full: "Salt water and other waste liquids may not be impounded and collected or disposed of by evaporation in excavated earthen pits. Exceptions may be granted after application to the agency. Produced salt water may be disposed of into sub-surface formations not productive of fresh water. All procedures of salt water disposal shall be approved by the agency." IOCC, *General Rules and Regula-tions*, pp. 34–35.

Injection wells are themselves objects of detailed regulation. Under typical rules,[23] they cannot be drilled or operated without explicit permission of the conservation commission. Such permission is forthcoming only if injection wells are drilled to approved salt water bearing strata and are so cased and operated that the injected brines cannot leak into fresh-water-bearing strata or otherwise do damage to valuable resources.

All states approve of salt water disposal by means of regulated underground injection. Otherwise, subject to the common standard of pollution avoidance, the various state regulations differ in significant detail. A few examples will illustrate the principal differences. Colorado's regulations provide that

. . . the owner shall take all reasonable precautions to avoid polluting streams and underground water. If useless liquid products of wells cannot be treated or destroyed, or if the volume of such products is too great for disposal by usual methods without damage, the Director must be consulted and the useless liquids disposed of by some method approved by him.[24]

Alaska's regulations allow salt water disposal by underground injection, dumping into the sea or tidewater, or "in any manner, approved by the Committee, which will not contaminate fresh water sources or endanger other natural resources."[25] Mississippi's regulations, also, permit the discharge of salt water into "bodies of water" where no pollution would result and when not prohibited by rules of any other regulatory authority (e.g., game and fish commission) having jurisdiction.[26] Indiana's regulations specify the use of earthen pits for temporary storage only, pending permanent disposal of brines underground, although the regulatory commission may authorize continued pit use where no pollution or other violation of the state public health code would result.[27] Statewide regulations in Texas, since January 1, 1969, prohibit the use of earthen pits to dispose of oil field brines.[28]

---

[23] For example, Corporation Commission of Oklahoma, *General Rules and Regulation*, Rules 813 and 815, pp. 76–77.

[24] Oil and Gas Conservation Commission of the State of Colorado, *Rules and Regulations*, Rule 323, pp. 18–19.

[25] Alaska, Department of Natural Resources, *Oil and Gas Conservation Regulations and Statute*, Rule 2165, p. 21.

[26] Mississippi State Oil and Gas Board, *Statewide Rules and Regulations, Amendments*, Order No. 245-56, p. 16.

[27] Indiana Division of Oil and Gas, *Rules and Regulations*, Rule 38, pp. 24–25.

[28] Railroad Commission of Texas, *Special Order Amending Rule 8 of the General Conservation Rules of Statewide Application* (Austin, April 3, 1967).

Control of surface subsidence

With removal of fluids and reduction of pressure inside an oil or gas reservoir, the weight of overlying strata tends to crush and compress the reservoir rock. Ordinarily the rock is strong enough to withstand the external pressure exerted upon it. In rare instances, however, the reservoir rock collapses with removal of fluids, allowing the entire overburden to subside. The subsidence at the surface may damage structures and, in areas adjacent to water, cause flooding. There is only one remedy short of prohibiting production from the affected reservoir: pressure maintenance through fluid reinjection.

Thus far, only California has experienced damaging subsidence. In reaction to a growing problem of subsidence in the Wilmington field, which in part underlies Los Angeles and Long Beach Harbor,[29] that state enacted control legislation in 1958. Under the terms of the legislation, known as the Subsidence Act,[30] the state oil and gas supervisor may approve voluntary unitization agreements for pressure maintenance to halt subsidence.[31] Such agreements may take effect with the consent of those persons entitled to 75 percent of the proceeds of production, and any city or county may exercise the power of eminent domain to acquire the properties of nonconsenting persons and commit such properties to a unit plan of pressure maintenance. If there is failure to secure voluntary agreements where a pressure maintenance program is required to check subsidence, the supervisor may compel unitization of the affected area upon agreement of the *working interest* owners entitled to 65 percent of proceeds gross of royalties. Although the basic purpose is the prevention of subsidence and associated surface damage, before compelling unitization the supervisor must find that the estimated cost of pressure maintenance will not exceed the estimated value of the resultant increase in oil and gas production.

Major legislative and regulatory developments since 1948

The regulations affecting external damages in petroleum production have not always been as detailed or rigorous as at present. The current

---

[29] By 1958, subsidence of as much as 25 feet had occurred in the center of the affected area, causing an estimated $90 million in damages to surface structures and harbor facilities. S. M. Roberts, "Oil Conservation Law and Program to Stop Land Subsidence at Long Beach, California," *IOCC Committee Bulletin* (June 1959), pp. 34–35.

[30] West's Ann. Calif. Codes, Public Resources (1956) 1970 Supp., art. 5.5.

[31] A successful program of pressure maintenance in the Wilmington Field has been in operation since 1959. Roberts, "Oil Conservation Law and Program to Stop Land Subsidence," p. 38.

regulations just outlined are the product of long experience, changing technology, and growing problems of damage to other resources as the industry has grown larger and geographically more extensive. In large measure, they are the product of developments since 1948.

As noted in chapter 3, petroleum conservation legislation prior to 1909 dealt largely with the casing and plugging of wells—with the control of external damages—as society sought to protect itself from the peculiar hazards created by a new industry. Then, with the rise of the automobile and massive discoveries in the Southwest, emphasis shifted for three decades to production control and other means of limiting waste of oil and gas. Finally, as the industry and the control system emerged mature from World War II, attention swung once again to problems of external damages. Legislative interest in averting such damages rose to a new peak in the fifties and early sixties, particularly in the major producing states.

The time was ripe. The great legislative and judicial battles over production control had been won; the basic pattern of regulation was set. The principal producing areas of the Midwest and Southwest had experienced decades of producing history, accumulating with them thousands of old fields producing salt water in growing proportion to oil and tens of thousands of abandoned wells inadequately cased and plugged under primitive, poorly enforced regulations. The technology of secondary recovery and underground waste disposal was well developed and widely known. Reservoir unitization and pressure maintenance through fluid injection were no longer novel. Not least, population growth, urbanization, industrialization, and agricultural irrigation created mounting demands for fresh water. The problem of damage to fresh water resources was recognized as real, expensive, and preventable.

Aside from new basic conservation statutes, enacted in twenty-one states since 1948,[32] legislation dealing with external damages during the period falls into four general categories: (a) acts extending the jurisdiction of petroleum conservation commissions over other resources, (b) acts authorizing the replugging of old wells, (c) acts prohibiting practices leading to pollution, and (d) acts facilitating salt water disposal. The most important of these acts will be briefly enumerated.

---

[32] Mississippi (1948), Arizona (1951), Colorado (1951), Illinois (1951), Indiana (major amendment of basic law, 1951), Washington (1951), Wyoming (1951), Montana (1953), Nevada (1953), North Dakota (1953), Oregon (1953), Alaska (1955), Utah (1955), Maryland (1956), Nebraska (1959), Kentucky (1960), Pennsylvania (1961), South Dakota (1961), New York (1963), Ohio (1965), and Missouri (1966).

Acts extending jurisdiction

In 1951, Ohio enacted a well law placing the drilling and plugging of wells under the supervision of the Division of Mines of the Department of Industrial Relations.[33] This act made provision for the regulation of well drilling outside coal bearing areas for the first time in Ohio. An Oklahoma act of 1955 extended broad powers to the Corporation Commission for the control of salt water and other waste disposal and for the prevention of fresh water pollution from such disposal.[34] In the following year, the legislature of Mississippi vested responsibility for the prevention of soil and water pollution resulting from petroleum operations in the Oil and Gas Board.[35] Texas in 1961 enacted a water pollution control bill regulating injection wells and giving jurisdiction over such wells in oil and gas operations to the Railroad Commission.[36] In a 1964 enactment, Ohio increased the authority of the chief of the Division of Mines to prevent water pollution and to make rules governing the disposal of salt water and other oilfield wastes.[37] Oklahoma in 1965 broadened the power of the Corporation Commission to control pollution, particularly with respect to salt water disposal in earthen pits.[38] And in the same year, New Mexico enacted a statute authorizing the Oil Conservation Commission to regulate oil and gas operations with a view to preventing waste of potash.[39]

Acts authorizing replugging of old wells

In 1949, a Kansas act authorized the Corporation Commission to replug abandoned wells that were causing fresh water pollution.[40] A similar act, passed by Michigan in 1951, authorized the supervisor of wells to enter private property to plug a well if the owner neglected to plug it properly.[41] An Ohio law of 1957 provided for the plugging at public expense of wells abandoned prior to the passage of the 1951 well law referred to above.[42] And an Oklahoma law of 1965 authorized volunteers, with approval of the Corporation Commission, to enter pri-

---

[33] Ohio Rev. Code Ann. (1965) §4159.02.
[34] Okla. Stat. Ann. (1969) tit. 52, §139.
[35] Miss. Code Ann. (1942) 1968 Supp., tit. 23, §6132-10.
[36] Vernon's Rev. Civ. Stat. of Texas (1962) tit. 102, art. 7621b.
[37] Ohio Rev. Code Ann. (1965) §4159.031.
[38] Okla. Stat. Ann. (1969) tit. 52, §§139, 140, and 142.
[39] N.M. Stat. Ann. (1953) 1969 Supp., §65-3-5.
[40] Kan. Stat. Ann. (1964) §55.139.
[41] Mich. Stat. Ann. (1967) §13.138(12).
[42] Ohio Rev. Code Ann. (1965) §4159.12.

vate lands with immunity from prosecution for the purpose of plugging or replugging leaking abandoned wells.[43]

Acts prohibiting practices leading to pollution

In 1953, Kansas enacted a law regulating disposal of wastes in wells and requiring the State Board of Health to maintain permanent records of maximum pressures established by it for such wells.[44] This act was followed in 1957 by a law specifically requiring that in drilling wells in Kansas surface casing be cemented in place below fresh water strata.[45] An Indiana act of 1957 prohibited the injection of potable ground water into strata containing nonpotable water without a permit from the Water Resources Division of the Department of Conservation.[46] And in the same year, Arkansas enacted a law prohibiting the disposal of salt water into any stream, lake, or pond.[47]

Acts facilitating salt water disposal

Arkansas has enacted two laws facilitating salt water disposal since 1948, one in 1957 and the other in 1959. The first authorized the compulsory creation of salt water disposal units where field-wide unitization agreements already existed and where 75 percent of the working and royalty interest owners consented.[48] The second granted credit against severance tax liability to help finance the cost of underground salt water disposal systems.[49]

Recent regulatory developments reflect the recognized problems and the legislation of the fifties and sixties. In general, these developments may be summarized as modernization of drilling and plugging regulations, firmer enforcement of such regulations, virtual outlawing of salt water disposal in streams, gradual elimination of unlined evaporation pits, and encouragement of salt water disposal by means of underground injection. By far the greatest regulatory attention has been devoted to problems of salt water disposal.

In 1956 and 1957, the Research Committee of the Interstate Oil Compact Commission made a study of brine production and disposal in

[43] Okla. Stat. Ann. (1969) tit. 52, §§309 to 317.
[44] Kan. Stat. Ann. (1964) §55-1004.
[45] Kan. Stat. Ann. (1964) §§55-136 to 137.
[46] Burns' Ind. Stat. Ann. (1960) §27–1315.
[47] Ark. Stat. Ann. (1947) 1969 Supp., §§53–211 to 212.
[48] Ark. Stat. Ann. (1947) 1969 Supp., §53–115.
[49] Ark. Stat. Ann. (1947) 1969 Supp., §§84–2113 to 2120.

the United States and Canada.[50] The committee reported widely varying conditions among the states: in the ratio of brine to oil produced, in the total volume of brine to be disposed of, in disposal methods, and in recent progress in reducing pollution-causing methods of disposal. Relatively little brine is produced in the Rocky Mountain region, for instance, and existing disposal in surface pits or injection wells is considered adequate to control pollution.[51] In the older producing states of the Midwest (Indiana, Illinois, and Kansas) and the Southwest (Oklahoma, Texas, Arkansas, and Louisiana), in contrast, total brine production is two to sixteen times total oil production, and the disposal problem is immense.[52] Because of the high humidity in Indiana and Illinois, surface evaporation of brines is inefficient; underground injection is the only satisfactory method of permanent disposal. Indiana reported that about 80 percent of produced brines were reinjected in 1957.[53] In Kansas, evaporation is more efficient, particularly in the western part of the state, but the presence of shallow fresh water strata makes surface pits a pollution hazard. As a result of intensified effort to eliminate pollution after the legislation of 1953, Kansas could by 1957 report that approximately 99 percent of produced brine were reinjected underground.[54] (The figure was approximately the same in 1963.[55]) In Oklahoma, Texas, Arkansas, and Louisiana, as of 1957, not nearly so much progress could be reported. Oklahoma reported that seeping pits and stream disposal were disallowed after 1955, and that in 1957 about 70 percent of produced brine was disposed of underground.[56] Texas reported that "most" brine was still disposed of in surface pits, although a trend to underground injection was in evidence.[57] In Arkansas, "a large quantity" of produced brine was dumped in streams;[58] in Louisiana, approximately one-third of produced brine, half of it in the northern portion of the state far removed from the sea, was disposed of in streams.[59]

Each of the southwestern states made further progress in pollution

---

[50] IOCC, Research Committee, *Production and Disposal of Oilfield Brines in the United States and Canada* (Oklahoma City: IOCC, 1960).

[51] Ibid., pp. 9, 53–54, 70.

[52] Ibid., pp. 6–7, 10–12, 20–21, 27–31, 35–42, 62–63, 65.

[53] Ibid., p. 23.

[54] Ibid., p. 31.

[55] Bruce F. Latta, "The Oil Field Pollution Control Program in Kansas," *IOCC Committee Bulletin* (June 1963), p. 4.

[56] IOCC, *Production and Disposal of Oilfield Brines*, pp. 62–63.

[57] Ibid., p. 65.

[58] Ibid., p. 6.

[59] Ibid., p. 42.

control after 1957. Oklahoma reduced the number of unlined pits in use by 80 percent in the five years 1958–63.[60] Beginning in 1961, and in cooperation with the Water Pollution Control Board, the Texas Railroad Commission mounted a campaign to eliminate surface pits contributing to soil and water pollution. As of October 1966 it had outlawed all surface pits in forty-one counties.[61] In April 1967 the commission issued a special order amending its statewide rules and regulations to prohibit, as of January 1, 1969, the use anywhere in the state of surface pits to dispose of oil field brines.[62] In 1958 the Arkansas Board of Conservation, under pressure from the federal Department of Health, Education, and Welfare to end pollution of interstate waters, ordered into effect a five-year plan to eliminate salt water disposal in streams in the Ouachita and Red River basins. The order required an annual reduction of net salt water production in the affected fields by 20 percent of the 1958 base. To assist operators in complying, the 1959 legislation allowed them to deduct depreciation and operating costs of underground disposal systems from severance tax liability, with a ceiling deduction of $105,000 in 1959 up to $370,000 in 1963 and subsequent years.[63] In 1964, as a first step in a statewide drive to end pollution of surface waters by oilfield operations, the commissioner of conservation in Louisiana moved to end stream disposal in Caddo Parish (northwest Louisiana). To enforce this order, in January 1966 the commissioner shut down 142 noncomplying wells.[64]

Thus, the fragmentary evidence available suggests that, while regulation to prevent pollution in petroleum operations is far from perfect, it progresses continuously. Adequate control of external damages within the next decade seems highly probable.

An evaluation of control of external damages

In evaluating control of external damages by petroleum conservation commissions, it is useful to distinguish between different possible intents or objectives. The apparent intent of pertinent regulations is to protect

[60] "Oilfield Pollution and What's Being Done About It," p. 81.

[61] *Oil and Gas Journal*, vol. 64 (October 17, 1966), p. 64.

[62] Texas Railroad Commission, *Special Order Amending Rule 8 of the General Conservation Rules of Statewide Application as recompiled April 16, 1964* (April 3, 1967).

[63] Sterling S. Lacy, Jr., "Salt Water Disposal Practices in Arkansas," *IOCC Committee Bulletin*, June 1963, pp. 24–25.

[64] "Louisiana Shutting Down Polluters," *Oil and Gas Journal*, vol. 64 (January 24, 1966), pp. 54–55.

other resources from damage, and to do so absolutely. The regulations do not appear to contemplate a range of degrees of damage, some portion of which is tolerable. Rather, any degree of damage appears to be unacceptable, and the regulations are formally designed to prevent the smallest degree. On the other hand, because regulations are imperfectly designed and enforced, in practice damages have been tolerated if they were not immediately and obviously costly to influential groups— farmers, industrialists, sportsmen, and municipalities, for instance. Judged on the basis of apparent intent, then, the regulations have thus far been less than satisfactory.

But the apparent intent itself is questionable. The purpose of conservation regulation, as we have repeatedly asserted, is to protect or increase human welfare. No resource is inherently superior to any other in giving satisfactions to human beings; and all production involves "destroying" resources in order to secure satisfaction-yielding products. The issue is whether that which is destroyed is worth more or less than that which is produced. In conservation regulation, the control of external damages should be designed not necessarily to prevent such damages absolutely, but to insure that the production of any given resource bears all of its social costs. If external damage, although physically measurable, is economically valueless, it should not be prevented at an economic cost. If external damage is economically valuable, it should not be prevented at a greater economic cost; rather, those causing the damage should be required to compensate those suffering the economic loss. Absolute prevention is justified only if the loss averted is worth at least as much as the necessary cost.[65]

Judged on the basis of genuine conservation intent, the (thus far) imperfect control of external damages is less easily condemned as unsatisfactory. The regional differences in regulation and the lagging but persistent adjustment of control measures to "felt needs" undoubtedly reflect a crude but continuous cost-benefit calculation by legislators and regulators. The new emphasis on pollution control in recent years, for instance, clearly stems from a rise in the economic value of damage relative to the economic cost of prevention. The merited criticisms of the control system are that (a) a lag in adjustment persists and (b) there is no systematic attempt to compare cost and benefit in the regulatory process.

Systematic cost-benefit analysis would permit intelligent discrimina-

[65] Of course, allowance must be made for the cost of determining costs and benefits. Where that cost is significant, absolute prevention may be the only feasible way of dealing with external damage.

tion in the control of external damages. It would identify, for particular localities, those damages that should be prohibited altogether because they cost more than preventive measures; and it would distinguish, for particular localities, those damages for which compensation should be required because they cost less than preventive measures. It would assure that petroleum production bears its full social costs, but not more. It thus would help assure an optimum rate of exploiting the total natural stock of petroleum resources.

9. Control of Production and Well Spacing

The principal conservation problem created by unregulated exploitation of petroleum deposits is the loss of otherwise recoverable oil and gas brought about by high initial rates of production from new reservoirs. Dense drilling poses a conservation problem partly because it implements high initial rates of production. But beyond that, dense drilling needlessly increases reservoir development costs and, because it is anticipated by explorers, artificially contracts the margin of profitable exploration. Consequently, control of well spacing lies with production control at the heart of conservation regulation.

Well spacing is regulated to some degree in all the producing states. However, the typical regulations only prescribe minimum spacing distances, these being subject to exception. A substantial range of choice usually is open to the developers of a new reservoir. The principal determinant of the spacing chosen in a new reservoir, given its depth and operating characteristics, is the incentive embodied in the prevailing system of controlling production. Accordingly, my first concern in this chapter is with production control. Except where specifically noted, the discussion pertains exclusively to crude oil production.

Types of production control

The first and simplest kind of production control is restriction of well density on the basis of uniform statewide rules. The feasible rate of production of a well is not proportionate to the acreage being drained. Therefore, the fewer the number of wells tapping a reservoir the lower is the maximum feasible rate of production from the reservoir at any given stage of depletion. By controlling the number of wells tapping a reservoir, spacing regulations limit the rate of production—conceivably, by coincidence in individual cases, to the level consistent with maximum ultimate recovery. Regulation of spacing is the basic method of controlling production in Illinois, Indiana, Ohio, Pennsylvania, Kentucky, and West Virginia. Under this method the rule of capture still effectively prevails, so operators have an incentive to drill wells as densely as regulations permit.

The second kind of production control is limitation of the output of each reservoir to its MER, or maximum rate of production consistent with no significant loss of ultimate recovery. In the usual case, formal restriction of production is imposed only upon specific finding by the regulatory commission that the unregulated rate of production from a reservoir is conducive to "waste" (i.e., is inconsistent with maximum ultimate recovery). The permissible rate of production is determined separately for each affected reservoir in the light of its distinctive operating characteristics, and each well is assigned its share of the allowable reservoir output. This, in addition to regulation of well spacing, is the basic approach to production control in Arkansas, Mississippi, Alaska, California (voluntary), Utah, Colorado, Wyoming, Montana, and Nebraska. Where operators may anticipate that the MER will be determined early in the life of each new reservoir and production allocated to wells in proportion to acreage drained, there is no incentive to drill more wells on a given acreage than can produce the proportionate share of the expected MER. Thus systematic production control on the basis of MER may lead to wider spacing than the minimum required under general spacing regulations.

The third and final kind of production control is restriction of area output to market demand (or to the capacity of transportation and market facilities, if smaller). The prospective purchases in a state or major subdivision are periodically determined by the regulatory authority, and the total is allocated among reservoirs and wells in proportion to their basic allowables. The basic allowables may in some instances be reservoir MERs or other special reservoir allowables, but usually they are derived from a statewide schedule of well allowables based on well depth and acreage drained. Restriction to market demand is the basic method of controlling production in Texas, Louisiana, New Mexico, Oklahoma, and Kansas,[1] which together produce about three-fourths of the nation's total output of liquid hydrocarbons. In those states the well spacing incentive reflects the structure of the depth-acreage allowable schedule in use, particularly the allowance for acreage drained per well. The spacing incentive embodied in the depth-acreage schedule of each of the above states will be discussed later in this chapter.

---

[1] Restriction of production to market demand is authorized in three other significant producing states—Alabama, Michigan, and North Dakota—but is not currently being practiced because of excess of demand over basic allowables.

Depth-acreage allowable schedules

The depth-acreage allowable schedules, or Yardsticks, in use in Texas, Louisiana, New Mexico, Oklahoma, and Kansas are reproduced in tables 4 through 12. Three schedules (tables 4 through 6) are effective in Texas: (a) the 1947 Yardstick, applicable to discoveries prior to 1 January 1965; (b) the 1965 Yardstick, applicable to discoveries on or after 1 January 1965; and (c) the offshore Yardstick, effective 1 January 1966. Five schedules (tables 7 through 9) are effective in Louisiana: (a) the depth-bracket schedule corresponding to the 40-acre column of table 7, applicable to onshore discoveries prior to 10 November 1960; (b) the entire depth-acreage schedule given in Table 7, applicable to onshore discoveries on or after 10 November 1960; (c) the "intermediate zone" depth-acreage schedule (table 8), effective 1 January 1967, applicable to wells in bay and marsh areas intermediate between onshore and offshore locations; (d) the depth-bracket

Table 4. Texas 1947 Allowable Yardstick

(barrels per day)

Depth	Acres per well				
(thousand ft.)	10	20	40	80	160
0.0–1.0	18	28	–	–	–
1.0–1.5	27	37	57	97	177
1.5–2.0	36	46	66	106	186
2.0–3.0	45	55	75	115	195
3.0–4.0	54	64	84	124	204
4.0–5.0	63	73	93	133	213
5.0–6.0	72	82	102	142	222
6.0–7.0	81	91	111	151	231
7.0–8.0	91	101	121	161	241
8.0–8.5	103	113	133	173	253
8.5–9.0	112	122	142	182	262
9.0–9.5	127	137	157	197	277
9.5–10.0	152	162	182	222	302
10.0–10.5	190	210	230	270	350
10.5–11.0	–	225	245	285	365
11.0–11.5	–	255	275	315	395
11.5–12.0	–	290	310	350	430
12.0–12.5	–	330	350	390	470
12.5–13.0	–	375	395	435	515
13.0–13.5	–	425	445	485	565
13.5–14.0	–	480	500	540	620
14.0–14.5	–	540	560	600	680

Source: IOCC, Governors' Special Study Committee, *A Study of Conservation of Oil and Gas in the United States, 1964* (Oklahoma City: IOCC, 1965), p. 71.

Table 5.   Texas 1965 Allowable Yardstick

(barrels per day)

Depth	Acres per well				
(thousand ft.)	10	20	40	80	160
0.0–2.0	21	39	74	129	238
2.0–3.0	22	41	78	135	249
3.0–4.0	23	44	84	144	265
4.0–5.0	24	48	93	158	288
5.0–6.0	26	52	102	171	310
6.0–7.0	28	57	111	184	331
7.0–8.0	31	62	121	198	353
8.0–8.5	34	68	133	215	380
8.5–9.0	36	74	142	229	402
9.0–9.5	40	81	157	250	435
9.5–10.0	43	88	172	272	471
10.0–10.5	48	96	192	300	515
10.5–11.0	–	106	212	329	562
11.0–11.5	–	119	237	365	621
11.5–12.0	–	131	262	401	679
12.0–12.5	–	144	287	436	735
12.5–13.0	–	156	312	471	789
13.0–13.5	–	169	337	506	843
13.5–14.0	–	181	362	543	905
14.0–14.5	–	200	400	600	1,000

Source: Texas Railroad Commission, *Special Order of Nov. 20, 1964, Amending Rule 45(A) of the Statewide Conservation Rules,* as recompiled April 16, 1964 (April 3, 1967).

schedule corresponding to the 40-acre column of table 9, applicable to offshore discoveries prior to 10 November 1960; and (e) the entire depth-acreage schedule given in table 9, applicable to offshore discoveries on or after 10 November 1960. Only one depth-acreage schedule is effective in each of the other states—New Mexico, Oklahoma, and Kansas (tables 10 through 12). The New Mexico schedule runs in terms of proportionate factors, which are multiplied by a variable "normal unit allowable" to determine the allowable production per well in barrels per day.

All of the schedules have in common an allowance for depth; i.e., allowable production in each spacing category (40 acres, 80 acres, etc.) increases with well depth. The increase is more than proportionate to depth. Thus, under the Texas 1947 Yardstick (table 4), the basic allowable for wells on 40-acre spacing ranges from 57 barrels per day at a depth interval of 1,000–1,500 feet to 133 barrels per day at a depth interval of 8,000–8,500 feet and to 560 barrels per day at a depth interval of 14,000–14,500 feet. In all cases, the allowance for depth is in consideration of the fact that well drilling and operating costs in-

Table 6. Texas Offshore Allowable Yardstick

(barrels per day)

Depth	Acres per well		
(thousand ft.)	40	80	160
0.0–2.0	200	330	590
2.0–3.0	220	360	640
3.0–4.0	245	400	705
4.0–5.0	275	445	785
5.0–6.0	305	490	865
6.0–7.0	340	545	950
7.0–8.0	380	605	1,050
8.0–9.0	420	665	1,150
9.0–10.0	465	730	1,260
10.0–11.0	515	800	1,380
11.0–12.0	565	875	1,500
12.0–13.0	620	950	1,625
13.0–14.0	675	1,030	1,750
14.0–15.0	735	1,115	1,880

Source: Texas Railroad Commission, *Special Order of Dec. 16, 1965, Amending the State-wide Conservation Rules by Adding Rule 45(A)(4).*

Table 7. Louisiana 1960 Allowable Schedule

(barrels per day)

Depth	Acres per well				
(thousand ft.)	10	20	40	80	160[a]
0.0–2.0	20	40	80	120	200
2.0–3.0	24	48	95	143	238
3.0–4.0	29	57	114	171	285
4.0–5.0	34	67	134	201	335
5.0–6.0	40	80	159	239	398
6.0–7.0	47	93	186	279	465
7.0–8.0	54	107	214	321	535
8.0–9.0	60	120	239	359	598
9.0–10.0	69	137	274	411	685
10.0–11.0	78	155	310	465	775
11.0–12.0	87	174	347	521	868
12.0–13.0	96	192	383	575	958
13.0–14.0	108	216	431	647	1,078
14.0–15.0	121	242	483	725	1,208
15.0–16.0	140	279	557	836	1,393
16.0–17.0	162	323	645	968	1,613
17.0–18.0	182	363	726	1,089	1,815
18.0–19.0	204	408	816	1,224	2,040
19.0–20.0	232	464	927	1,391	2,318
20.0–21.0	265	529	1,057	1,586	2,643

Source: IOCC, *Conservation of Oil and Gas,* p. 66; Louisiana Department of Conservation, *Statewide Order No. 29–H* (24 May 1960).

[a] The maximum acreage credit for allowable purposes in Lousiana in 90 acres. However, this column, based on the acreage credit formula in use, is included for comparability with other states' schedules.

Table 8. Louisiana Intermediate Zone Allowable Schedule

(barrels per day)

Depth	Acres per well				
(thousand ft.)	10	20	40	80	160
0.0–2.0	26	52	104	144	248
2.0–3.0	31	62	124	172	296
3.0–4.0	37	74	148	205	353
4.0–5.0	44	87	174	241	415
5.0–6.0	52	104	207	287	494
6.0–7.0	61	121	242	335	577
7.0–8.0	70	139	278	385	663
8.0–9.0	78	156	311	431	742
9.0–10.0	89	178	356	493	849
10.0–11.0	101	202	403	558	961
11.0–12.0	113	226	451	625	1,076
12.0–13.0	125	249	498	690	1,188
13.0–14.0	140	280	560	776	1,336
14.0–15.0	157	314	628	870	1,498
15.0–16.0	181	362	724	1,003	1,727
16.0–17.0	210	420	839	1,162	2,001
17.0–18.0	236	472	944	1,307	2,251
18.0–19.0	265	531	1,061	1,469	2,530
19.0–20.0	301	603	1,205	1,669	2,874
20.0–21.0	344	687	1,374	1,903	3,277

Source: Louisiana Department of Conservation, *Supplement to Statewide Order No. 151–A* (1 Jan. 1966).

crease more than proportionately to depth. Higher drilling and operating cost is also the reason for larger allowables for wells in the intermediate zone of Louisiana and in offshore areas of Texas and Louisiana.[2]

Except for the Louisiana schedules applicable to discoveries prior to 10 November 1960, all of the schedules also make an allowance for acreage drained per well; that is, the allowable production per well increases (but not necessarily proportionately) with acreage drained per well. Thus, under the Texas 1947 Yardstick the allowable production per well in the 1,000–1,500 feet depth interval increases from 27 barrels per day for wells on 10-acre spacing to 177 barrels per day for wells on 160-acre spacing. In all cases, the allowance for acreage per well is in consideration of the fact that wider spacing, other things being equal, increases the time required to deplete a reservoir and thus increases the payout period on well investments. At least in the cases of the newer Texas and Louisiana schedules, the allowance for acreage drained per well is designed to encourage wide spacing while reducing

[2] The order creating Louisiana's intermediate zone cites "costs of operating and the (hurricane) risk involved in operating" as its justification. Louisiana Department of Conservation, *Supplement to Order No. 151-A* (1 January 1966).

Table 9. Louisiana Offshore Allowable Schedule

(barrels per day)

| Depth | Acres per well | | | | |
(thousand ft.)	10	20	40	80	160
0.0–2.0	48	97	193	233	426
2.0–3.0	54	107	214	262	476
3.0–4.0	60	119	238	295	533
4.0–5.0	66	133	265	332	597
5.0–6.0	74	148	296	376	672
6.0–7.0	83	166	331	424	755
7.0–8.0	95	190	379	486	865
8.0–9.0	104	208	416	536	952
9.0–10.0	116	232	463	600	1,063
10.0–11.0	128	256	512	667	1,179
11.0–12.0	140	280	559	733	1,292
12.0–13.0	151	303	605	797	1,402
13.0–14.0	167	334	668	884	1,552
14.0–15.0	184	367	734	976	1,710
15.0–16.0	208	415	830	1,109	1,939
16.0–17.0	236	471	942	1,265	2,207
17.0–18.0	263	527	1,053	1,416	2,469
18.0–19.0	292	584	1,167	1,575	2,742
19.0–20.0	327	654	1,307	1,771	3,078
20.0–21.0	367	735	1,469	1,998	3,467

Source: IOCC, *Conservation of Oil and Gas,* p. 66; Louisiana Department of Conservation, *Statewide Order No. 29–H* (24 May 1960).

the allowable rate of production per unit area. Consider, for example, the case of a reservoir discovered in the depth interval of 14,000–14,500 feet and subject to the Texas 1965 Yardstick (table 5). To save the cost of an additional deep well on each 160-acre tract, operators may choose 160-acre rather than 80-acre spacing although the top allowable rate of production per 160-acre tract would be 1,000 barrels per day with 160-acre spacing and 1,200 barrels per day with 80-acre spacing.

The formulas employed in making allowance for acreage drained differ widely among the several depth-acreage schedules. In the Texas 1947 Yardstick one barrel per day of additional production is allowed for each additional acre drained. In the Texas 1965 Yardstick a minimum spacing of 40 acres is aimed at, particularly at intermediate and greater depths, the allowable rate of production for more densely spaced wells declining in proportion to acreage drained. The allowable rate of production for less densely spaced wells increases sharply, but not in exact proportion to acreage drained. Louisiana's 1960 depth-acreage schedule (table 7) also induces a minimum spacing of 40 acres: one

Table 10. New Mexico Schedule of Proportionate Factors

Depth (*thousand ft.*)	Acres per well		
	40	80	160
0.0–5.0	1.00	–	–
5.0–6.0	1.33	2.33	4.33
6.0–7.0	1.77	2.77	4.77
7.0–8.0	2.33	3.33	5.33
8.0–9.0	3.00	4.00	6.00
9.0–10.0	3.77	4.77	6.77
10.0–11.0	4.67	5.67	7.67
11.0–12.0	5.67	6.67	8.67
12.0–13.0	6.75	7.75	9.75
13.0–14.0	8.00	9.00	11.00
14.0–15.0	9.33	10.33	12.33
15.0–16.0	10.78	11.78	13.78
16.0–17.0	12.33	13.33	15.33
17.0–18.0	14.00	15.00	17.00

Source: IOCC, *Conservation of Oil and Gas,* p. 68; New Mexico Oil Conservation Commission, *Rules and Regulations* (1965), Rule 505.

well on a 40-acre tract is allowed to produce as much per day as two wells on 20 acres each or four wells on 10 acres each. The 80-acre allowable is 50 percent larger than the 40-acre allowable, and the 160-acre allowable is 75 percent larger than the 80-acre allowable.[3] The New Mexico schedule (table 10) makes allowance for acreage drained by adding one proportionate factor for each 40 acres in excess of the basic minimum of 40 acres per well. Thus, in the 5,000–6,000 feet interval a well on 40 acres has a proportionate factor of 1.33, a well on 80 acres has a proportionate factor of 2.33, and a well on 160 acres has a proportionate factor of 4.33.[4] In Oklahoma's depth-acreage schedule (table 11) the 20-acre allowable is 125 percent of the 10-acre allowable, the 40-acre allowable is 125 percent of the 20-acre allowable, and so on through the 80-acre allowable; but the 160-acre allowable is 180 percent of the 80-acre allowable. Kansas (table 12) provides the same allowable for wells on 10-acre and 20-acre spacing. For wells on 40-acre spacing the allowable is 1.00 barrel per day for each 100 feet

[3] The 160-acre allowable is computed from the acreage-credit formula in use in Louisiana. However, in practice 90 acres is the largest acreage for which allowable credit is given.

[4] North Dakota employs the same proportionate factors for 40-acre spacing as New Mexico, but it increases the proportionate factors for wider spacing in exact proportion to acreage drained. IOCC, *A Study of Conservation of Oil and Gas in the United States, 1964* (Oklahoma City, 1965), p. 69.

Table 11.   Oklahoma Allowable Schedule

(barrels per day)

Depth	Acres per well				
(thousand ft.)	10	20	40	80	160
1.8–2.0	25	31	39	–	–
2.8–3.0	30	38	48	–	–
3.8–4.0	35	44	55	–	–
4.8–5.0	40	50	63	79	142
5.8–6.0	47	60	75	94	169
6.8–7.0	57	70	88	110	198
7.8–8.0	67	80	101	126	227
8.8–9.0	77	95	119	149	268
9.8–10.0	90	113	141	176	317
10.8–11.0	115	144	180	225	405
11.8–12.0	153	191	239	299	538
12.8–13.0	203	254	317	398	716
13.8–14.0	253	316	395	494	889
14.8–15.0	303	379	473	593	1,067

Source: IOCC, *Conservation of Oil and Gas*, p. 70; Oklahoma Corporation Commission, *General Rules and Regulations* (1961), Rule 303.
Note: Condensed version. Complete schedule is in 200-ft. intervals.

of depth, rising to 1.25 barrels per day for wells on 80 acres, and to 1.50 barrels per day for wells on 160 acres.

In summary, the various depth-acreage allowable schedules are similar in general structure, permitting increasing production per well with increasing depth and increasing acreage per well; but in the specific allowances made for depth and acreage they differ substantially.[5] The differences will be examined more thoroughly later in this chapter.

The mechanics of restricting production to market demand

The depth-acreage allowable schedules in use in Texas, Louisiana, Oklahoma, Kansas, and New Mexico specify only the basic maximum allowables of the affected wells (or, in the case of New Mexico, the basic proportionate relationships among allowables). The actual effective allowables during a period in these states are limited by previous official estimates of "market demand" for the period. Prospective market demand is estimated once each month. New Mexico is divided ad-

---

[5]For a more detailed treatment of the various depth-acreage schedules see Wallace F. Lovejoy and Paul T. Homan, *Economic Aspects of Oil Conservation Regulation* (Baltimore: Johns Hopkins Press for Resources for the Future, 1967), pp. 141–53.

Table 12. Kansas Allowable Schedule

(barrels per day)

Depth	Acres per well				
(thousand ft.)	10	20	40	80	160
0.0–4.0	25	25	–	–	–
4.0–4.5	31	31	43	54	65
4.5–5.0	37	37	48	60	72
5.0–5.5	43	43	53	66	80
5.5–6.0	48	48	58	73	87
6.0–6.5	52	52	63	79	95
6.5–7.0	56	56	68	85	102
7.0 and above	60	60	73	91	110

Source: IOCC, *Conservation of Oil and Gas*, p. 66; Kansas Corporation Commission, *General Rules and Regulations* (1958), Rule 82–2–109.

ministratively into two market areas, the northwest and the southeast,[6] and market demand is estimated separately for each area. In the other states studied the coverage of the estimate is statewide. Each state estimate is made independently of the others.

The typical procedure in estimating prospective market demand is as follows. Approximately two weeks before the beginning of the period for which an estimate is to be made, the regulatory commission conducts a public hearing. At the hearing, with the Bureau of Mines monthly consumption forecast and data on inventories before it, the commission receives formal "nominations" (statements of intentions to buy) from the principal oil purchasers in the state. It also receives any other pertinent testimony from those present or represented. For example, an independent producer may testify that he is unable to find a market for all of his allowed production, or a refiner-purchaser may testify that inventories of crude oil are above or below normal for the season. General opinions may be expressed as to prospective demand in the state. Purchasers may be questioned if their nominations differ markedly from those of the preceding period or from the current Bureau of Mines forecast. Throughout the proceedings, the prospective price of crude oil is ignored. Purchasers' nominations make no mention of price. The implicit assumption in the hearing is either that price will remain unchanged or that demand is so inelastic with respect to price in the short run that prospective price has negligible bearing on prospective purchases.

In the light of all the information made available to it, the commis-

---

[6] Local use aside, the production of the northwest is marketed in the Pacific region, while the production of the southeast is marketed in the Gulf and mid-continent regions.

sion then forms its judgment as to the probable quantity of oil to be demanded in the state (or area in New Mexico) during the forthcoming period. This quantity, adjusted for expected changes in inventory, becomes the target rate of production which, in turn, corrected for estimated underproduction of allowables,[7] becomes the announced total allowable for the state (or area) during the forthcoming period.[8]

The next step is to relate the total allowable to the basic maximum allowable for the state (or area). The basic maximum allowable is the sum of: (a) maximum production of fields or wells assigned special allowables or permitted to produce at capacity, such as water-flood fields, discovery wells, statutory marginal wells, and stripper wells; (b) the MERs in fields subject to MER restriction; and (c) the top allowables specified for wells in fields subject to the statewide depth-acreage schedule, such as the Texas Yardstick. If the allowable required to match estimated market demand exceeds the basic maximum allowable of the state (or area), then the latter—in total and in each of its separate components—limits production during the affected period. If the allowable required to match estimated market demand is less than the basic maximum allowable, on the other hand, then the former limits total production during the affected period and must be allocated to the various fields and wells in the state (or area).

The allocation involves two steps. First, the fields and wells exempt from market-demand restriction, such as capacity water-flood fields or discovery wells, are allotted their capacity rates of production or their exempt special allowables as applicable. The sum of the exempt allotments is then subtracted from the total allowable estimated to match market demand, and the remainder is allocated to nonexempt fields and wells in proportion to their respective basic maximum allowables. The proportionate allocation to nonexempt fields and wells in Texas, Louisiana, and Oklahoma is accomplished by means of a market demand factor, a decimal fraction representing the ratio of the total nonexempt share of allowed production to the total nonexempt basic allowable, which is multiplied by each well's basic allowable to compute its actual allowable for the effective period. In Kansas, which has a statutory

---

[7] In any given period, numerous wells are unable to produce their allowables because of undercapacity or shutdown for repairs.

[8] In a simple correlation analysis of monthly data, 1946–60, Mitchell found that in Texas variation in nominations explains 74 percent of variation in allowables or, alternatively, variation in Bureau of Mines forecasts explains 79 percent of variation in allowables. Alfred C. Mitchell, *Market Demand and Proration of Texas Crude Petroleum* (Austin: Bureau of Business Research, the University of Texas, 1964), p. 31.

minimum allowable of 25 barrels per day for wells on standard spacing of 10 acres or more, pools (reservoirs) are classified on the basis of the average capacity per well, and the allowables of the wells in each separate pool category are proportionately adjusted, subject to the 25-barrel minimum, as necessary to permit the desired aggregate rate of production. In New Mexico, a "normal unit allowable" in barrels per day is determined monthly for each of the two market areas; the normal unit allowable is then multiplied by the proportionate factor[9] of each non-exempt well to determine the well's allowable for the month.

An individual well's allowable, reflecting its share of market demand, is subject to further reduction if necessary to comply with state or field rules specifying the maximum permissible gas-oil ratio. Thus, as explained earlier, a well's allowable typically would be reduced in proportion to the excess of the actual ratio over the specified maximum.[10]

The exemptions from market-demand restrictions are quite important, especially in Texas, Oklahoma, Kansas, and New Mexico. The proportion of total crude oil production accounted for by exempt wells in each state varies, of course, with the degree of restraint on nonexempt wells, but the figures for 1963 are indicative of the recent past. In that year, 43 percent of production in Texas came from exempt sources. The corresponding proportions in the other market-demand states were 58 percent for Oklahoma, 47 percent for New Mexico, 61 percent for Kansas, and 20 percent for Louisiana.[11]

The exemptions are of several kinds. First, all of the market-demand states except Louisiana have special allowables for wells designated discovery wells. Except in Kansas, the discovery allowables are free of market-demand restriction. The Texas discovery allowable schedule, shown in table 13, applies to all wells drilled in a new field until 24 months from discovery have passed or the eleventh well is drilled, whichever occurs first. The Oklahoma discovery allowable schedule, shown in table 14, applies to all wells drilled in a new field until the indicated number of days from discovery have passed. The Kansas discovery allowable is simply 1.5 times the regular allowable for wells in a given depth-acreage category. It applies to all wells drilled in a new field until 18 months from discovery have passed or the eleventh well is drilled, whichever occurs first. New Mexico, finally, offers the successful wildcatter a bonus allowable in addition to the regular allowable.

---

[9] See table 10.
[10] See chapter 3, footnote 43.
[11] U.S. Department of the Interior, Office of Oil and Gas, *An Appraisal of the Petroleum Industry of the United States* (Washington, 1965), p. 26.

Table 13. Texas Discovery Allowable Schedule

(barrels per day)

Depth (*thousand ft.*)	Allowable	Depth (*thousand ft.*)	Allowable
0.0–1.0	20	9.0–9.5	200
1.0–1.5	40	9.5–10.0	200
1.5–2.0	40	10.0–10.5	210
2.0–3.0	60	10.5–11.0	225
3.0–4.0	80	11.0–11.5	255
4.0–5.0	100	11.5–12.0	290
5.0–6.0	120	12.0–12.5	330
6.0–7.0	140	12.5–13.0	375
7.0–8.0	160	13.0–13.5	425
8.0–8.5	180	13.5–14.0	480
8.5–9.0	180	14.0–14.5	540

Source: IOCC, *Conservation of Oil and Gas*, p. 71.

The bonus is five barrels per foot of depth, to be produced over a period of two years. Thus, a 10,000-foot discovery well would get 50,000 barrels of bonus oil, or $50,000/(2 \times 365)$ barrels per day in addition to the regular allowable for two years. A double bonus is granted for the first or deepest discovery in a county.[12]

Second, all of the market-demand states except Louisiana assign special allowables to wells in pressure-maintenance, water-flood or other secondary recovery projects. The special allowables may be the capacity of the affected wells (as in certain water-flood fields in Texas), uniform allowables adopted throughout the state or area for the category of project (as in water-flood fields in New Mexico and Oklahoma), or allowables set on an individual field basis after a hearing to determine the most efficient rate of production (as in certain pressure-maintenance projects in Oklahoma).

Third, all of the market-demand states exempt certain low-capacity wells and fields from market-demand restriction. As previously noted, Kansas has a statutory minimum daily allowable of 25 barrels per well on standard spacing, and Texas defines by statute a category of "marginal" wells which are free of production restraint based on market

---

[12] The significance of discovery allowables was sharply increased in 1966. In that year Texas increased the number of wells eligible per new field from five to ten and extended the maximum duration from 18 to 24 months; Kansas increased the number of wells eligible per new field from four to ten and extended the maximum duration from 12 to 18 months; Oklahoma increased its discovery allowable by 20 percent; and New Mexico introduced its bonus system. *Oil and Gas Journal*, vol. 64 (6 June 1966), p. 75, and (5 September 1966), p. 86.

Table 14. Oklahoma's Discovery Allowable Schedule

(barrels per day)

Depth (*thousand ft.*)	Allowable	Number of days effective
1.8–2.0	30	270
2.8–3.0	36	340
3.8–4.0	42	410
4.8–5.0	48	480
5.8–6.0	56	570
6.8–7.0	68	660
7.8–8.0	80	770
8.8–9.0	92	880
9.8–10.0	108	1,000
10.8–11.0	138	1,030
11.8–12.0	184	1,050
12.8–13.0	244	1,050
13.8–14.0	304	1,050
14.8–15.0	364	1,050

Source: IOCC, *Conservation of Oil and Gas,* p. 69; allowables adjusted for the effect by Corporation Commission Order No. 62631, 27 May 1966, increasing allowables 20 percent. *Note:* Condensed version. Complete schedule is in 200-ft. intervals.

demand.[13] Texas exempts, in addition, numerous small fields, designated "county regular" fields, in twenty-five North Texas counties, and certain small piercement salt dome fields. Oklahoma partially exempts a large number of wells and fields designated "unallocated." These are wells and fields held by the commission not to require specific production restraint to prevent waste or to protect correlative rights. The affected wells may produce at capacity, subject to one limitation: the daily production of an unallocated well may not exceed the smallest allowable of the allocated, or regulated, wells. Thus if the market demand factor is low enough, the allowable output of the more productive unallocated wells is affected by market-demand restriction. Louisiana and New Mexico in effect exempt any well incapable of producing the regular allowable for its depth-acreage class, for such a well is assigned an allowable equal to its capacity (subject to the gas-oil ratio rule).

The exemptions from market-demand restriction are designed to encourage exploration, pressure maintenance, and secondary recovery, and to prevent the premature abandonment of low-capacity wells and fields. They undoubtedly contribute to these ends but, as the relative importance of production from exempt sources clearly indicates, they help account for the often severe restraint imposed on the nonexempt sources when demand is depressed relative to capacity.

[13] For the statutory definition of marginal wells in Texas, see pp. 114–16.

Market demand production restriction since 1948

Table 15 indicates the pattern of *nominal* production restriction in the major market-demand states since 1948. The table shows the annual average of monthly market demand factors in Texas, Louisiana, New Mexico, and Oklahoma from 1948 to 1967. (The method of production restriction in Kansas does not permit the calculation of a market demand factor that is comparable from year to year.) Multiplied by basic maximum allowables, such as those given in depth-acreage schedules, these factors determine per well allowables in barrels per day.

Although comparable data are not available for the earlier years in Louisiana and Oklahoma, two features of the data in table 15 stand out. The first is a pronounced downward trend in the market demand factors from the earlier years to about 1960–63. (Note, however, the rise in New

Table 15. Annual Average of Monthly Market Demand Factors: Texas, Louisiana, New Mexico, and Oklahoma, 1948–67

(*percent*)

Year	Texas	Louisiana	New Mexico[a]	Oklahoma
1948	100%	b	63%	c
1949	65	b	61	c
1950	63	b	69	c
1951	76	b	74	c
1952	71	b	68	c
1953	65	90%	63	c
1954	53	61	57	c
1955	53	48	57	60%
1956	52	42	56	53
1957	47	43	56	52
1958	33	33	49	45
1959	34	34	50	41
1960	28	34	49	35
1961	28	32	49	31
1962	27	32	50	35
1963	28	32	54	31
1964	28	32	54	28
1965	29	33	56	27
1966	34	35	65	38
1967	41	38[d]	74	50

Sources: Respective state conservation commissions.

[a] Southeast area only. Normal unit allowables converted to market demand factor based on 70 barrels per day as maximum normal unit allowable.

[b] No fixed allowable schedule.

[c] Comparable data not available.

[d] Not exactly comparable with preceding figures because of the introduction in this year of the new "intermediate zone" allowable schedule, which effectively increased the base to which the market demand factor applied.

Mexico's market demand factor from 1948 to 1951.) The second is a marked drop in the market demand factors during business recessions, as in 1948–49, 1953–54 and 1957–58. The downward trend was so pronounced that the market demand factors show little or no tendency to rise during post-recession periods of business recovery and expansion. Only in the middle sixties does the trend seem to reverse and market demand factors respond to general business growth.

It may be noted also that in any given year the state market demand factors differ significantly from each other. Nothing much can be made of this fact, however, because the market demand factors are not comparable among states, for two reasons. First, the different state factors are multiplied by quite different basic allowable schedules to arrive at per well allowables; and the basic allowable schedules bear no consistent relationship, as among reservoirs or states, to capacity or efficient rates of production. Second, because of wide differences among states in exemptions from market-demand restriction, a given allowable per nonexempt well represents a different degree of restriction relative to capacity or to efficient production rates in each state.

No data are available that would permit us to compare allowed rates of production with efficient rates of production in each state. It is possible, however, to compare allowed rates of production with capacity for the years since 1954. (Estimates of productive capacity by state are not available for the years prior to 1954.) Table 16 shows the ratios of

Table 16. Ratio of Crude Oil Output to Productive Capacity: Texas, Louisiana, New Mexico, Oklahoma, and Kansas, 1954–67

(percent)

Year	Texas	Louisiana	New Mexico	Oklahoma	Kansas
1954	71%	85%	91%	82%	92%
1955	72	87	99	83	88
1956	72	80	93	84	88
1957	70	69	93	83	88
1958	60	59	89	79	88
1959	63	63	92	79	90
1960	60	67	90	77	87
1961	60	65	88	79	88
1962	59	68	83	82	90
1963	62	69	84	84	89
1964	63	68	89	86	89
1965	64	66	92	87	91
1966	67	69	96	98	95
1967	70	69	98	101	97

Sources: Capacity—Productive Capacity Committee, Independent Petroleum Association of America; *Output*—U.S. Bureau of Mines.

Note: Capacity estimated as of 1 January of each year. Output is for the full year.

crude oil output to productive capacity[14] in the five major market-demand states from 1954 to 1967. It may be seen that during the period covered Texas exercised the greatest degree of production restraint relative to capacity, followed by Louisiana, Oklahoma, Kansas, and New Mexico in that order. The rate of capacity utilization in Kansas is remarkably stable throughout the period. In the other states the rate of capacity utilization shows sensitivity to business recessions (note particularly the decline in 1957–58 and the recoveries in 1954–55 and 1958–59) and exhibits some downward trend from 1955 to 1961 or 1962. An upward trend in the capacity utilization rates is noticeable after 1962. In all years the rates of capacity utilization are much larger than the corresponding market demand factors (table 15), a fact that reflects primarily the extent of exemptions from market-demand restriction and secondarily the relation of basic allowable schedules to capacity.

Some perspective on rates of capacity utilization in the major market-demand states is provided by comparing them with rates of capacity utilization in other important producing states. Table 17 shows the ratio of crude oil output to productive capacity in Mississippi, Colorado, Wyoming, Montana, and Utah for the years between 1954 and 1967; the data are distinctly different from those in table 16. Table 17 reveals that (a) most of the rates of capacity utilization are in the neighborhood of 100 percent, particularly after 1957;[15] (b) there is no downward trend from the earlier to the later years; and (c) there is no consistent response to business recessions and recoveries. The pattern of the data suggests that variation in rates of capacity utilization in the non-market-demand states primarily reflects temporary divergencies between rates of growth of producing capacity and rates of growth of pipeline and refining facilities in local areas.

To some extent, trends in rates of capacity utilization reflect trends in well spacing in new reservoirs. Other things being equal, wider spacing results in less short-run capacity than denser spacing. For this and

---

[14] Productive capacity is defined as "the average rate of production from existing wells that could be maintained for a period of from 6 to 12 months without further development and with no significant loss of ultimate recovery ... [and assuming] no substantial modification of producing facilities or operating methods." "Report of the IPAA Productive Capacity Committee," mimeographed (April 1965), p. 1. "Crude oil" for purposes of both production and capacity includes lease condensate.

[15] Because capacity is defined here as sustained ability, as of the first of the year, to produce for 6 to 12 months with no significant loss of ultimate recovery, measured capacity utilization rates can exceed 100 percent, particularly if actual capacity is growing throughout the affected year.

Table 17. **Ratio of Crude Oil Output to Productive Capacity: Mississippi, Colorado, Wyoming, Montana, and Utah, 1954–67**

(*percent*)

Year	Mississippi	Colorado	Wyoming	Montana	Utah
1954	97%	115%	85%	78%	119%
1955	106	93	83	73	85
1956	98	92	88	96	96
1957	93	89	92	100	80
1958	100	86	97	85	136
1959	119	90	100	97	110
1960	104	100	105	97	102
1961	104	100	102	107	82
1962	104	91	94	110	94
1963	104	95	100	97	108
1964	98	95	98	100	87
1965	103	97	96	106	92
1966	89	101	94	104	100
1967	88	100	90	96	98

Sources: Capacity—Productive Capacity Committee, Independent Petroleum Association of America; *Output*—U.S. Bureau of Mines.
Note: Capacity estimated as of 1 January of each year. Output is for the full year.

other reasons, the postwar trend in well spacing is significant for purposes of this study.

Trends in well spacing since 1948

The usual well spacing regulation, which specifies minimum distances between adjacent wells and between a well and the nearest property line, anticipates regular geometric spacing with a certain minimum-sized area drained by each well. In 1948, the typical minimum area per well required in new oil reservoirs was 20 acres. But experience under the Petroleum Administration for War (PAW) regulation during World War II had demonstrated the technical feasibility and economic advantages of 40-acre spacing in a wide variety of situations. Consequently, the regulations adopted under most of the new state conservation laws enacted since 1945 have required a minimum of 40-acre spacing; and the older producing states have gradually amended their regulations correspondingly. Today, 40 acres is the typical minimum area per well, with 80 acres or more required in some cases.

The trend toward wider minimum spacing in state regulation is significant, of course, for it represents the direction in which practice is moving. But a regulatory minimum does not precisely determine spacing in any state. In the first place, exceptions may be granted to the regulatory minimum spacing. Since commissions rely primarily upon the adversary nature of hearings to bring out all relevant facts, they tend to grant exceptions when operators are unanimous, or nearly so, in requesting them. In the second place, a regulatory minimum in no way limits wider spacing. Operators are free to respond to economic incentives in requesting wider-than-minimum spacing; and if they are unanimous, or nearly so, commissions are likely to grant their requests. The result, therefore, is not some uniform spacing in new reservoirs reflecting a given state's basic regulation, but rather a *distribution* of spacings reflecting the variety of situations confronting operators in each year's crop of new reservoirs in a given state.

In connection with its 1964 study, the IOCC Governors' Special Study Committee surveyed recent oil well spacing orders issued by commissions in a number of regulating states. The results for selected years, 1950–62, in the principal states surveyed are given in table 18. Data are not available for the earlier postwar years in some states, but the data that are available show a marked trend toward wider spacing, particularly after 1955.

The data for Louisiana, New Mexico, Oklahoma, and Texas are especially significant. In 1950 and 1955 Louisiana spaced several new fields on 20 acres or less, but none on 160 acres or more. In 1960 and 1962 the number on 20 acres or less was larger but the proportion was smaller, and both the number and the proportion on 80 acres and 160 acres or more increased markedly. Just between 1955 and 1962 the modal spacing of new fields in Louisiana rose from 40 acres to 80 acres. In New Mexico the effective minimum spacing throughout the period covered was 40 acres. After 1955 the number of new fields spaced on 80 acres became significant, and in 1962 four new fields were spaced on 160 acres or more. The shift in the spacing distribution in Oklahoma between 1955 and 1962 was dramatic. In the former year 115 new fields were spaced on 20 acres or less, as compared with thirty-seven on 40 acres and only two on 80 acres. In the latter year the pattern was essentially reversed. The number of new fields on 20 acres or less had fallen to fifty-seven, while the number on 80 acres rose to 104. Three new fields in Oklahoma were spaced on 160 acres or more in 1962. The post–World War II trend in oil well spacing in Texas is quite similar to that in Oklahoma. In 1950 thirty new fields were spaced on 20 acres or less, twenty-four new fields on 40 acres, and none on 80 acres or more. By 1962 the number on 20 acres or less had fallen to five, while the number on 40 acres rose to fifty-five, and the number on 80 acres or more to forty-four. There is reason to believe that the trend to wider spacing in these states still continues, and that as of this writing (1970) the modal spacing of new oil fields is 80 acres.

Table 18.   Distribution of New Oil Fields by Well-Spacing Category: Selected States, 1950, 1955, 1960, and 1962

				(*no. of fields*)
State and year	20 acres or less	40 acres	80 acres	160 acres or more
Colorado				
1950	na	na	na	na
1955	0	23	0	0
1960	0	0	0	0
1962	0	1	0	0
Kansas				
1950	na	na	na	na
1955	na	na	na	na
1960	3	30	3	0
1962	2	33	15	0
Louisiana				
1950	2	20	7	0
1955	4	10	6	0
1960	10	23	12	3
1962	8	17	40	5
Montana				
1950	na	na	na	na
1955	1	0	10	1
1960	1	1	1	1
1962	3	4	1	4
New Mexico				
1950	0	na[a]	1	0
1955	0	na[a]	0	0
1960	0	na[a]	10	0
1962	0	na[a]	12	4
North Dakota				
1950	na	na	na	na
1955	0	1	4	0
1960	0	0	3	6
1962	0	0	0	0
Oklahoma				
1950	21	18	0	0
1955	115	37	2	0
1960	42	53	41	0
1962	57	90	104	3
Texas				
1950	30	24	0	0
1955	31	44	19	0
1960	14	69	22	0
1962	5	55	38	6
Wyoming				
1950	0	1	0	0
1955	1	9	4	2
1960	0	0	8	0
1962	0	1	8	1

Source: IOCC, *Conservation of Oil and Gas*, p. 59.
na—Not available.   [a] All fields not spaced on 80 or 160 acres.

(Also evident in the postwar period is a trend toward wider spacing of gas wells. The data produced by the IOCC Governors' Special Study Committee indicate that the modal spacing in new gas fields rose from 160 acres in 1950 to 640 acres in 1962.[16])

As indicated earlier, not all of the trend toward wider spacing in new oil fields, particularly above 40 acres, can be attributed to direct regulatory restraint. It is apparent that economic incentives play a major role; that in choosing one well density over another operators weigh incremental well cost against incremental present value of expected proceeds (cash flow) from production.[17] As rational businessmen, they choose the well density that promises to maximize present value net of well costs, future outlays and receipts being discounted at the minimum acceptable rate of return. Well costs are determined by drilling technology, the unit costs of inputs, depth, location, and the given geological situation. Expected proceeds from production are determined by expected prices and operating costs, expected tax treatment of income and, given reservoir operating characteristics, permissible producing rates under regulatory restraint. In the major market-demand states, permissible producing rates in new fields are usually derived from the applicable depth-acreage allowable schedules.

Spacing incentives in depth-acreage allowable schedules

On the premise that in a given reservoir operators prefer the well density that maximizes the present value of expected proceeds net of well costs, I have estimated the incentives embodied in the several state depth-acreage allowable schedules by computing and comparing the net present values resulting from various densities under different assumptions as to market demand factor and recoverable reserves per acre.[18] The results indicate the well density that would be chosen at each depth under the market demand and recoverable reserves conditions assumed.

The two basic components of net present value are (a) the present value of expected proceeds (cash flow) from production and (b) well costs by depth. Computation of each requires some explicit assump-

---

[16] IOCC, *Conservation of Oil and Gas*, p. 58.

[17] See chapter 5, figs. 6 and 7 and associated text.

[18] This procedure was suggested by that of the Texas Industry Advisory Committee which designed the 1965 Texas Yardstick. "Statement of the Committee before the Texas Railroad Commission," mimeographed (July 16, 1964).

tions.[19] The assumptions employed in computing the present value of expected proceeds are:

1. Oil production declines at a constant percentage rate from the initial allowable to one barrel per day per well.[20] The initial allowable is taken from the applicable depth-acreage schedule. Discovery allowables are disregarded.

2. Future outlays and receipts are discounted at 10 percent per year.

3. Associated gas revenues are disregarded.

4. All prices, costs, tax rates, and market demand factors are expected to remain constant over well life.

5. Oil price: $3.00 per barrel.

6. Royalty, including override: 17.5 percent of gross.

7. Severance and property taxes: 7.5 percent of net after royalty.

8. Percentage depletion: 27.5 percent of net after royalty or 50 percent of net income before tax, whichever is smaller.

9. Depreciation is taken on a unit-of-production basis (fixed amount per barrel, given depreciable value).

10. Depreciable value per well: 30 percent of gross well cost (see below) plus $5,000 to $12,000 for surface equipment, depending on depth.

11. Income tax rate: 50 percent.

12. Operating cost per well, onshore:

Depth (thousand ft.)	Cost per year (thousand dollars)
2	2.4
4	2.8
6	3.4
8	4.2
10	5.2
12	6.4
14	7.6
16	9.0

[19] My assumptions are similar to those employed by the Texas Industry Advisory Committee.

[20] The decline rate (percent per year) is calculated from the standard formula for the sum of a geometric series: $s = a/d[1 - (1 - d)^n]$, where s = recoverable reserves per well, a = initial annual allowable, n = number of years to abandonment and d = decline rate. As n becomes large, d approaches a/s. No significant error is introduced by taking $d = a/s$, as is done in our computations. The number of years to abandonment thus becomes a dependent variable in our analysis.

13. Operating cost per well, offshore: three times onshore cost.

14. Prices, operating costs, and severance and property taxes are assumed to be the same in all states and areas.

The assumptions employed in computing well costs by depth are:

1. All wells are assumed to be drilled at time zero.

2. Well drilling costs by depth derived from Fisher's regressions on sample data from the Joint Association Survey of 1959.[21] Costs are estimated separately for each state and area. Texas offshore costs are assumed to be the same as Louisiana offshore costs.

3. Seventy percent of well drilling costs are assumed to be "intangible,"[22] hence deductible for income tax purposes as current expense. At the assumed tax rate of 50 percent the immediate tax saving is, thus, 35 percent of drilling cost; hence the net cost at time zero is 65 percent of the gross cost.

4. Costs of surface equipment are assumed to range (in $1,000 increments per 2,000 feet) from $5,000 for the shallowest to $12,000 for the deepest wells.

These assumptions do not necessarily describe the typical situation in any state or area. They are believed to be reasonable, however, for the purpose at hand, which is to show how different well densities are induced at different depths, or under different market demand or recoverable reserve conditions, given the applicable depth-acreage allowable schedule. I hardly need add that, since each reservoir presents a unique situation, the following results of my computations offer no guide in practical decision making.

Consider first the case of the Texas 1947 Yardstick (table 4). Assuming that the initial well allowable based on that schedule reflects a market demand factor of 60 percent, and further assuming that recoverable reserves are 12,500 barrels per acre,[23] figure 15 shows the net present

---

[21] Franklin M. Fisher, *Supply and Costs in the U.S. Petroleum Industry: Two Econometric Studies* (Washington: Resources for the Future, 1964), pp. 122–31.

[22] Intangible costs include expenditures for labor, fuel, materials, supplies, tool rental, and repairs in connection with drilling and equipping productive wells. For a thorough discussion of percentage depletion and the tax treatment of various costs in the petroleum industry, see Stephen L. McDonald, *Federal Tax Treatment of Income from Oil and Gas* (Washington: The Brookings Institution, 1963), especially pp. 8–26.

[23] Of course, actual recoverable reserves per acre are different for each reservoir and vary widely. This factor is held constant in the computation in order to bring out the effect of the other variables. The effect of varying recoverable reserves per acre is indicated by a comparison of figure 17 with the other figures.

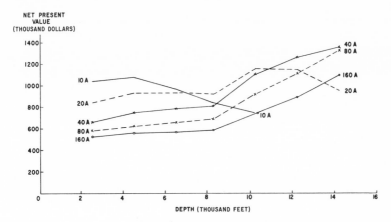

Figure 15.   Texas 1947 Yardstick: Net present value of cash flow after tax by depth (160-acre tract; 12,500 barrels per acre; 60 percent market demand factor; 10 percent discount after tax).

values of a 160-acre tract with wells on various alternative spacings drilled to various alternative depths. Each curve (labeled 10 acres, 20 acres, etc.) shows how net present value at that spacing varies with depth. At any given depth, the highest curve (representing the greatest present value) indicates the spacing which would be preferred. Thus, at depths less than 7,000 feet, 10-acre spacing would be preferred; between depths of 7,000 feet and 11,000 feet, 20-acre spacing would be preferred; and at depths greater than 11,000 feet, 40-acre spacing would be preferred. At no depth within the range covered would 80-acre or 160-acre spacing be chosen. The figure suggests that if operators were completely free to select well spacing, and wells drilled were distributed evenly by depth, about a third of the wells would fall into each of the spacing categories—10 acres, 20 acres, and 40 acres.

Figure 16 is based on the same assumptions as figure 15, except that the market-demand factor is now assumed to be only 30 percent. Of course, given the same discount rate all the net present values are lower now, since the exhaustion of the same recoverable reserves requires more time. In addition, wider spacing is induced at some depths. Thus, the preference now shifts from 10 acres to 20 acres at 5,500 feet (vs. 7,000 feet in figure 15); and from 20 acres to 40 acres at 10,500 feet (vs. 11,000 feet in figure 15). This is because with a lower market demand factor, smaller increments to present value of expected proceeds result from additional basic allowables per tract gained through denser spacing; the incremental present value of expected proceeds becomes equal to the incremental well cost sooner (at wider spacing).

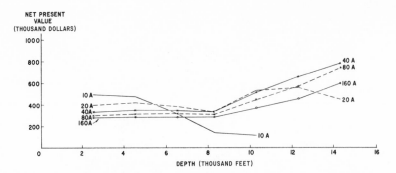

Figure 16. Texas 1947 Yardstick: Net present value of cash flow after tax by depth (160-acre tract; 12,500 barrels per acre; 30 percent market demand factor; 10 percent discount after tax).

Similar reasoning makes it apparent that wider spacing is induced by lower prices, higher operating costs, higher well costs, or higher tax rates, other things being equal. It may be noted also that since the net present value of developed tracts represents the lump-sum return to exploration, a lower market demand factor, by reducing net present values, discourages exploration.[24]

Figure 17 is based on the same assumptions as figure 15, except that the assumed recoverable reserves are now only 6,250 barrels per acre. The reduced amount of recoverable oil reduces all net present values; but not proportionately, since given initial allowables shorten the time required for exhaustion. Significantly wider spacing is induced by lower recoverable reserves. Thus, 10-acre spacing is preferred only up to depths of 3,500 feet, 20-acre spacing at depths between 3,500 and 6,000 feet, 40-acre spacing at depths between 6,000 feet and 9,000 feet, and 80-acre spacing at all depths greater than 9,000 feet. The wider spacing is induced because with smaller recoverable reserves depletion time is reduced at any given well density, and smaller increments to present value of expected proceeds result from additional tract allowables gained through denser spacing. Put another way, shorter depletion time at any given well spacing lessens operators' gain from shortening depletion time still further by means of denser spacing and larger initial allowables.

The analysis reflected in figures 15–17 helps explain two things. First,

---

24 On markedly supramarginal exploration prospects, a reduced anticipated market demand factor merely has the effect of reducing the lease bonus offered to the landowner. On barely supramarginal or marginal prospects, however, it has the effect of discouraging exploration.

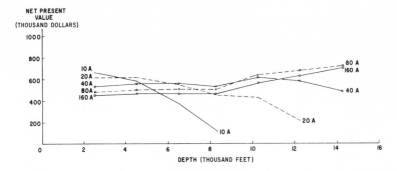

Figure 17.   Texas 1947 Yardstick: Net present value of cash flow after tax by depth (160-acre tract; 6,250 barrels per acre; 60 percent market demand factor; 10 percent discount after tax).

why in Texas in recent years (prior to the adoption of the 1965 Yardstick) there has been a *distribution* of spacing densities in new fields, many fields being spaced on acreages far greater than the regulatory state-wide minimum. Given the allowable schedule, the distribution of wells by depth and other factors affecting their cost, and the distribution of discoveries by size of recoverable reserves, a certain distribution of preferred spacings is created. Second, the analysis helps explain why the average spacing in new fields has become greater in recent years, particularly since 1955. Lower market demand factors and greater average depth of new wells have certainly contributed to this result. Still other causes may have been operating. Lower prices after 1957, if not matched by reduced operating costs, would have worked for wider spacing, as would higher unit costs of well drilling inputs not offset by

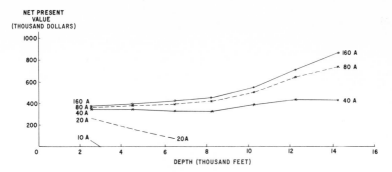

Figure 18.   Texas 1965 Yardstick: Net present value of cash flow after tax by depth (160-acre tract; 12,500 barrels per acre; 30 percent market demand factor; 10 percent discount after tax).

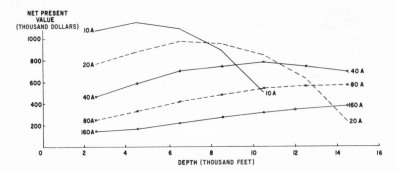

Figure 19.   Louisiana 1953 schedule: Net present value of cash flow after tax by depth (160-acre tract; 12,500 barrels per acre; 30 percent market demand factor; 10 percent discount after tax).

technological improvement. Similarly, decreasing recoverable reserves per acre in new discoveries would have induced wider average spacing. Unfortunately, data on which to base firm conclusions as to these latter factors are lacking.

The introduction in 1965 of the new Texas Yardstick (table 5) radically changed the pattern of spacing incentives in that state. Figure 18, which is based on the assumptions of 12,500 barrels of recoverable reserves per acre and a market demand factor of 30 percent, shows that under the new Yardstick the preferred spacing is 160 acres for all depths above 2,500 feet. However, the differences in net present value among 40-acre, 80-acre, and 160-acre spacings are very small at depths below 4,500 feet; so one of the denser spacings might be preferred in some practical situations at the shallower depths. A comparison of figure 18 with figure 16, which is based on the same reserves and market demand assumptions, shows that the net present value at the preferred spacing is higher under the 1965 Yardstick than under its 1947 counterpart for all depths above 5,000 feet. The new Yardstick should, thus, stimulate exploration at the greater depths, market demand and other factors remaining the same.[25]

Louisiana, also, introduced a new allowable schedule during the period 1948–68. From 1953 to 1960 Louisiana employed a schedule corresponding to the 40-acre column in table 7. The spacing incentives embodied in that schedule are indicated in figure 19, which is based on assumptions of recoverable reserves of 12,500 barrels per acre

---

[25] Figures based on different reserves and market demand assumptions relative to the 1965 Yardstick will not be presented, since they would only suggest again the conclusions drawn from figures 15 through 17.

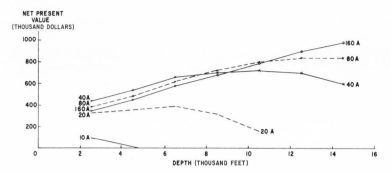

Figure 20. Louisiana 1960 schedule: Net present value of cash flow after tax by depth (160-acre tract; 12,500 barrels per acre; 30 percent market demand factor; 10 percent discount after tax).

and a market demand factor of 30 percent. It appears that under the assumptions the 1953 allowable schedule induced 10-acre spacing at depths up to 8,000 feet, 20-acre spacing at depths between 8,000 feet and 11,000 feet, and 40-acre spacing at depths above 11,000 feet. Note also that at the preferred spacings the net present values decline from the lesser to the greater depths. Since exploration costs increase with depth, the 1953 Louisiana allowable schedule apparently discouraged deep exploration relative to shallow exploration.

The situation in Louisiana was dramatically changed by the introduction of the 1960 allowable schedule (table 7). Figure 20, reflecting the same assumptions as figure 19, indicates a preferred spacing of 40 acres at depths up to 8,000 feet, 80 acres at depths between 8,000 feet and 11,000 feet, and 160 acres at depths above 11,000 feet. The net present values at the preferred spacings rise from the lesser to the greater depths, thus providing an incentive to exploration which varies in the same direction as exploration costs. It is interesting to note, however, on comparing the 1953 and 1960 allowable schedules, that the 1960 schedule reduced all net present values below 11,000-feet depths. The reason is that the new schedule drastically reduced the relatively high tract allowables previously obtainable with 20-acre or 10-acre spacing.

Assuming recoverable reserves of 12,500 barrels per acre and a 30 percent market demand factor, the New Mexico allowable schedule (table 10) apparently induces spacing of 40 acres at all depths (figure 21).[26] However, if the assumed amount of recoverable reserves per

[26] Strictly interpreted, the figure indicates a preferred spacing of 160 acres in a narrow range of depths around 6,500 feet. Note that the 80-acre and 160-acre curves begin only at 6,500 feet.

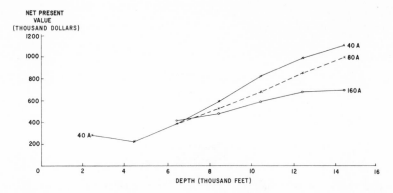

Figure 21. New Mexico schedule: Net present value of cash flow after tax by depth (160-acre tract; 12,500 barrels per acre; 30 percent market demand factor; 10 percent discount after tax).

acre is reduced to 6,250 barrels, the preferred spacing becomes 80 acres at depths above 8,000 feet (not shown). No doubt the distribution of new discoveries in New Mexico by volume of reserves per acre helps explain the few fields spaced on 80 or 160 acres in recent years.

Figure 22 shows the pattern of net present values reflecting the Oklahoma allowable schedule (table 11), assuming recoverable reserves of 12,500 barrels per acre and a 30 percent market demand factor. The chart indicates that 20-acre spacing would be preferred at depths up to 5,000 feet, 40-acre spacing at depths between 5,000 and 6,500 feet, and 160-acre spacing at depths above 6,500 feet.[27] The apparent exploration incentive is quite low at depths below 10,000 feet.

Figure 23, reflecting the Kansas allowable schedule (table 12), conveys a radically different picture. Under the same assumptions as to recoverable reserves and market demand factor, 10-acre spacing apparently would be preferred at depths up to 7,000 feet, 40-acre spacing at depths between 7,000 and 7,500 feet, 80-acre spacing at depths between 7,500 and 9,500 feet, and 160-acre spacing at depths above 9,500 feet. The apparent exploration incentive is very high at the lesser depths but declines steeply to about 8,000 feet and disappears at about 12,000 feet. The principal reason for the high net present values at the lesser depths is the 25-barrel minimum daily allowable per well prevailing in Kansas. Neither density of spacing (if approved by the commission) nor restriction of market demand factor can reduce this allowable per well. Given well costs, the sheltered allowable thus encourages

[27] Note that the 80-acre and 160-acre curves begin only at 6,500 feet.

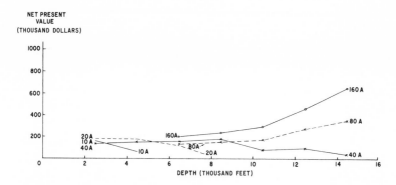

Figure 22. Oklahoma schedule: Net present value of cash flow after tax by depth (160-acre tract; 12,500 barrels per acre; 30 percent market demand factor; 10 percent discount after tax).

applications for dense spacing; and to the extent that approvals can be anticipated, exploration at shallow depths is strongly stimulated.

It remains now to compare the spacing incentives embodied in the Texas and Louisiana offshore allowable schedules (tables 6 and 9). Figure 24, reflecting the usual recoverable reserve and market demand assumptions, shows that in Texas the preferred spacing would be 40 acres for depths up to 4,500 feet, 80 acres for depths between 4,500 and 7,000 feet, and 160 acres for depths above 7,000 feet. Figure 25, reflecting the same assumptions, shows that in Louisiana the preferred spacing would be 40 acres for depths up to 9,000 feet, 80 acres for depths between 9,000 and 10,000 feet, and 160 acres for depths above

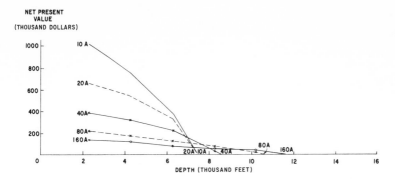

Figure 23. Kansas schedule: Net present value of cash flow after tax by depth (160-acre tract; 12,500 barrels per acre; 30 percent market demand factor; 10 percent discount after tax).

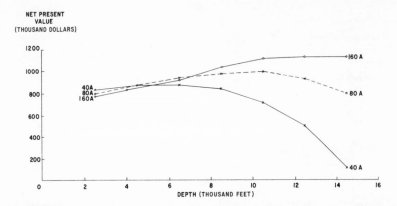

Figure 24.   Texas offshore schedule: Net present value of cash flow after tax by depth (160-acre tract; 12,500 barrels per acre; 30 percent market demand factor; 10 percent discount after tax).

10,000 feet. The net present values at preferred spacings are well above those onshore; but, of course, exploration costs offshore are higher than those onshore.

I have noted several times that an apparent exploration incentive is embodied in the various state allowable schedules (in combination with state well drilling costs). It is interesting to compare those incentives. Figure 26, based on the assumptions of 12,500 barrels per acre recoverable reserves and a 30 percent market demand factor, shows the net present values at preferred spacings in the major market-demand states (onshore only). At depths below 5,000 feet Kansas holds out the largest exploration incentive, followed by Louisiana (1960 schedule),

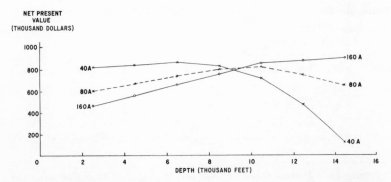

Figure 25.   Louisiana offshore schedule: Net present value of cash flow after tax by depth (160-acre tract; 12,500 barrels per acre; 30 percent market demand factor; 10 percent discount after tax).

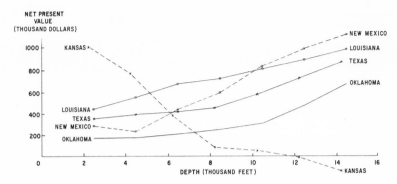

Figure 26. Net present value of cash flow after tax at optimum spacing (160-acre tract; 12,500 barrels per acre; 30 percent market demand factor; 10 percent discount after tax).

Texas (1965 Yardstick), New Mexico, and Oklahoma in that order. Between 5,000 and 10,000 feet the Kansas incentive falls to last place while that of New Mexico rises toward first place; the incentives of Louisiana, Texas, and Oklahoma remain in the same order, that of Louisiana leading all the other states. At depths above 10,000 feet New Mexico offers the largest incentive, followed in order by Louisiana, Texas, Oklahoma, and Kansas. At all depths the difference between the first and last state is at least five hundred thousand dollars per 160-acre tract. In all states except Kansas the exploration incentive at least doubles from the lesser to the greater depths, this pattern being consistent with rising exploration costs from lesser to greater depths.

The implications of the comparison in figure 26 must be qualified with several observations. First, exploration costs may differ substantially among states, perhaps in such a way that the apparent incentive differences among states is reduced. Second, the computations underlying all of the foregoing charts are based on the assumption that prices, operating costs, and severance and property taxes are the same in all states; this, of course, is not strictly true. Third, the well costs used in the underlying computations are statewide averages for each depth; there is undoubtedly a good deal of dispersion of well costs at each depth within states. Fourth, on supramarginal prospects the differences in exploration incentives are absorbed partly by differences in lease bonuses per acre; to this extent it is the landowner's income rather than exploration itself that suffers from a low incentive.[28] Nonetheless, the differences in computed incentives are so large that it must be assumed

[28] Because of uncertainty in exploration, it would be coincidental if an incentive differential were absorbed precisely by the lease bonus.

that the allocation of exploration effort among states is at least marginally affected by the differences in allowable schedules.

An evaluation of production and well spacing control

In several respects, state regulation of production and well spacing has made valuable contributions to oil conservation. First, both limitation of well density and control of production on the basis of MER preclude the grosser physical losses associated with unrestrained drilling and production. Restriction of production to MER is an especially useful conservation device. While genuine conservation would permit some loss of ultimate recovery in order to avoid an economically more important loss of value caused by lengthened recovery time, the waste of value under MER regulation could scarcely ever equal that which would occur in the absence of any production control. To the extent that MERs in practice reflect the economic cost of time, they may differ little from optimum rates of production. Moreover, systematic control of production on the basis of MER induces a typical well density which, being anticipated by explorers, in turn induces a rate of exploration that may closely approximate the optimum.

Second, regulation of production on the basis of market demand, which will be criticized extensively in chapter 11, makes some contributions to genuine conservation. Although it introduces some at least partially offsetting costs, it precludes the massive losses of ultimate recovery resulting from unrestrained production. Only at the greater depths are the maximum reservoir allowables provided by depth-acreage schedules likely to exceed MERs; and in such instances MERs may be imposed to displace the regular schedule as the basis of allowables. Additionally, regulation on the basis of market demand is a positive device for preventing discrimination in purchases within and among fields, for assuring all producers an access to the market, and for limiting the amount of surface storage. It thus contributes to conservation by averting some socially unnecessary costs resulting from inefficient reservoir drainage, arbitrary allocation of production among reservoirs, and excessive surface storage. Even the price stabilizing effects of market-demand regulation may make some contribution to conservation, for, as pointed out in chapter 6, short-run prices in the absence of regulation tend to be unstable to a socially undesirable degree, because of the (socially unnecessary) negative marginal user cost of competitive extraction.[29]

Third, given regulation based on market demand, the depth-acreage

---

[29] See pp. 95–96.

allowable schedule has proved to be a workable administrative device. However arbitrary in structure it may be, it is an inexpensive substitute for the complicated and time-consuming process of determining individual reservoir MERs. As a constant for long periods of time, it provides an element of certainty in the prospects of explorer-developers. And, in its typical form, it induces far wider spacing than would prevail without regulation, particularly in the leaner fields, at the greater depths, and under the lower market demand factors.

Finally, it should be noted that state regulation of production and well spacing is susceptible to change in ways that generally must be regarded as improvements. Since the end of World War II, the typical minimum spacing standard has been approximately doubled, the two leading states have modified their depth-acreage schedules to induce spacing much wider than the minimum, and most of the states enacting new conservation laws have omitted provision for production restraint based on market demand while including provision for restraint based on MER.[30] Furthermore, the inducements built into depth-acreage allowable schedules have led to wider spacing as wells have gone deeper and market demand factors have fallen lower. The system, thus, has not been entirely rigid in form or effects.

Granted that present approaches to controlling production and well spacing contribute in several ways to oil conservation, they are subject to criticism on a number of grounds. First, statewide rules that specify some minimum acceptable distance between wells, or some minimum acceptable acreage per well, are essentially arbitrary. In no state or area is there some single well density which, on sound conservation grounds, divides the appropriate from the inappropriate. As explained in chapter 5, the appropriate—that is to say, the optimum—well density varies from one reservoir to another. Codetermined with the optimum planned rate of production, the optimum well density in a reservoir depends upon the unique conditions of that reservoir, notably its depth, recoverable reserves per acre, drive, and other operating characteristics. In principle, there is no well density which may not be appropriate under some circumstances.[31] Nor, it follows, is wider spacing always preferable to closer spacing. Only when at the allowed or preferred rate of production closer spacing would result in excess capacity is wider spacing clearly superior. It is because this condition of latent excess capacity has

---

[30] See the chronology of legislation since 1948 in the Appendix.
[31] The effect of a minimum spacing rule is probably not great in practice, because of administrative exceptions, incentives for operators to use wider-than-minimum spacing, and the practice (in Texas and North Dakota, notably) of requiring early development in new fields on sufficiently wide spacing to allow flexibility in the final spacing pattern adopted.

obtained in the market-demand states over most of the postwar period that we can regard the trend to wider spacing as an improvement.

Second, regulation of production on the basis of MER is not ideal. The MER of a reservoir is not necessarily its optimum rate of production. As usually interpreted by regulators, the MER is that rate of production which, if exceeded, would result in some (technically) avoidable loss of ultimate recovery. So interpreted, the MER is designed to avoid physical waste and makes no allowance for either the economic cost of time or the relationship of present to expected costs and prices. Unlike the optimum rate of production, the MER is unresponsive to those changes in the cost of capital and in the relationship of present to expected marginal net revenues which ordinarily occur during the life of a reservoir in a continuously developing economy. Even if the MER should approximate the optimum rate in the first years of production from a reservoir, it would not do so continuously throughout reservoir life in the face of changing economic conditions and prospects. Nonetheless, the MER is undoubtedly the most valid and useful single concept employed in oil conservation regulation. Particularly if a secular rise in oil prices is expected, so that a special premium is placed on future relative to present production, the MER of a reservoir need not differ greatly from the optimum rate of production. Moreover, as the earlier quotation from Buckley[32] suggests, it would involve no great change in concept to incorporate the economic cost of time into the determination of MERs.

Third, the depth-acreage allowable schedules employed in the major market-demand states are largely without foundation in conservation principles. Well allowables vary directly with depth and acreage drained, and their pattern generally induces wider spacing at greater depths. But the resultant reservoir allowables bear no systematic relationship to (hypothetical) MERs, or even to recoverable reserves per acre. The allowables in deep, lean reservoirs may greatly exceed (hypothetical) MERs, while those in shallow, rich reservoirs may fall markedly short of (hypothetical) MERs.[33] Only by coincidence do the allowable sched-

---

[32] See chapter 2, footnote 18 and associated text.

[33] Under the 1947 Texas Yardstick, at the preferred spacing and with a 30 percent market demand factor, allowed production the first year from a reservoir at 2,000 feet containing 12,500 barrels per acre would be approximately 4 percent of recoverable reserves, while that from a reservoir at 14,000 feet containing 6,250 barrels per acre would be approximately 25 percent of recoverable reserves. The corresponding figures based on the 1965 Yardstick are 1 percent and 11 percent. Of course, where the MER is less than the schedule allowable the regulatory commission may adopt the former as the basis of allowable production.

ules induce the optimum well density and initial rate of production. Given depth and recoverable reserves per acre in a reservoir, induced well density is related not to reservoir operating characteristics, but to the pattern of well allowables and expected market demand factors. Well density tends to be optimal, not with respect to reservoir conditions but with respect to the regulatory restraints imposed. Furthermore, there is no reason in conservation principles for increasing well allowables with depth or adverse location (offshore). This feature of depth-acreage allowable schedules distorts the allocation of exploration and production among locations of varying cost. It encourages the exploitation of relatively high-cost opportunities at the expense of relatively low-cost opportunities. The effect is to increase the cost of oil consumed at any point in time and to hasten artificially the substitution of other energy sources for oil. The optimum utilization of petroleum resources requires that production move progressively over time from lower-cost to higher-cost locations as technology improves or as oil prices rise with growing scarcity.

Fourth, the mixed pattern of spacing-production regulation distorts the allocation of exploration and production among states. As noted earlier in this chapter, the different depth-acreage schedules employed in the several market-demand states create different levels of exploration incentive. On marginal prospects at least, some states are favored at the expense of others, not because of natural advantages, but because of specific features of allowable schedules. A similar distortion of incentives occurs between the market-demand states and non-market-demand states. The difference in basis of production regulation (e.g., allowable schedule and market demand vs. MER) creates an artificial cost difference which, on marginal prospects at least, affects the allocation of productive activity among states. Since MER and associated spacing regulation generally allows more nearly optimal producing conditions than other forms of regulation, exploration and production in the MER states is favored in relation to those states using market demand or simply minimum spacing as the basis of production restraint.

Fifth, the exemptions from market-demand production restriction distort the allocation of productive activity within the affected states. Special discovery allowables of the type employed in Texas and Kansas, which apply to a limited number of wells for a limited period, give relative encouragement to exploration where prospects are small and wholly controlled by a single lessee. Under these conditions the discoverer can quickly drill the exact number of wells to maximize the size and term of the discovery allowable; while where prospects are large and divided into many leaseholds, competition for available oil leads to quick expiration of the discovery allowable as lessees drill more than the permissible number of wells. The exemption of statutorily defined "marginal" wells or provision for a minimum well allowable gives relative encouragement to exploration where prospects are lean, promising limited capacity per well; and the exemption or special treatment of secondary recovery projects obviously favors secondary recovery relative to exploration for new primary capacity. All these incentive distortions are intensified to the extent that market-demand production restriction stabilizes prices. To that extent, the exempt categories of production are free from either quantity or price effects of fluctuating demand, and the full burden of adjustment to fluctuations falls on the nonexempt categories. Thus, in yet another way high-cost oil is favored at the expense of low-cost oil, long-run marginal cost is raised, and the resource life of petroleum is shortened. The optimum utilization of petroleum resources requires that different reservoirs and types of production compete for available markets on the basis of real costs undistorted by special exemptions or restrictions. Over time, lower-cost oil should be consumed first, followed by higher-cost oil as technology progresses or oil prices rise with increasing scarcity.

Sixth, the regulatory adjustment of output to quantity demanded, regardless of the price, in the market-demand states leaves the price to be independently set by refiner-buyers (who may also be producer-sellers) on the basis of some long-run consideration such as overall rate of return on investment. In free, competitive markets price continually gravitates to the level at which quantity willingly supplied equals quantity willingly demanded—where the cost of the last unit supplied just equals the value to consumers of the last unit demanded. The schedules of supply and demand in effect determine what the price will be; and at the determined price, under certain ideal conditions, the net satisfactions derived from the product in question are maximized.[34] But under market-demand regulation of oil production, the going price independently set determines quantity demanded and allowed production is then forcibly equated with that quantity. No excess supply or demand is allowed to develop that would cause price to fall or rise for competitive reasons. In the short run at least, price is denied its function of clearing markets, of equating quantity willingly supplied with quantity willingly demanded. Price becomes simply a device for influencing the incomes of buyers and sellers.

We must be cautious in going further than that. True, forcible restraint of production implies that allowed production is less than the quantity which would be willingly supplied; that the cost of the last unit

[34] See pp. 64–67.

supplied is less than the value to consumers of the last unit demanded. This, in turn, implies that price under market-demand restraint is always too high. But because of the negative marginal user cost of unrestrained extraction,[35] the amounts competitive operators are willing to supply in the short run at given prices are always too great in a social sense. An excess of quantity willingly supplied over quantity willingly demanded at the going price is, therefore, no evidence that the going price is too high in a social sense. My present point is not the excessively high price but that under market-demand production restriction the market for oil contains no mechanism for equating a socially appropriate quantity supplied with the quantity demanded. Price simply cannot perform its proper function under market-demand regulation.

Seventh, the system of regulation in the major market-demand states, in association with industry pricing practices, evidently tends to produce and perpetuate excess capacity, which burdens the industry with unnecessary costs, artificially discourages exploration, and shortens the resource-life of oil and gas. Excess capacity results in part from depth-acreage allowable schedules that, in some depth and recoverable reserve situations, induce the drilling of more wells than are required to produce the allowed output. It is only by coincidence that capacity just equals allowables at the preferred spacing in any reservoir. More fundamentally (and truistically), excess capacity is produced and perpetuated by prices that for the long run are too high and too resistant to downward adjustment. Prices at any level are supported by the restriction of output to market demand; and if capacity grows faster than demand at a given supported level, the burden of providing a disincentive to further expansion of capacity falls on reduced allowables for nonexempt wells. Exempt categories of production (e.g., secondary recovery) in the market-demand states and all operations in the non–market-demand states are free meanwhile to respond to undiminished price incentives.[36] If profitable opportunities are abundant in the exempt categories and non–market-demand states, total capacity may continue for a long while to grow faster than demand as nonexempt capacity slowly shrinks with depletion of the affected reservoirs; for exempt production, expanding with exempt capacity, displaces nonexempt production without destroying nonexempt capacity. Such a process, fed by a backlog of secondary recovery opportunities in older producing states and fresh exploration opportunities in Mississippi and the Rocky Mountain states, may largely explain the growing degree of excess capacity in the market-

---

[35] See pp. 98–99.
[36] Actually, as we shall see below, prices in the non–market-demand states are imperfectly supported by production restriction in the market-demand states.

demand states from 1948 until after the first significant postwar price declines in 1958–61. The effect was intensified, of course, by the concurrent growth of imports based on a persistent differential between foreign and domestic prices.

It must be observed that excess capacity has proved of value to the United States in three wars and two Middle East crises since 1941.[37] It has permitted sharp increases in production on short notice with modest price increases.[38] Some degree of excess capacity in normal times may be a desirable objective of public policy. Even assuming this is so, the amount, durability, and location of the excess capacity resulting from market-demand regulation are only by coincidence at any point in time consistent with given aims of public policy. Furthermore, one may question the propositions that the costs of the excess capacity as presently created are less than the benefits, that there are no less costly means of maintaining the desired level of excess capacity, and that the costs should be borne by the public as consumers rather than as taxpayers. Since excess capacity is an undesigned product of conservation regulation, there is a strong presumption of the superiority of a distinct program specifically designed to maintain and finance genuine reserve capacity in desired amounts and locations.

The foregoing seven criticisms may be summarized in one. The prevailing system of conservation regulation, particularly in the market-demand states, induces or permits certain inefficiencies in the exploitation of petroleum resources. The margins of both development and exploration are needlessly contracted, so that the long-run supply of oil is reduced below its optimum level. Consequently, price is higher than the optimum at every point in time, and the resource-life of oil and gas—the time remaining before substitute energy sources absorb their markets—is unduly shortened. However much it may improve over a condition of no regulation at all, the prevailing system fails to provide a framework within which the benefits from oil and gas may be maximized before they cease to be economic resources.

In further evaluation: some observations on crude oil prices

I have frequently alluded to the price stabilizing effects of market-demand regulation. These effects are undeniable, but it may be useful to observe some statistical evidence. Table 19 shows the annual averages of crude oil prices and market demand factors in Texas, 1948–66.

---

[37] With this in mind, many industry spokesmen prefer the term "reserve capacity."
[38] Given limited excess refinery capacity, excess crude oil producing capacity has chiefly permitted increased exports to allies or substitution of domestic for imported crude oil when normal third-country supplies have been curtailed.

Table 19. Crude Oil Prices and Market Demand Factors in Texas: Annual Averages, 1948–66

Year	Crude oil price	Market demand factor
	(*dollars per bbl*)	(*percent*)
1948	2.61	100%
1949	2.59	65
1950	2.59	63
1951	2.58	76
1952	2.58	71
1953	2.73	65
1954	2.84	53
1955	2.84	53
1956	2.83	52
1957	3.11	47
1958	3.06	33
1959	2.98	34
1960	2.96	28
1961	2.97	28
1962	2.99	27
1963	2.97	28
1964	2.96	28
1965	2.96	29
1966	2.97	34

Sources: American Petroleum Institute (API), *Petroleum Facts and Figures*, biennial, 1959–67; and Texas Railroad Commission.

Note that crude oil prices remained approximately constant in the periods 1948–52,[39] 1954–56 and 1959–66, rising to new levels in 1952–54 and 1956–59. Market demand factors were relatively constant in the periods 1949–53, 1954–56 and 1958–65, falling to new plateaus in 1953–54 and 1956–58. Except for the period of price ceilings, 1951–52, and the recent period of accelerating demand in 1966, stable prices are associated with stable market demand factors and rising prices with falling market demand factors.[40] It appears that until 1966 market demand factors have had to be adjusted downward to support each new level of prices. Moreover, market demand factors fell sharply in the recessions of 1948–49, 1953–54 and 1957–58, while prices fell only slightly in the first and third recessions and rose in the second. Apparently prices have been cyclically insensitive to demand and adjustments in market demand factors have largely compensated for variations in demand.

[39] Prices were subject to regulatory ceilings in 1951–52.
[40] The use of annual averages tends to conceal the behavior of market demand factors in the months just preceding or coincident with changes in prices. The generalization here may not hold for month-to-month relations.

Crude oil prices have been only slightly less stable in the other major producing states. Table 20 shows the prices of crude oil in selected states as percentages of Texas prices, 1948–66. Fluctuations in these percentages represent variations in *relative* prices, Texas prices being the base. The two bottom lines in the table give, respectively, the mean price relative for each state and the average deviation from the mean in each state expressed as a percentage of the mean. The latter percentage indicates the degree of variation in relative prices. It can be seen that the degree of variation is relatively low in the market-demand states of Louisiana, New Mexico, Oklahoma, and Kansas, and relatively high in the major non–market-demand states, particularly Montana, Mississippi, and California. Apparently regional markets are sufficiently insulated from each other by distance and rigidities in pipeline routes that relative prices are affected to some extent by purely local supply and demand conditions. The price stability resulting from market-demand regulation in the practicing states is not communicated in full to the non–market-demand states. California is almost entirely insulated from the other producing regions, and it shows the second highest degree of variation in relative prices. It is especially noteworthy that relative prices in California declined in each of the recessions, 1948–49, 1953–54, 1957–58, and 1960–61. None of the non–market-demand states shows a definite trend in relative prices since 1948, which suggests that factors affecting prices in the long run are similar in all states.

As stated earlier, it is truistic that the creation and persistence of excess capacity is fundamentally due to prices that are too high and too resistant to reductions in the long run. If at the first signs of excess capacity prices fell in the affected region, marginal exploration, development, and secondary recovery prospects would be dropped or postponed, abandonments would be accelerated, and the growth of capacity would be checked. Demand would be attracted from other regions, leading to price reductions and capacity adjustments there. The aggregate quantity demanded would grow more rapidly, if demand has any price elasticity whatever, and eventually the initial excess capacity would be eliminated in all regions. Appropriate price adjustments would by this process eliminate excess capacity (except that induced purely by the structure of depth-acreage allowable schedules)[41] regardless of market-demand regulation of output, provided only that regulatory commissions responded passively to nominations in setting aggregate allowables. Apparently the commissions do so respond to nominations. I

---

[41] Price reductions, by inducing wider spacing, also would to some extent reduce excess capacity arising from the structure of allowable schedules.

Table 20. Relative Price of Crude Oil, Selected States, 1948–66

(percent of Texas price)

Year	Market-demand states				Non-market-demand states				
	Louisiana	New Mexico	Oklahoma	Kansas	Colorado	Wyoming	Montana	Mississippi	California
1948	102.7%	93.9%	98.9%	99.6%	98.1%	89.3%	98.9%	92.3%	92.7%
1949	102.7	94.2	98.8	99.6	98.5	88.0	99.6	95.0	87.3
1950	102.7	93.8	99.2	99.2	98.5	83.4	97.3	89.2	83.4
1951	102.7	94.6	99.6	99.6	98.4	83.3	95.7	86.8	87.2
1952	101.9	94.6	99.2	99.2	98.8	84.5	87.2	86.4	86.4
1953	102.9	96.3	98.9	98.5	99.3	86.8	79.9	86.4	91.2
1954	103.2	96.8	98.2	98.4	97.5	86.3	77.4	88.0	89.7
1955	103.2	96.1	97.9	98.6	97.5	84.9	79.6	86.6	88.0
1956	103.5	97.2	98.2	98.6	98.2	86.2	91.2	86.6	92.6
1957	106.8	96.1	97.4	96.8	97.1	85.5	86.8	93.6	98.1
1958	106.5	97.4	96.7	98.0	94.7	85.3	86.6	93.5	94.8
1959	106.0	95.6	98.0	97.7	97.3	83.9	85.9	95.3	85.6
1960	106.1	96.3	98.6	98.0	98.0	84.8	81.4	95.6	83.1
1961	106.1	96.3	98.0	97.3	97.0	84.2	81.5	94.9	81.8
1962	105.4	96.3	97.7	97.3	96.3	83.3	80.9	93.0	83.6
1963	105.1	97.0	98.0	98.0	97.0	84.2	82.2	92.9	83.5
1964	105.1	97.0	98.0	98.6	97.3	85.5	82.1	90.2	82.1
1965	104.7	94.9	97.6	98.6	97.3	84.4	82.1	89.2	80.4
1966	104.7	95.6	98.0	99.3	98.0	86.2	82.2	89.2	79.1
Mean	104.3	95.8	98.3	98.4	97.7	85.2	86.7	91.0	86.7
Relative deviation	1.4	1.0	0.6	0.7	0.8	1.5	6.1	3.5	4.4

Source. Computed from basic data in API, *Petroleum Facts and Figures*, biennial, 1959–67.

conclude, therefore, that although market-demand regulation of output is necessary to support a price level that generates excess capacity, it is not a sufficient condition of such a level; the other essential ingredient is the price policy (or policies) of crude oil buyers.

It is not possible to make a simple generalization about the price policies of crude oil buyers. Policies differ from company to company and from time to time in the same company. We can only identify some common elements. They are as follows: (a) Basically, buyers (who may also be producer-sellers) seek to achieve and maintain an overall rate of return on investment that they regard as commensurate with risks assumed. (b) Buyers readily accept opportunities to earn higher-than-target rates of return, provided the required actions do not markedly disturb established buyer-seller relations, significantly attract competitive entry, or risk a price war. (c) In the belief that the relevant supply and/or demand schedules are quite inelastic with respect to price, buyers react to lower-than-target rates of return by lowering prices at which they buy and/or raising prices at which they sell, subject to the qualifications to element (b) above. (d) Buyers avoid a price structure as among fields or as among sellers within fields that sellers or governmental agencies (including conservation commissions) might regard as discriminatory.

To these observations an important tax consideration can be added. In fields or market areas where buyers produce about 80 percent or more of the oil they buy, it is profitable for such buyers to transfer net income from transportation and refining to production by overpricing crude oil relative to products. This increases the benefits of percentage depletion, which is based on the wellhead value of oil, and thus reduces the effective tax rate on aggregate net income.[42] The artificial overpric-

---

[42] The net tax benefit is diminished somewhat where severance taxes are based on wellhead value. Ignoring severance taxes, the formula for a break-even transfer of income from transportation and refining to production is:

$$-\Delta P(1 - t) = X \Delta P(1 - t + tp)$$

where: ΔP = change in crude oil price;
      X = fraction of purchases produced by buyer;
      t = nominal income tax rate;
      p = percentage depletion rate.

Substituting 50 percent for the tax rate and 27.5 percent for the percentage depletion rate, we get a break-even value for X of .78. Where X is larger than .78, therefore, the gain as oil producer from a crude oil price increase (right-hand side of the equation) would exceed the loss as transporter-refiner (left-hand side of the equation). For an extended discussion of percentage depletion in association with production control, see A. E. Kahn, "The Depletion Allowance in the Context of Cartelization," *American Economic Review*, vol. 54 (June 1964) pp. 286–314.

ing of oil is most feasible, obviously, in those fields or market areas where all or nearly all of the buyers are important producers. Other buyers in such areas may in the short run match the artificially high prices to avoid producer charges of discrimination, but in the long run they presumably would withdraw to fields or areas not dominated by integrated producer-buyers. In any case, subject to other considerations of price policy, special tax provisions applying to oil and gas production may impart an upward bias to crude oil prices, at least in some fields or market areas.[43] This bias may reflect itself partly in the downward inflexibility of crude oil prices relative to product prices.

The above elements of price policy have the following implications regarding price-making and price behavior: (a) Proximately, crude oil prices are based on the net-back from given product prices. Net-back pricing is reflected primarily in the structure of prices by type of crude and location. (b) Ultimately, both crude oil and product prices are based on full costs (at some assumed level of output) plus a "normal" rate of return on investment. Cost-plus pricing is reflected primarily in the average level of prices over time.[44] The interests of integrated

[43] It may be observed that any integrated company whose aggregate production in all areas is 80 percent or more of its refinery runs from all areas has an interest in raising all crude oil prices at the expense of transportation-refining margins until the combined effects of percentage depletion and the expensing of intangible development costs eliminate the company's entire income tax liability. However, in the absence of collusion among integrated companies, it is not clear how the interest can be made effective unless for each company purchasing areas and producing areas coincide; for it is in the immediate interest of each company to seek lower prices in those areas where it produces less than 80 percent of its purchases.

[44] After this was written, the following quotation from an executive of a leading integrated company came to my attention:

"As a first step [in determining offered wellhead prices], the Manufacturing Department, taking into account its projected knowledge of probable product prices and knowing the types of crude oil necessary for the requirements of each refinery and the refining costs, analyzes the various types of oil to determine how much it can pay for each type and still make a fair profit from its operations. This is done just as if the Manufacturing Department were an independent refining company. All of the principles of practical economics are taken into account.

"Second, we consider the possible sources of supplies, in relation particularly to the costs of transporting them to the refineries.

"Third, we must consider the important element of competition, and competition is keen. If our price is less than that paid by our competitors we may not be able to purchase our requirements. If we pay more than our competitors, our costs may be such that we cannot compete in the product market. This is why, because of stiff competition, both in the crude oil and product markets, prices have a tendency to be parallel. It is not because of collusion, or conservation

producer-buyers account for cost-plus pricing of crude oil; and the same interests may occasionally demand reduction of a price below cost-plus to discourage producer entry into the affected market area. (c) In the non–market-demand states, price tends to the level which equates long-run supply with demand. In equilibrium, therefore, price equals cost-plus without excess capacity.[45] In the market-demand states, on the other hand, a cost-plus target price determines quantity demanded, to which output is forcibly adjusted. If the target price lies above the long-run supply schedule, excess capacity develops, unit cost rises, and the target price may be raised still further. In equilibrium, price equals cost-plus with substantial excess capacity. (d) In market areas dominated by integrated producer-buyers, crude oil prices tend to be higher relative to product prices and more resistant to reduction than in other areas. The difference is moderated by the desire of producer-buyers to avoid attracting additional producers and of all buyers to avoid charges of

---

regulations, but because of competition. This, too, involves principles of practical economics.

"Lastly, Phillips knows that the future domestic supply of oil depends upon the continuous and active exploration for new reserves on the part of the whole industry, including the independents. The independent is highly important in this respect. Such exploration depends almost entirely upon a price for the oil that will pay the cost of exploration, development and operation, plus a fair return for the cost and risk involved. This, too, is a basic principle of practical economics. It follows that to the extent competition and other cost factors permit, Phillips attempts to adjust the price paid for crude oil upward to accomplish this very important objective.

"I repeat that the other companies must follow the same pattern, because their prices are competitive and thus more or less parallel."
John M. Houchin, "The Attorney General's 1967 Interstate Oil Compact Report—An Industry Viewpoint from 35 Years of Experience," *The Oil and Gas Compact Bulletin*, vol. 26 (December 1967), p. 22.

Houchin stoutly denies that integrated companies artificially raise the price of crude oil to increase the benefits of percentage depletion, again citing the behavior of his company but inferring that other companies behave similarly since prices are "comparable" (p. 21). He adds, however: "It so happens, however, that Phillips' net domestic crude oil production is less than 40 percent of the crude oil requirements for its domestic refineries. It would certainly be poor business for Phillips to raise the price paid for the portion of its requirements purchased from others in exchange for the much smaller return from the depletion tax savings from higher prices for its own production. I am not an economist, but I can figure that one out." No doubt he could also figure out that if his company's ratio of production to refinery runs were 80 percent or more, the dictates of good business would lead to different pricing behavior.

[45] The long-run supply schedule is in effect a cost-plus schedule; for it gives the quantities willingly supplied in the long run at different prices.

discrimination. (e) Crude oil prices tend to be cyclically sensitive to variation in product demand only in those market areas dominated by nonintegrated buyers. Even in such areas price fluctuations are moderated by the desire of buyers to avoid disturbing established buyer-seller relations.

The above implications of common elements in price policy throw some light on observed price behavior. We attach special significance to implications (b) and (c), for they would explain both successive upward movements of crude oil prices in the first twelve years of the post–World War II period in association with growing excess capacity and the confinement of persistent excess capacity to the market-demand states. However, the price reductions of 1957–60 suggest the existence of a critical level of excess capacity which if exceeded triggers price reductions. With excess capacity above the critical level, integrated companies with strong producer orientation may accept lower prices as necessary to limit entry and further growth of excess capacity; while companies with a strong buyer orientation can satisfy their interest in lower prices without fear of losing connections or otherwise jeopardizing long-run supply of crude oil.

It is sometimes popularly supposed that the petroleum industry and the regulatory commissions together constitute a profit-maximizing, though open-ended, cartel of national scope. There are, indeed, some cartel-like features of the regulatory system in the market-demand states, notably the control of total output, the allocation of the total on the basis of formula among producers, and the protection of weaker producing units from market instability. But in several key respects the system fails to qualify as a comprehensive cartel arrangement. First, the system does not formulate, and has no machinery for formulating, price objectives. Buyers independently set prices, which vary in level and flexibility among states and regions. Any motivation of buyers to collude is weakened by the fact that in given fields or market areas different buyers have different price interests depending on whether they are predominantly producer-buyers or predominantly refiner-buyers. Second, the system does not formulate, and has no machinery for formulating, total output objectives. Subject to MER, capacity, or allowable schedule restraints, total output is free to adjust to quantity demanded as the latter may be affected by changes in either demand intensity or price; and price is free to adjust to either excess supply or excess demand in the non–market-demand states. Finally, the system contains no machinery for administrative allocation of output among states. The mutual adjustment of demand, supply, and price in each of the non–market-demand states determines their respective rates of output, while passive adjustment of allowables to quantities demanded (as reflected in buyers' nominations)[46] in each of the market-demand states determines their respective rates of output. Increase in either relative capacity or relative demand in the non–market-demand states increases their relative shares of total national output. Increase in relative nominations, which might reflect the location of new producing capacity owned by a producer-buyer or of new pipeline or refinery facilities owned by a refiner-buyer, increases the share of one market-demand state relative to the others. Contrary to some popular impressions, the Bureau of Mines demand forecasts by state are not state output quotas, and the Interstate Oil Compact Commission participates in no way in the allocation of total national output among states.

In sum, the prevailing system of petroleum conservation regulation is to be criticized not because it is a scheme to extract monopoly prices from the consuming public (although it does help to keep prices above their optimum level),[47] but because it induces or fails to eliminate wastes in the utilization of the nation's total petroleum resources.[48]

---

[46] No one has ever suggested that buyers conspire to determine the allocation of nominations among states.

[47] The statement in parentheses is not necessarily inconsistent with the proposition that prices under the prevailing system of regulation are lower than they would be in the absence of regulation. Indeed, in my judgment, wastes (and unit costs) in the absence of regulation were far greater than those under existing regulation. The point is simply that wastes (and unnecessary costs) remain when they could be eliminated.

[48] For an effort to quantify the wastes, see M. A. Adelman, "Efficiency of Resource Use in Crude Petroleum," *Southern Economic Journal*, vol. 31 (October 1964), pp. 101–22.

10. Unitization and Unit Operation of Reservoirs

The matter of external damages aside, and given the extension of surface private property rights to underlying minerals, the conservation
problem in petroleum production arises out of the joint effects of two
conditions: (a) the existence of two or more owners of operating interests in the surface overlying a single reservoir and (b) the fluid, hence
migratory, nature of reservoir contents.[1] These two conditions create
the incentive, which we have symbolized in the negative marginal user
cost of competitive extraction, to drill wells more densely, to extract
fluids more rapidly, and to allow to escape or to leave unrecovered more
gas and oil than is appropriate from the point of view either of the
operators as a whole or of society at large. Both conditions are essential
to the conservation problem; neither alone would create it. If *either*
there were one owner of operating interests in each reservoir *or* the contents of a reservoir were solid, then there would be no opportunity for
drainage across property lines and the incentive symbolized in the negative marginal user cost of competitive extraction would be nonexistent.
Each operator would then bear the full cost burden of unrecovered
minerals and enjoy the full income benefits of extraction properly distributed over time. Consequently, given competitive markets, each
operator in pursuing his own economic interest would choose the well
density, rate of extraction, and degree of ultimate recovery that would
maximize expected net benefits to society; in other words, each operator would voluntarily practice true conservation.

As we have seen thus far, conservation regulation as practiced by the
several states seeks not so much to create conditions under which private operators would voluntarily conserve petroleum as to restrain
private operators from responding fully to the incentives they have to

---

[1] The "rule of capture" may be regarded as a third element in the circumstances
that create the problem of petroleum conservation, but that rule itself arises out
of the two conditions named, which, respectively, necessitate a definition of individual property interest in minerals produced from a common supply and
make it impossible to establish the source of mineral particles brought to the
surface of a given tract.

violate conservation. It seeks to restrain the density of wells, the rate of extraction, the loss of gas—even the uses to which gas may be put. For the purpose, legislatures and commissions devise a host of detailed rules which, to be administratively feasible, must have broad applicability throughout a given state and must at least partly disregard the infinite variation of conditions from one reservoir to another. Consequently, the rules may fail to require the optimum well density or rate of extraction or degree of ultimate recovery in any reservoir. Rules designed to cover special cases, to bolster weak economic interests, to protect correlative rights indirectly, or to offset disincentives created by other rules add not only to the complexity and cost of administration but also to the potential for inefficient resource use.

Unitization of reservoirs, in contrast, strikes directly at the root cause of the conservation problem. It seeks effectively to eliminate the multiplicity of competing interests for purposes of operating a common reservoir, while retaining separate interests for purposes of sharing equitably in common costs and benefits. It creates a consolidated private interest which coincides with the public interest in conservation, thus enlisting the powerful force of profit-motivated private enterprise in a public cause, while directly by contract protecting correlative rights. It obviates the necessity for numerous negative rules and allows well density, the rate of extraction, the disposition of associated gas, and other matters relating to conservation to be adapted flexibly to the circumstances of each reservoir. Unitization is, in short, a positive instrument of petroleum conservation.

The conservation logic of unitization and unit operation of reservoirs has been recognized by knowledgeable men, both inside and outside the petroleum industry, for roughly half a century. Yet, despite rapid growth of the practice in recent years, unitization is still quite limited in application; and in no state has it supplanted the detailed negative regulation described in the preceding three chapters. Obviously, there must be disadvantages of or obstacles to the practice. After a fuller discussion of the nature and advantages of unitization, presented in connection with treatment of facilitating state laws, I shall consider those disadvantages or obstacles and their implications.

The nature of unitization and unit operation

Unitization is defined as "the practice of unifying the ownership and control of an actual or prospective oil or gas pool by the issuance or assignment of units or undivided interests in the entire area with provision for development and operation by an agent, trustee or committee representing all holders of undivided interests therein."[2] Thus unitization connotes unit operation, which means "the carrying on of development and production of a field, pool or area thereof as a geological unit under one control, with or without the exchange of transfers of undivided interests."[3] Hereinafter I shall use the term unitization to imply and include unit operation.

Williams distinguishes between two types of unitization agreement, the first involving the merger of titles in leases and the second involving the pooling of interests in production.[4] In the former, which is characteristic of early practice, there is an exchange of assignments among lessees so that each lessee becomes a cotenant of each tract in proportion to his ascribed interest in the whole unitized area. This, apparently, is the device contemplated in the definition of unitization quoted above. In the other type of agreement, now the more common, each lessee retains full title to his lease, but title in production is pooled and each lessee shares in total production and expenses in proportion to the percentage interest ascribed to his tract. In either case, the royalty owner receives compensation on the basis of production attributed by agreement to his land.

By virtue of the unitization agreement, the unit becomes a legal entity with the right to make contracts and to sue and be sued as such. It thus takes on some of the attributes of a corporation. Under existing state and federal law, however, units are not taxed as corporations. Each owner of interest is responsible for state or federal income tax at personal or corporate rates as applicable on his share of net income. The percentage depletion allowance applies to each owner's share of gross income as if that share were produced on the owner's specific tract. Similarly, intangible development costs, which for tax purposes may be treated as current expense, are proportionately allocated among leases. Unitization thus creates no tax disadvantages.[5]

The unitization agreement, once executed, is binding upon each maker and his heirs and assigns for the term of the agreement, usually

---

[2] Robert E. Hardwicke, *Antitrust Laws et al.* v. *Unit Operation of Oil and Gas Pools* (New York: American Institute of Mining and Metallurgical Engineers, 1948), p. 191, quoting Mid-Continent Oil and Gas Association, *Handbook on Unitization of Oil Pools* (1930), p. 15.

[3] Hardwicke, *Antitrust Laws*, p. 191.

[4] R. M. Williams, "The Negotiation and Preparation of Unitization Agreements," *First Annual Institute on Oil and Gas Law and Taxation* (Dallas: Southwest Legal Foundation, 1949), pp. 86–87.

[5] Ibid., p. 88.

the remaining economic life of the affected reservoir. Thus owners may bequeath, sell, or collateralize their interests without terminating or altering the agreement or operations under it.

Since the essence of unitization is provision for unified operating control, the agreement must provide for a central management. Typically an operator with a major interest in the unitized area is designated unit operator or unit manager and acts on behalf of the operators as a whole. Alternatively or in addition, the unitization agreement may provide for an operating committee on which all operators are represented, each with a vote in proportion to his interest in the unit. Where the agreement provides for both a unit manager and an operating committee, the committee may stand to the manager much as a board of directors stands to the chief executive officer of a corporation. In any case, the individual owner of an operating interest surrenders separate managerial discretion, although he may retain some voice in decisions made for the unit as a whole.

Usually the most difficult part of a unitization agreement is that which specifies the basis of relative participation in costs and benefits. If unitization takes place, as it typically does, after substantial exploration and development have occurred, there may have to be some initial adjustment among the parties to allocate past investment outlays on an equitable basis. Then provision must be made for allocating further capital outlays, operating costs, and proceeds from production. Rarely does a single simple basis of allocation, such as proportionate share of productive acreage, satisfy all the parties. Quite aside from the desire of each owner of interest to maximize his share of the net benefits, the problem of allocation is complicated by existing lease and credit obligations; by variability of thickness, porosity, and permeability of host rock within the reservoir; and by differences in the value of minerals beneath each tract depending on the specific plan of operation contemplated, particularly when a significant amount of gas is associated with oil. Not surprisingly, then, many different bases of participation are found in existing agreements,[6] although the most common, either singly or in combination with others, are productive acreage, amount of recoverable oil or gas in place, and value of oil or gas in place.[7] Where agreements are made early in the life of reservoirs, provision is generally made for

---

[6] In one study of extant agreements, forty-two different bases of participation were distinguished. A. A. Khan and H. H. Power, "An Analysis and Comparison of Engineering Bases of Participation in Unit Agreements," *IOCC Committee Bulletin*, December 1960, p. 101.

[7] Stuart E. Buckley, ed., *Petroleum Conservation* (Dallas: American Institute of Mining and Metallurgical Engineers, 1951), p. 283.

adjustment of relative shares as additional knowledge about reservoir conditions is acquired through further development and operation.

The unitization agreement ordinarily contains or is supplemented by an agreement on a general plan of operation for the unit. This plan indicates the type of drive to be selected, the manner of creating or supplementing the selected drive, the number and locations of additional wells to be drilled, the number and locations of existing wells to be plugged or converted to injection wells, the rate of oil and/or gas production, the handling of associated gas, and the disposal of salt water or other waste materials. Where gas liquids extraction or injection of dry gas or liquids is contemplated, the unitization agreement may also provide for joint ownership and operation of the necessary processing and compressor facilities by the parties to the agreement.

Although all aspects of extraction, including the facilities and processes of injection to improve the efficiency of extraction, are normally covered by the unitization agreement, marketing per se is not. The usual agreement provides for payment of each lessee's share of oil or gas in kind, leaving the lessee to make his own marketing arrangements.[8] This procedure allows the individual producer to make or to maintain an association with a preferred buyer, while protecting himself against possible challenge under federal antitrust laws.[9]

In sum, unitization converts a multiplicity of interests in a common reservoir to a single interest for purposes of extractive operations, and at the same time fixes the shares of participants in common net benefits. What then profits the unit as a whole profits each participant proportionately.

The possible benefits of unitization[10]

The general benefit of unitization has already been indicated: by eliminating the negative marginal user cost of competitive extraction, unitization creates a consolidated private interest that coincides with the public interest in efficient resource use, so that the pursuit of private profit in

[8] Williams, "Negotiation and Preparation of Unitization Agreements," p. 91.

[9] In the only antitrust action ever brought against a unit, *United States of America* v. *Cotton Valley Operators Committee* (77 F. Supp. 409, 339 U.S. 972), dismissed without trial on a procedural technicality, the complaint was not against the unit agreement for production, but against certain alleged practices in processing and marketing products. For a thorough discussion of this case and its implications, see Hardwicke, *Antitrust Laws*, pp. 135–37, 211–28, 329–30.

[10] The discussion in this section does not take into consideration existing regulations. These would preclude some of the possible benefits of unitization.

petroleum extraction becomes an instrument of conservation.[11] Unitization opens the way, in the interest of conservation, to allow each reservoir, whether an oil or a gas reservoir, to be developed and operated so as to maximize at all times its net present value to its owners. The following specific benefits accrue in the first instance to private operators and royalty owners; but corresponding to each is an equivalent public benefit accruing to the users at large of the nation's total product.

1. Within the limits imposed by prior drilling and current regulation, unitization permits the joint selection, for the affected reservoir, of the optimum rate of production (which implies the optimum degree of ultimate recovery) and the optimum number of wells. More precisely, it permits the selection of that combination of planned time-distribution of production and number of wells that promises to maximize the net present value of the affected reservoir at the time of decision. The gain to the operators as a whole (and to society) is the excess of this maximum present value over the present value that would result from either free competitive extraction, or competitive extraction constrained by general spacing rules combined with MER, or a depth-acreage allowable schedule. The gain in relation to free competitive extraction would usually be quite large, while that in relation to wide spacing and MER regulation might be quite small. In any case, this benefit is diminished by dense drilling, rapid production, and dissipation of reservoir pressure before unitization occurs.

The benefit of optimizing the rate of production and the number of wells in each reservoir may usefully be viewed as the summation of a number of more specialized benefits.

a. Unitization permits the deliberate selection of the most efficient available natural drive. For example, in an oil reservoir in which the dominant drive is dissolved gas expansion, the rate of production may deliberately be reduced to allow a naturally subordinate (but more efficient) water drive to become dominant. This would be done by a unit management if the present value of additional recovery exceeded the loss of present value caused by lengthening the period of recovery. Under competitive extraction constrained by a depth-acreage allowable schedule, in contrast, each operator would seek to forestall adverse drainage by producing as rapidly as permitted, and the dominant drive (and efficiency of recovery) would be determined arbitrarily by the resultant aggregate rate of withdrawal.

b. Unitization permits or facilitates supplementation of the se-

---

[11] Of course, in making this statement the problem of external damages is not taken into account.

lected natural drive. For example, where the selected drive in an oil reservoir is gas-cap expansion, pressure in the reservoir may be maintained by closing all wells tapping the cap and reinjecting into the cap such dissolved or channeled gas as may be produced unavoidably with oil through other wells; and the gas cap may be made even more effective by injecting into it gas acquired from another source. Some such procedure would be followed by a unit management if the present value of additional oil recovery exceeded the loss of present value caused by additional costs and delay in marketing the gas used for injection. Owners of shut-in gas-cap wells would be compensated by their shares in oil (and eventually gas) produced within the unit as a whole. The procedure described would not usually be feasible under constrained competitive extraction. No individual operator in the oil-producing portion of the reservoir could hope to capture more than a fraction of the benefits of reinjecting associated gas produced through his wells; and owners of gas-cap wells would have to be allowed to produce and market some gas from the cap in order to protect their correlative rights.[12]

c. Unitization permits or facilitates the creation of an artificial drive. For example, in oil reservoirs where the only available natural drive (e.g., dissolved gas expansion) is quite inefficient or exhausted, it may be possible to create an artificial drive by in situ combustion or by injecting water, steam, gas, detergents, solvents, or some combination of fluids. Such methods of drive creation are usually efficient only if combustion occurs or fluids are injected at one end of the reservoir, driving oil toward wells at the opposite end, or if combustion or injection is conducted throughout the reservoir in a geometric pattern under a plan of cooperative action. With unitization, full benefits can be weighed against full costs of the operation, and correlative rights can be protected, regardless of the resultant pattern of fluid migration within the reservoir. Without unitization, on the other hand, each operator must weigh his own costs against his own prospective benefits; and since no individual operator could expect to capture the entire benefits of his independent efforts to create an artificial drive, such efforts would be inhibited. Without unitization,

---

[12] The most common regulatory practice in situations of this sort is to allow competing oil and gas producers to withdraw concurrently volumetrically equivalent (under reservoir conditions) amounts of hydrocarbons. This solution is recognized as not entirely satisfactory for purposes of either achieving conservation or protecting correlative rights. William J. Murray, Jr., "Engineering Aspects of Unit Operation," *Third Annual Institute of Oil and Gas Law and Taxation*, 1952, p. 15.

projects of drive creation which, taken as a whole, would more than pay for themselves might never be undertaken.

d. Unitization permits the optimum use of associated gas. Cap gas may be produced concurrently with oil or retained in the reservoir until recovery is completed; dissolved gas may be produced with oil or allowed to come out of solution in the reservoir to form an artificial cap; produced gas, with or without liquids extraction, may be flared, marketed as produced, or reinjected into the reservoir to assist oil recovery and be later marketed. Unitization permits the deliberate selection of that use or combination of uses that promises to maximize the present value of the reservoir as a whole. Without unitization, in contrast, the only procedure that is economically feasible for the individual operator and compatible with correlative rights may be to produce gas concurrently with oil and either flare the gas or market it as produced.

Regulation as typically practiced attempts a compromise solution, which may raise or lower the value of a given reservoir relative to a situation of unrestrained extraction. As previously explained, in order to restrain the rate of exhaustion of reservoir pressure, regulations generally limit the ratio of gas to oil at which a well may produce without penalty. To protect the correlative rights of gas well owners without unnecessarily exhausting reservoir pressure, field rules governing reservoirs under gas-cap drive commonly allow oil wells below the cap and gas wells tapping the cap to withdraw hydrocarbons at volumetrically equivalent rates. In addition, most state regulations restrain in some degree the flaring of gas produced in association with oil. The Texas commission, notably, has in numerous instances flatly prohibited gas flaring, enforcing its prohibition by shutting down oil production in the affected reservoirs until some beneficial use could be made of produced associated gas. The usual effect in such instances has been to force unitization for purposes of some injection plan,[13] which might or might not be economical.[14] Thus regulation as practiced regarding associated gas may at best reduce the wastes of free competitive extraction without eliminating them altogether (as with volumetrically equal withdrawal of gas and oil), and at worst actually create wastes that are greater than those averted (as with forced uneconomical reinjection). Unitization permits wastes in the use of associated gas to be totally eliminated.

[13] Williams, "Negotiation and Preparation of Unitization Agreements," pp. 71–72.
[14] Here is an instance in which insistence on preventing "physical waste" may result in a net loss of satisfactions to society.

e. Unitization permits the flexible adjustment of the rate of output from either oil or gas reservoirs to maximize present value continuously. To the extent that direct production regulations permit, a unit management may alter the rate of production to conform with new optimums as relevant current and prospective conditions change. For instance, if current prices should fall relative to expected future prices, it would be in the interest of the operators as a whole (and of society) to reduce the current rate of output with a view to increasing future rates of output and perhaps extending the life of all reservoirs. The opposite reaction would be appropriate in response to a decline in expected future prices (as a result, say, of a technological innovation in exploration) relative to current prices. Unitization, thus, permits continuous "tracking" of a changing optimum rate of output in a dynamic economy. With extraction as presently regulated, on the other hand, each operator would find it in his interest to produce continuously at the maximum rate permitted, regardless of changes in current relative to expected future prices (or costs), in order to avoid adverse drainage. The maximum rate of output permitted under MER regulation would be unresponsive to changes in the relationship of current to expected future prices (or costs); while that permitted under market-demand regulation would be appropriately responsive only as the price changes were associated with consistent changes in current quantities demanded.[15]

f. Unitization permits the selection of the optimum number of wells in an oil or gas reservoir, the optimum number implying the optimum locational pattern of wells drilled and operated for either extraction or injection purposes. Subject to the constraints imposed by (i) spacing regulation, (ii) drilling prior to unitization, and (iii) remaining ignorance of reservoir limits and operating characteristics, a unit management may select that number and location of wells which, in association with the jointly chosen time-distribution of extraction, would maximize the present value of the reservoir net of well costs at the time of decision. Ultimate spacing need not be on a regular geometric pattern, since the correlative rights of lessees and landowners are directly protected by the terms of relative participation in the unitization agreement. If more than the optimum number of wells are drilled prior to unitization, or if they are drilled after

---

[15] An appropriate change in the maximum permitted rate of output would occur if, for example, a rise in expected future prices were the result of a shift in demand from present to future. On the other hand, no change in the maximum permitted rate of output would occur if the rise in expected future prices were the result of reduced expected future supply.

unitization in order to define the reservoir and its characteristics, operating costs may be reduced and some salvage realized by closing the undesired wells. Redundant producing wells may also be converted to injection wells, either initially or at intervals in reservoir life as the interface between driving and driven fluids migrates past them. Without unitization, in contrast, the number of wells drilled in a reservoir would depend on state-wide spacing rules, or the estimated requirement on each lease to produce a proportionate share of an expected MER, or the inducements embodied in the applicable depth-acreage allowable schedule. Such a number would coincide with the optimum only by coincidence. Because of the problem of adverse drainage across property lines, there would be inadequate incentive under constrained competitive extraction to close redundant wells or to convert old producing wells to injection wells.

g. Unitization permits the optimum investment in surface equipment. To the extent that such equipment is an integral part of the well, this point is already covered in the above discussion of the optimum number of wells. Beyond that, equipment that is separable from the well, such as separators and storage tanks, may be consolidated into units of the most economical size, each serving a number of wells. Concentration of producing wells in the optimum locations and consolidation of storage facilities may also minimize the necessary investment in gathering pipelines. In short, unitization allows operators in a common reservoir to avoid the duplication of equipment otherwise made necessary by competition for available oil and regulation of output on an individual well or lease basis.

In addition to allowing optimization of the rate of production and the number of wells in each reservoir, unitization confers other benefits in oil and gas production.

2. Unitization permits dry gas recycling for liquids recovery in retrograde condensate reservoirs. As explained in chapter 2,[16] hydrocarbons that under surface conditions are divisible into natural gas and light liquids are often encountered in deep, high-temperature reservoirs in a single gaseous phase. As this "wet" gas is extracted, pressure in such a reservoir tends to drop toward a critical level at which the liquids would condense and distribute themselves throughout the reservoir in such low concentration as to make them unrecoverable. Maintenance of reservoir pressure above the critical level, however, allows the liquids to be conducted to wells in the gaseous phase and condensed under conditions permitting full recovery. In the absence of an adequate water drive, the

[16] Chapter 2, section on "Production from Unassociated Gas Reservoirs."

required pressure maintenance may be accomplished by reinjecting produced gas that has been stripped of its liquid content. To avoid diluting the remaining wet gas and thereby reducing the efficiency of the recovery process, the dry gas must be injected in one area of the reservoir so that it drives the wet gas toward wells in other areas. Dry gas thus migrates across the reservoir, gradually displacing wet gas. When displacement is complete, or nearly so, the dry gas now filling the reservoir may be produced for sale or other beneficial use through the usual process of pressure depletion. Clearly, the procedure described would not be feasible under competitive extraction, even if the aggregate rate of extraction were restrained by individual well allowables. The reservoir must be managed as a unit, at least during the period of liquids recovery, by using some wells for extraction and others for injection, and protecting the correlative rights of each owner of interest by agreement as to relative participation in net benefits. The necessary unitization agreement may also provide for joint ownership and operation of the plant required for liquids extraction and compression of residual dry gas.

3. Unitization reduces the problem of waste disposal in oil and gas production. In the first place, unitization of a reservoir permits the early closing of wells that begin to produce substantial quantities of brine with hydrocarbons, while protecting the correlative rights of affected owners by the agreement covering relative shares in total reservoir output. Consequently, less brine is produced at any given stage of reservoir depletion, and a smaller drop in reservoir pressure is experienced with any given rate of hydrocarbon recovery. In the second place, unitization facilitates the disposal of such waste liquids as may be unavoidably produced. For example, waste disposal may be combined with pressure maintenance by collecting brine from all producing wells in a reservoir and reinjecting it into the producing formation below the water-oil interface.[17] Even if some other plan of disposal is followed, unitization may reduce costs by enabling the acquisition and operation of facilities of the most economical size and type for use in common by all operators in a reservoir.

4. Unitization obviates the necessity for regulation of gas-oil ratios and gas flaring, thus saving administrative and compliance costs. As explained above, a unit management would make the optimum use of associated gas from the point of view both of reservoir operators as a

[17] As the experience in the East Texas Field indicates, cooperative action short of unitization may be sufficient for a successful program of combined waste disposal and pressure maintenance. There salt water is collected by a company created for the purpose and reinjected below the water-oil interface. Producers pay for the disposal service and benefit from the resulting pressure maintenance.

whole and of society at large. That being so, regulation of gas use in unitized reservoirs would be either redundant or pernicious, and in either case unnecessarily costly to operators and society.

5. Unitization obviates the necessity for a regulatory authority to restrict the rate of output from a reservoir and to allocate the reservoir allowable among operators, thus in another way saving administrative and compliance costs. As already explained, a unit management would at every point in time choose a reservoir rate of output which, given current and expected future prices and costs, would be optimal from the point of view both of operators as a whole and of society at large. This rate of output implies the optimum degree of ultimate recovery, so regulatory restraint to increase this degree would be harmful to all concerned. The chosen rate of output also implies use of the optimum drive and the distribution of production among wells in a manner consistent with that drive. Since relative shares in benefits are provided for in the unitization agreement, allocation of allowable production to protect correlative rights would be unnecessary. There would be no competitive extraction and therefore no need to restrain individual operators to prevent drainage across property lines or wasteful surface storage. If the chosen volume of output could not be marketed in full—because, say, of temporarily limited transportation capacity—the unit management could reduce reservoir output accordingly, so that the sum of operators' shares in output would be equal to the quantity demanded. Purchaser discrimination among operators in the same reservoir would thus be prevented.[18] If purchasers responded to potential excess supply by lowering posted prices (and if discounted expected future prices did not fall equally), the optimum current rate of output in each affected reservoir would be reduced; and the indicated decline in current output would limit the reduction in prices necessary to equate quantity supplied with quantity demanded. Without unitization, the problem of adverse drainage would prevent individual operators from responding appropriately to price reductions. Consequently, given the price policies of purchasers, prices would be more unstable than they would under unitization.[19]

6. If unitization of new discoveries can be anticipated by explorers, the margin of profitable exploration is extended and the sum of lease

---

[18] Unitization of reservoirs would do nothing, of course, to prevent purchaser discrimination among reservoirs.

[19] In technical terms, unitization increases the elasticity of supply, thus reducing the degree of price fluctuation associated with given fluctuations in demand and supply schedules. See chapter 6, section on "The Supply of Crude Oil—Short Run."

bonus and royalties payable to landowners for access to each supramarginal prospect is raised. Unitization does this by making the present value of each new oil or gas reservoir at discovery higher than it would be under either free or constrained competitive extraction. If other conditions are satisfied (e.g., competitive capital markets and free entry into and exit from the petroleum industry), unitization thus promotes the optimum level of exploration—the optimum rate of exploitation of the remaining natural stock of petroleum deposits.

7. Finally, if unitization were permitted to embrace the marketing of reservoir output, still other benefits would be possible. Cooperative marketing would make it impossible for purchasers to discriminate with respect to price paid to different operators in a reservoir. It would permit sellers to bargain more effectively with buyers over price and other terms of sale. By increasing the volume that might be assured to any purchaser, it would make it easier to attract buyers and pipeline connections to new reservoirs. It would more easily accommodate long-term delivery contracts, which might also be useful in attracting independent buyers and pipelines into a market area. Finally, it would facilitate sales to distant refineries by making it easier to meet minimum tender requirements of common carrier pipelines.[20] These benefits would accrue in the first instance to producers in unitized reservoirs; but by making petroleum markets more competitive and efficient and by attracting independent capital into petroleum exploration and production, they would ultimately accrue in the form of larger, cheaper supplies to society at large.

State encouragement of voluntary unitization

As the foregoing discussion should amply indicate, the possible benefits of unitization to oil and gas producers are large and numerous. Most of them—particularly those relating to well costs, pressure maintenance, and secondary recovery—have been widely understood at least since World War II. Understanding has grown progressively with experience. These facts alone would account for much of the growth of voluntary unitization in the postwar period. But, in addition, voluntary unitization has been encouraged by the state conservation commissions and legislatures.

Official encouragement has taken at least three forms. First, regula-

---

[20] A minimum tender is the minimum-sized shipment that a common carrier is obliged to accept from an independent shipper.

tory officials have helped disseminate information and promote understanding, particularly through the relevant committees of the IOCC.
In this and in other, more direct, ways they have indicated their sym-
pathy. None, to my knowledge, has ever offered opposition to voluntary
unitization. Second, conservation commissions have adapted spacing
and production regulations to accommodate unitized projects. In particular, they have granted special allowables to pressure maintenance
and secondary recovery projects, permitted the closing of redundant
wells with transfer of allowables to other wells in unitized areas, and
placed extraordinary restraints on production to preserve pressure and
to protect correlative rights in reservoirs in the (sometimes long) process of being unitized. Third, the legislatures of all the producing states
except Kansas, Kentucky, Maryland, Michigan, Ohio, Tennessee, Virginia, and West Virginia have enacted statutes explicitly sanctioning
voluntary unitization.[21] Of special concern in such legislation has been
the desire to remove all fear that voluntary unitization of petroleum
reservoirs might be found to be in violation of state antitrust laws. In
any case, no unitization agreement has ever been challenged under state
antitrust laws.

The flavor of most legislation sanctioning voluntary unitization is indicated in the following excerpt from the IOCC model statute.

An agreement for the unit or cooperative development or operation of a
field, Pool, or part thereof, may be submitted to the Commission for approval as being in the public interest or reasonably necessary to prevent
Waste or Protect Correlative Rights. Such approval shall constitute a complete
defense to any suit charging violation of any statute of the State relating
to trusts and monopolies on account thereof or on account of operations
conducted pursuant thereto. The failure to submit such an agreement to the
Commission for approval shall not for that reason imply or constitute evidence that the agreement or operations conducted pursuant thereto are in
violation of laws relating to trusts and monopolies.[22]

Wyoming provides an example of a very similar statutory provision.

An agreement for water flooding, repressuring or pressure-maintenance
operations, cycling or recycling operations, including the extraction and

---

[21] None of the excepted states has any laws prohibiting unitization or otherwise
making it of doubtful legality. Kansas and Michigan have laws under which
minority interests may be required to join a unitization agreement approved by
a majority of interest owners in a reservoir.

[22] IOCC, Legal Committee, *A Form for an Oil and Gas Conservation Statute*
(1959), sec. 8.

separation of liquid hydrocarbons from natural gas in connection therewith, or for carrying on any other method of unit or co-operative development or operation of a field or pool or a part of either, is authorized and may be performed, and shall not be held or construed to violate any of the Statutes of this State relating to trusts, monopolies, or contracts and combinations in restraint of trade, if after notice and a public hearing, the agreement is approved by the Commission as being in the public interest for conservation and reasonably necessary to increase ultimate recovery or to prevent waste of oil and gas. Such agreements shall bind only the persons who execute them, and their heirs, successors, assigns, and legal representatives.[23]

The statutes of New Mexico and Texas, however, represent two contrasting extremes in their approach to sanctioning voluntary unitization. The New Mexico statute says simply:

Whenever it appears that the owners in any pool have agreed upon a plan for the spacing of wells, or upon a plan or method of distribution of any allowable fixed by the Commission for the pool, or upon any other plan for the development or operation of such pool, which plan, in the judgment of the Commission, has the effect of preventing waste as prohibited by this act and is fair to the royalty owners in such pool, then such plan shall be adopted by the Commission with respect to such pool; however, the Commission upon hearing and after notice, may subsequently modify any such plan to the extent necessary to prevent waste as prohibited by this act.[24]

The Texas statute, on the other hand, requires numerous findings by the commission before it may approve voluntary agreements.

Subject to approval of the Railroad Commission of Texas (hereinafter called Commission), as hereinafter set out, persons owning or controlling production, leases, royalties or other interests in separate properties in the same oil field, gas field, or oil and gas field, may voluntarily enter into and perform agreements for the following purposes:

(A) To establish pooled units necessary to effect secondary recovery operations for oil and gas, including those known as cycling, recycling, repressuring, water flooding, and pressure maintenance, and to establish and operate cooperative facilities necessary for said secondary recovery operations;

(B) To establish pooled units and cooperative facilities necessary for the conservation and utilization of gas, including those for extracting and separating the hydrocarbons from the natural gas or casinghead gas and returning the dry gas to a formation underlying any lands or leases committed to the agreement.

---

[23] Wyo. Stat. Ann. (1957) 1967 Repl. Vol., ch. 6, art. 1, §30-222.
[24] N.M. Stat. Ann. (1953) §65-3-14e.

Such agreements shall not become lawful nor effective until the Commission finds, after application, notice and hearing:

1. Such agreement is necessary to accomplish the purposes specified in (A) or (B) or both; that it is in the interest of the public welfare as being reasonably necessary to prevent waste, and to promote the conservation of oil or gas or both; and that the rights of the owners of all the interests in the field, whether signers of the unit agreement or not, would be protected under its operation;

2. The estimated additional cost, if any, of conducting such operation will not exceed the value of additional oil and gas so recovered, by or on behalf of the several persons affected, including royalty owners, owners of overriding royalties, oil and gas payments, carried interests, lien claimants and others as well as the lessees;

3. Other available or existing methods or facilities for secondary recovery operations and/or for the conservation and utilization of gas in the particular area or field concerned are inadequate for such purposes;

4. The area covered by the unit agreement contains only such part of the field as has reasonably been defined by development, and that the owners of interest in the oil and gas under each tract of land within the area reasonably defined by development are given an opportunity to enter into such unit upon the same yardstick basis as the owners of interests in the oil and gas under the other tracts in the unit.[25]

The Texas statute is unusual also in that it contains a number of prohibitions or limitations on the contents of approved unitization agreements, specifically:

All agreements executed hereunder shall be subject to any valid order, rule, or regulation of the Commission relating to location, spacing, proration, conservation, or other matters within the authority of the Commission, whether promulgated prior to or subsequent to the execution of such agreement, and no such agreements shall attempt to contain the Field Rules for the area or field, that being solely the province of the Commission; and no such agreement shall provide for nor limit the amount of production of oil and gas from the unit properties, that being the province of the Commission.

No such agreement shall provide, directly or indirectly, for the cooperative refining of crude petroleum, distillate, condensate, or gas, or any by-product of crude petroleum, distillate, condensate or gas. The extraction of liquid hydrocarbons from gas, and the separation of such liquid hydrocarbons into propanes, butanes, ethanes, distillate, condensate, and natural gasoline, without any additional processing of any of them, shall not be considered to be refining.

[25] Vernon's Rev. Civ. Stat. of Texas (1962) tit. 102, art. 6008b.

No such agreement shall provide for the cooperative marketing of crude petroleum, condensate, distillate or gas, or any by-products thereof.[26]

These prohibitions obviously restrict the kinds of benefits that may be derived from unitization in Texas. In particular, they deny to operators in a unitized reservoir the benefits discussed above with respect to the optimum rate of production and cooperative marketing, and possibly also those with respect to well spacing, gas-oil ratios, and gas flaring. Nonetheless, it is clear from the historical context of this legislation that the lawmakers intended to facilitate voluntary unitization by giving the requisite agreements express legal sanction.

Obstacles to voluntary unitization

Given the substantial benefits of unitization and official encouragement of voluntary agreements, why is voluntary unitization not virtually universal? The answer, of course, is that there are in many instances substantial obstacles to total concurrence by owners of interest in the necessary plan of operation and scheme of benefit distribution. The following list is not necessarily exhaustive, but it indicates the principal obstacles encountered.[27]

1. *Real or imagined legal obstacles.* Leases may have been written so as to prohibit cross assignment, pooling of production, or other acts necessary to effect a plan of unit operation. Owners of interest may fear taxation of a unit as a corporation or loss of tax benefits (e.g., percentage depletion) available to them as individuals or separate corporate entities. Operators may fear prosecution under state or federal antitrust laws.

2. *Ignorance.* Some of the affected parties may lack knowledge of the principles of reservoir mechanics underlying a proposed plan of unit operation. Even with knowledge of principles, some may feel that reservoir data available to them provide an inadequate basis for intelligent decisions; they may feel uncertain about possible costs and benefits. Some may lack knowledge of tax laws and statutes exempting approved unitization agreements from the terms of antitrust laws.

3. *Mistrust.* Lacking adequate first-hand knowledge, some owners of interest may mistrust those promoting a unitization agreement and offer-

---

[26] Ibid.

[27] The list presented here is a modified version of one found in Stuart Buckley, ed., *Petroleum Conservation* (Dallas, American Institute of Mining and Metallurgical Engineers, 1951), pp. 287–92.

ing to inform the ignorant of the benefits that will accrue to them. Out of some real or imagined past wrong, some operators or royalty owners may refuse to do business of any kind with certain individuals or companies.

4. *Difficulty in contacting all owners of interest.* The number of operators in a reservoir is usually rather small, and all of them can normally be contacted without difficulty. But royalty owners may be numerous and widely scattered geographically. Titles may be unclear or in litigation in some instances. Consequently, it may be time-consuming and expensive to secure all the necessary signatures to a voluntary unitization agreement.

5. *Fear of reduced current income.* Some owners of interest in a reservoir may fear that a unit plan of operation, while promising significant long-run benefits, would result in short-run losses of income. Such possible losses may be unacceptable because, for instance, of current credit obligations or high-valued alternative uses of funds.

6. *Pride of ownership and operational control.* Many individuals, whether landowners or operators, derive satisfactions from tangible evidences of ownership and control. Such individuals may choose to have operating wells on their property, even at the expense of some pecuniary income, rather than participate in a plan under which production would be concentrated in wells located elsewhere in the reservoir. Independent operators may feel a sense of identity loss in merging their leases with others under a unit plan to be managed by a competitor or some major company. Such operators may also fear the consequences of sacrificing independence of action—say, in representing their particular interests before a conservation commission.

7. *Loss of operating experience.* Operators other than the unit manager may anticipate that further reservoir development and operation will be conducted by the manager's own (company) personnel. In such an event, the nonmanaging operators might sacrifice valuable geological knowledge, and their work crews, while losing useful experience, might be held together pending new assignment only at considerable expense.

8. *Increased trouble and expense in management.* Where a unit plan contemplates management by an operating committee, decision-making might be cumbersome and productive of irritating personal conflicts within the committee. Disagreements over proposed operations might be frequent, leaving some operators continuously dissatisfied with the conduct of reservoir operation. Some operators may prefer to avoid all such nuisances, even at the cost of some pecuniary income, by withholding their consent to a voluntary unitization agreement.

9. *Profitable obstructionism.* Some operating or royalty interests,

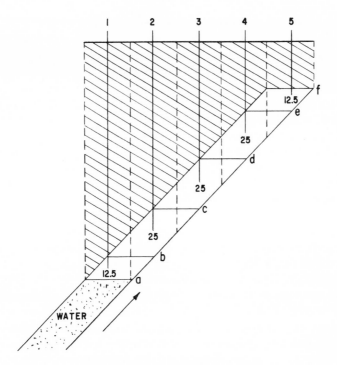

Figure 27.   Illustration of structural advantage.

knowing that the inclusion of their property is essential to the success of a proposed plan of unit operation, may take advantage of their position to make exorbitant demands as the price of their consent. Such tactics, even if moderated in the end, may at best cause costly delay in effecting the plan.

10. *Structural advantage.* Particularly in reservoirs under water or gas-cap drive, the migration of oil during reservoir life may be extensive. The driving fluid pushes oil toward wells at the opposite end of the reservoir, the remotest wells being the last to cease production. The wells toward which oil or gas is driven are said to have structural advantage, for during their life they are enabled to produce oil or gas to some multiple of the volume originally in place beneath the tracts on which they are located. The wells nearest the driving fluid have a corresponding structural disadvantage.

The principle is illustrated in figure 27,[28] which represents a cross-section of a tilted reservoir under water drive. As oil production occurs

[28] Adapted from Buckley, *Petroleum Conservation*, p. 239.

through wells 1–5, the water-oil interface, originally at level a, migrates upward and to the right, first passing well 1 (level b), then well 2 (level c), etc., until the recoverable oil is exhausted (level f). Of total recoverable oil in the reservoir, tracts 1 and 5 each have 12.5 percent originally in place beneath them; while tracts 2, 3, and 4 each have 25 percent. It is readily seen that, by the time the water-oil interface has migrated to level b, each well, producing at a given rate, will have produced 2.5 percent ($\frac{1}{5} \times$ 12.5 percent) of the total recoverable oil, and well 1 will no longer have access to the oil zone. When the interface has migrated to level c, wells 2–5 will each have produced an additional 6.25 percent ($\frac{1}{4} \times$ 25 percent) of the recoverable oil, and well 2 will no longer be able to produce. Carrying this calculation to its ultimate conclusion, we find that well 1 will produce 2.5 percent of the total; well 2, 8.75 percent; well 3, 17.08 percent; well 4, 29.58 percent; and well 5, 42.08 percent. These figures, especially for wells 1, 2, and 5, differ substantially from the corresponding percentages of recoverable oil originally in place, well 5 having a tremendous structural advantage.

It is clear that if production in the manner described is the alternative, the owner of well 5 would never voluntarily enter into a unitization agreement that would adequately protect the correlative rights of the owners of wells 1 and 2. If the owner of well 5 will accept no reduction in the oil accruing to him as his share, the prospective gains in recovery efficiency from unit operation must be substantial for the owner of well 1 to derive a significant benefit. As for the plan of operation, the owner of well 5 would object to, while the owner of well 1 would strongly favor, a plan involving a switch from water to assisted gas-cap expansion drive, which would reverse the structural advantages and alter the bases of bargaining over relative shares. Similarly, the owner of well 3 would most strongly favor a plan involving a combination water and gas-cap expansion drive. In short, where structural advantage is important, some owners must be prepared to sacrifice either principle (correlative rights) or income if a voluntary unitization agreement is to be effected.

Some of the obstacles to voluntary unitization, such as ignorance and imagined legal obstacles, can be overcome by means of adequate collection of reservoir data and thorough educational efforts by those promoting the agreement. Some, such as pride of ownership and loss of operating experience, can be overcome with appropriate adjustments in the proposed plan of operation and management. But some, such as mistrust, profitable obstructionism, and structural advantage, do not readily yield to any reasonable means of persuasion. Where such obstacles are present, a degree of compulsion may be necessary to effect a timely and useful unitization agreement.

Statutory or "compulsory" unitization

In recognition of both the benefits of unitization and the (often unreasonable) obstacles to voluntary unitization agreements, twenty-one states, beginning with Oklahoma in 1945, have enacted statutes authorizing conservation commissions to exercise a degree of compulsion in completing unitization agreements.[29] In general, these statutes provide that the respective conservation commissions may order reservoirs to be unitized when some (majority) percentage of both operating and royalty interests have agreed upon an acceptable plan. Thus, a minority is compelled to accept unitization,[30] although the possibility of compulsion may cause some parties at interest to volunteer more readily. An acceptable plan is, generally, one that will increase ultimate recovery or prevent waste as defined in the basic conservation statutes, will protect the correlative rights of all affected property owners, and is economically feasible.

There is no better way to indicate the content and tone of the compulsory unitization statutes than to quote from several of them. Because of its influence on numerous state laws, we begin with the pertinent section of the IOCC model statute:

7.1 The Commission upon its own motion may, and upon the application of any interested person shall, hold a hearing to consider the need for the operation as a unit of one or more Pools or parts thereof in a field.

7.2 The Commission shall make an order providing for the unit operation of a Pool or part thereof if it finds that:

7.2.1 such operation is reasonably necessary to increase substantially the ultimate recovery of Oil or Gas; and

7.2.2 the value of the estimated additional recovery of Oil or Gas exceeds the estimated additional cost incident to conducting such operations.

7.3 The order shall be upon terms and conditions that are just and reasonable and shall prescribe a plan for unit operations that shall include:

7.3.1 a description of the Pool or Pools or parts thereof to be so operated, termed the unit area;

7.3.2 a statement of the nature of the operations contemplated;

---

[29] The states are: Alabama, Alaska, Arizona, Arkansas, California (to control surface subsidence only), Colorado, Florida, Georgia (with respect to gas condensate), Indiana, Kansas, Louisiana, Michigan, Mississippi, Nebraska, Nevada, New York, North Dakota, Oklahoma, Oregon, South Dakota, and Washington.

[30] Only the Washington statute requires no specific percentage agreement by the ownership interests in oil reservoirs. In Alabama and Louisiana, the commission may require unitization for the purpose of gas cycling in condensate reservoirs without consent of any of the ownership interests.

7.3.3 an allocation to the separately owned tracts in the unit area of all the Oil and Gas that is produced from the unit area and is saved, being the production that is not used in the conduct of operations on the unit area or not unavoidably lost. The allocation shall be in accord with the agreement, if any, of the interested parties. If there is no such agreement, the Commission shall determine the relative value, from evidence introduced at the hearing, of the separately owned tracts in the unit area, exclusive of physical equipment, for development of Oil and Gas by unit operations, and the production allocated to each tract shall be the proportion that the relative value of each tract so determined bears to the relative value of all tracts in the unit area;

7.3.4 a provision for the credits and charges to be made in the adjustment among the Owners in the unit area for their respective investments in wells, tanks, pumps, machinery, materials, and equipment contributed to the unit operations;

7.3.5 a provision providing how the costs of unit operations, including capital investments, shall be determined and charged to the separately owned tracts and how said costs shall be paid, including a provision providing when, how, and by whom the unit production allocated to an Owner who does not pay the share of the cost of unit operations charged to such Owner, or the interest of such Owner, may be sold and the proceeds applied to the payment of such costs;

7.3.6 a provision, if necessary, for carrying or otherwise financing any Person who elects to be carried or otherwise financed, allowing a reasonable interest charge for such service payable out of such Person's share of the production;

7.3.7 a provision for the supervision and conduct of the unit operations, in respect to which each Person shall have a vote with a value corresponding to the percentage of the costs of unit operations chargeable against the interest of such Person;

7.3.8 the time when the unit operations shall commence, and the manner in which, and the circumstances under which, the unit operations shall terminate; and

7.3.9 such additional provisions that are found to be appropriate for carrying on the unit operations, and for the protection of Correlative Rights.

7.4 No order of the Commission providing for unit operations shall become effective unless and until the plan for unit operations prescribed by the Commission has been approved in writing by those Persons who, under the Commission's order, will be required to pay at least _____% of the costs of the unit operation, and also by the owners of at least _____% of the production or proceeds thereof that will be credited to interests which are free of cost, such as royalties, overriding royalties, and production payments, and the Commission has made a finding, either in the order providing for unit operations or in a supplemental order, that the plan for unit operations has been so approved. . . . If the Persons owning required percentage of interest in the unit area do not approve the plan for unit operations within a period of six (6) months from the date on which the order providing for unit operations is made, such order shall be ineffective, and shall be revoked by the Commission unless for good cause shown the Commission extends said time. . . .

7.8 All operations, including, but not limited to, the commencement, drilling, or operation of a well upon any portion of the unit area shall be deemed for all purposes the conduct of such operations upon each separately owned tract in the unit area by the several Owners thereof. The portion of the unit production allocated to a separately owned tract in a unit area shall, when produced, be deemed, for all purposes, to have been actually produced from such tract by a well drilled thereon. Operations conducted pursuant to an order of the Commission providing for unit operations shall constitute a fulfillment of all the express or implied obligations of each lease or contract covering lands in the unit area to the extent that compliance with such obligations cannot be had because of the order of the Commission.

7.9 The portion of the unit production allocated to any tract, and the proceeds from the sale thereof, shall be the property and income of the several Persons to whom, or to whose credit, the same are allocated or payable under the order providing for unit operations.[31]

As the compulsory unitization statutes of Colorado and New York are almost identical to the pertinent section of the IOCC model statute, neither will be quoted here. They may be noted, however, for their contrasting requirements as to the percentage of affected property owners who must consent to a unitization agreement before the conservation commission may order it in effect. New York's statute specifies approval by 60 percent of interest owners, Colorado's by 80 percent.[32]

Alaska's statute contains somewhat different language, including some interesting factors to be considered in determining equitable shares in unit production.

[31] IOCC, *A Form for an Oil and Gas Conservation Statute*, sec. 7.
[32] McKinney's Consol. Laws of N. Y. (1967) Conservation Law, art. 3-A, §79; *Colo. Rev. Stat.* (1963) 1965 Supp., §100-6-16.

(a) To prevent, or to assist in preventing waste, to insure a greater ultimate recovery of oil and gas, and to protect the correlative rights of persons owning interests in the tracts of land affected, these persons may validly integrate their interests to provide for the unitized management, development and operation of such tracts of land as a unit. Where, however, they have not agreed to integrate their interests, the department, upon proper petition, after notice and hearing, has jurisdiction, power and authority, and it is its duty to make and enforce orders and do the things necessary or proper to carry out the purposes of this section.

(b) If upon the filing of a petition by the department and after notice and hearing, all in the form and manner and in accordance with the procedure and requirements provided in this section, the department finds that (1) the unitized management, operation and further development of a pool or portion of a pool is reasonably necessary in order to effectively carry on pressure control, pressure maintenance or repressuring operations, cycling operations, water flooding operations, or any combination of these, or any other form of joint effort calculated to substantially increase the ultimate recovery of oil and gas from the pool; (2) one or more of the unitized methods of operation as applied to the pool or portion of it is feasible, and will prevent waste and will with reasonable probability result in the increased recovery of substantially more oil and gas from the pool than would otherwise be recovered; (3) the estimated additional cost, if any, of conducting such operations will not exceed the value of the additional oil and gas so recovered; and (4) the unitization and adoption of one or more of the unitized methods of operation is for the common good and will result in the general advantage of the owners of the oil and gas rights within the pool or portion of it directly affected, it shall make a finding to that effect and make an order creating the unit and providing for the unitization and unitized operation of the pool or portion of it described in the order, upon the terms and conditions, as may be shown by the evidence to be fair, reasonable, equitable, and which are necessary or proper to protect, safeguard and adjust the respective rights and obligations of the several persons affected, including royalty owners, owners of overriding royalties, oil and gas payments, carried interests, mortgages, lien claimants and others, as well as the lessees. . . .

(c) The order of the department shall define the area of the pool or portion of it to be included within the unit area and prescribe with reasonable detail the plan of unitization applicable to it. . . . The plan of unitization for each unit and unit area shall be one suited to the needs and requirements of the particular unit dependent upon the facts and conditions found to exist with respect to it. In addition to other terms, provisions, conditions and requirements found by the department to be reasonably necessary or proper to carry out the purpose of this chapter and subject to the further requirements of this section, each plan of unitization shall contain fair, reasonable and equitable provisions for

(1) the efficient unitized management or control of the further development and operation of the unit area for the recovery of oil and gas from the pool affected. . . .

(2) the division of interest or formula for the apportionment and allocation of the unit production, among and to the several separately owned tracts within the unit area, such as will reasonably permit persons otherwise entitled to share in or benefit by the production from such separately owned tracts to produce and receive, instead thereof, their fair, equitable and reasonable share of the unit production or other benefits of it; a separately owned tract's fair, equitable and reasonable share of the unit production shall be measured by the value of each such tract for oil and gas purposes and its contributing value to the unit in relation to like values of other tracts in the unit, taking into account acreage, the quantity of oil and gas recoverable from it, location on the structure, its probable productivity of oil and gas in the absence of unit operations, the burden of operations to which the tract will or is likely to be subjected, or so many of these factors, or such other pertinent engineering, geological or operating factors as may be reasonably susceptible of determination. . . .

(d) No order of the department creating a unit and prescribing the plan of unitization applicable to it becomes effective until the plan of unitization has been signed or ratified in writing, or approved by the lessees of record of not less than 62.5 per cent of the unit area affected by it and by the owners of record of not less than 62.5 per cent (exclusive of royalty interests owned by lessees or by subsidiaries of any lessee) of the normal one-eighth landowner's royalty interest in and to the unit area, and the department has made a finding either in the order creating the unit or in a supplemental order that the plan of unitization has been so signed, ratified or approved. . . .

(i) Property rights, leases, contracts and all other rights and obligations shall be regarded as amended and modified to the extent necessary to conform to the provisions and requirements of this chapter and to any valid and applicable plan of unitization or order of the department made and adopted under this chapter, but otherwise remain in effect.[33]

The operative sections of the Arkansas statute are notable for their simplicity and brevity.

C-1. Upon the filing of a petition as hereinafter provided, the Commission, after notice, shall hold a public hearing to consider the need for the

33 Alas. Stat. Ann. (1962) §31.05.110.

operation as a unit of an entire pool, or any portion thereof, to prevent waste, to increase ultimate recovery of oil and/or gas and to protect correlative rights. . . .

C-2. If, after hearing and considering the petition and evidence offered in support thereof, the Commission finds that:

(a) The proposed unit agreement has, or counterparts thereof have, been executed by persons, who, at the time of filing the petition, owned of record legal title to at least an undivided seventy-five per cent interest in the right to drill into and produce oil and/or gas from the total proposed unit area and by persons, who, at the time, owned of record legal title to seventy-five per cent of royalty and overriding royalty payable with respect to oil and/or gas produced from the entire unit area, and that,

(b) Unit operation of the pool, or any portion thereof, proposed to be unitized, is reasonably necessary to prevent waste, to increase ultimate recovery of oil and/or gas and to protect correlative rights, and that,

(c) The value of the additional oil and/or gas to be recovered from the proposed unit area as a result of the proposed unit operation will exceed the additional cost incident to conducting such operation, it shall issue an order requiring unit operation in accordance with the terms of the proposed unit operating agreement. Such order and the provisions of the unit operating agreement shall, thereafter, be effective as to and binding upon each person owning an interest in the unit area or in oil and/or gas produced therefrom or the proceeds thereof.[34]

Finally, we note the Louisiana laws empowering the conservation commission to effect involuntary unitization of oil or gas reservoirs. First, there is the section of the general conservation statute that authorizes the commission to unitize a retrograde condensate reservoir without the prior consent of any interest owners.

In order to prevent waste and to avoid the drilling of unnecessary wells, the commissioner shall, after notice and upon hearing, and his determination of feasibility, require the recycling of gas in any pool or portion of a pool productive of gas from which condensate or distillate may be separated or natural gasoline extracted, and promulgate rules to unitize separate ownership and to regulate production of the gas and reintroduction of the gas into productive formations after separation of condensate or distillate, or extraction of natural gasoline, from the gas.[35]

Then there is the separate involuntary unitization act applying to oil and gas reservoirs generally.

[34] Ark. Stat. Ann. (1947) 1969 Supp., tit. 53, §§115(C-1) and (C-2).
[35] La. Rev. Stat. (1969) tit. 30, §5-B.

Without in any way modifying the authority granted to the Commissioner of Subsection B of Section 9 of this Title 30 to establish a drilling unit or units for a pool and in addition to the authority conferred in Subsection B of this Section 5, the Commissioner of Conservation, upon the application of any interested party, also is authorized and empowered to enter an order requiring the unit operation of any pool or a combination of two pools in the same field, productive of oil or gas, or both, in connection with the institution and operation of systems of pressure maintenance by the injection of gas, water or any other extraneous substance, or in connection with any program of secondary recovery; and the Commissioner is further authorize, and empowered to require the unit operation of a single pool in any situation where the ultimate recovery can be increased and waste and the drilling of unnecessary wells can be prevented by such a unit operation. In connection with such an order of unit operation, the Commissioner shall have the right to unitize, pool and consolidate all separately owned tracts and other property ownerships. Any order for such a unit operation shall be issued only after notice and hearing and shall be based on findings that (1) the order is reasonably necessary for the prevention of waste and the drilling of unnecessary wells, and will appreciably increase the ultimate recovery of oil or gas from the affected pool or combination of two pools, (2) the proposed unit operation is economically feasible, (3) the order will provide for the allocation to each separate tract within the unit of a proportionate share of the unit production which shall insure the recovery by the owners of that tract of their just and equitable share of the recoverable oil or gas in the unitized pool or combination of two pools, and (4) at least three-fourths of the owners and three-fourths of the royalty owners, such three-fourths to be in interest as determined under (3) hereof, shall have approved the plan and terms of unit operation, such approval to be evidenced by a written contract or contracts covering the terms and operation of said unitization signed and executed by said three-fourths in interest of said owners and three-fourths in interest of the said royalty owners and filed with the Commissioner on or before the day set for said hearing. The order requiring the unit operation shall designate a unit operator and shall also make provision for the proportionate allocation to the owners (lessees or owners of unleased interests) of the costs and expenses of the unit operation, which allocation shall be in the same proportion that the separately owned tracts share in unit production. The cost of capital investment in wells and physical equipment and intangible drilling costs, in the absence of voluntary agreement among the owners to the contrary, shall be shared in like proportion; provided that no such owner who has not consented to the unitization shall be required to contribute to the costs or expenses of the unit operation, or the cost of capital investment in wells and physical equipment and intangible drilling costs, except out of the proceeds of production accruing to the interest of such owner out of production from such unit operation. . . .[36]

Note that both of the Louisiana statutes quoted make reference to the prevention of unnecessary well drilling as a legitimate basis of involuntary unitization. The act that applies to oil and gas reservoirs generally is unusual also in that it protects nonconsenting owners from having to contribute to capital costs and expenses of operation other than from the proceeds of production accruing to such owners. Nonconsenting owners in Louisiana are thus sheltered from some risk that must be borne by others.

It is interesting that the IOCC model statute and all of the individual state statutes condition involuntary unitization upon, among other things, the value of the estimated additional recovery of oil and gas exceeding the estimated additional cost incident to unit operations. The requirement that benefits (of whatever kind) exceed costs is entirely proper, of course. What is interesting is the imposition of this requirement in the case of involuntary unitization[37] but not in the case of physical waste prevention generally or in the case of external damage prevention, each of which involves involuntary action by oil and gas operators. I can only guess at the reason for this inconsistency. Perhaps it reflects a growing appreciation of economic factors between the time the leading conservation (waste prevention) statutes were enacted and the time most involuntary unitization laws were passed.

Developments since 1948

In the history of conservation legislation, the postwar period, particularly the fifties and sixties, may fairly be labeled the era of statutory or compulsory unitization. As earlier noted, Oklahoma enacted the first involuntary unitization statute in 1945. In 1951, this act was amended to reduce certain restrictions on the conservation commission.[38] Also in 1951, the constitutionality of the act was upheld in *Palmer Oil Corp.* v. *Phillips Petroleum Co., et al.,*[39] an appeal being dismissed by the U.S. Supreme Court. This decision opened the way for action in other states. In 1951, Indiana amended its basic conservation law of 1947 to au-

---

[36] La. Rev. Stat. (1969) tit. 30, §5-C.
[37] Recall that the requirement is also present in the Texas voluntary unitization statute.
[38] Okla. Stat. Ann. (1969) tit. 52, §§286 and 287.
[39] 204 Oklahoma 543, 231 P.2nd 997 (1951).

thorize the state Oil and Gas Commission to study the feasibility of and to order unit operations.[40] Between 1951 and 1963, five states enacted basic conservation laws along the lines of the IOCC model, including provisions for compulsory unitization of oil or gas reservoirs: Washington (1951), Nevada (1953), Alaska (1955), South Dakota (1961) and New York (1963). Between 1951 and 1967, twelve additional states supplemented their existing conservation laws with compulsory unitization statutes: Arkansas (1951), Alabama (1957), California, with respect to surface subsidence (1958), Michigan (1959), Louisiana (1960), Oregon (1961), Arizona (1962), Mississippi (1964), Colorado (1965), Nebraska (1965), North Dakota (1965) and Kansas (1967).[41] Note that most of the laws in significant producing states were enacted after 1957.

Not surprisingly, the concentration of unitization legislation after 1957 has been associated with accelerated growth in the number of unitized and cooperative projects in the United States. Data are available only for the years 1948–62.[42] These show that the number of projects increased from approximately 130 in 1948 to about 325 in 1957; then soared, reaching 1,550 in 1962. As of the latter year, unitized projects accounted for approximately 480 million barrels of oil production, or 18 percent of the national total. If the trends from 1957 to 1962 are projected to 1967, the number of unitized projects in that year was approximately 2,900, producing about 750 million barrels of oil, 24 percent of the national total. While the projection to 1967 cannot be accepted literally, these data indicate that unitization of oil reservoirs in the United States is rapidly growing, both absolutely and relatively.[43]

An evaluation of states' encouragement of unitization

As the content and tone of this study thus far should have indicated, I regard the states' encouragement of reservoir unitization, particularly the enactment of involuntary unitization statutes, as most desirable. Without apparent exception, the several conservation commissions and

---

[40] For additional details and legal references regarding this and the following cited legislation, see the Appendix.

[41] As explained above, under these laws, except for Washington's, unitization may be compulsory only for a minority of interest owners, ranging from 20 percent to 40 percent of the total.

[42] The data cited are from IOCC, *A Study of Conservation of Oil and Gas*, p. 62.

[43] No data are available on trends in unitization of gas reservoirs.

state legislatures have recognized that unitization confers certain conservation benefits that cannot be had in any other way; and many of
them have considered these benefits of sufficient importance to justify a
degree of compulsion in effecting unitization agreements. This recognition and appraisal of unitization benefits represents a critical advance in
the progress of petroleum conservation, one which opens new avenues
of development in future.

On the negative side, several observations can be made. First, it is
disappointing that after more than two decades of favorable experience
with involuntary unitization in other states, some of the more important
producing states—notably Texas, California (except with reference to
surface subsidence), New Mexico, Wyoming, and Illinois[44]—still lack
compulsory unitization laws of the IOCC type. Second, it is regrettable
also that, with the exceptions noted, the states enacting such laws have
approached unitization as a special, even extraordinary, tool of conservation requiring the consent of a majority of the affected interest
owners. I do not object to the implication that unitization and unit operation should benefit the operators as a whole in a reservoir. On the
contrary, such benefit (which has a counterpart for society at large)
should be the requisite of unitization. I object, rather, to placing the
burden of initiative and persuasion on private operators. The consequent expense and time requirement at best delays and at worst prohibits desirable unitization projects. Third, the involuntary unitization
statutes, except Louisiana's, seem to anticipate only one type of benefit:
increased ultimate recovery. This is, indeed, an important type of benefit flowing from unit operations; but it is not the only type. As we have
seen, other benefits include saving of well and equipment expense,
optimizing the time-distribution of recovery, facilitating waste disposal,
obviating the necessity for certain detailed regulations (e.g., gas-oil
ratios), and directly protecting correlative rights. Unnecessary restriction of the legitimate purposes of unitization unnecessarily limits the
growth of unitization and consequent benefits. Finally, there seems nowhere to be an understanding that unitization is a *fundamental* solution
of the conservation problem at the reservoir level; that private pursuit
of profit under unitization *substitutes* for regulation in all respects except that pertaining to external damages. Unitization is not just another
tool to be added to the others already in use; it is a tool to replace other,
less satisfactory ones. Until this is understood, unitization will be unduly limited in application and petroleum conservation will remain less
than complete.

[44] The five states named produce about 60 percent of the nation's output of crude
oil.

PART IV

FOR THE FUTURE

11. Some Proposals

It remains for me to spell out the proposals for change in conservation regulation suggested by the foregoing analysis. Following a brief summary evaluation of existing regulation, I shall propose some changes that would represent improvements in their own right and, more importantly, would serve as steps toward the ideal in conservation regulation.

Summary evaluation of existing regulation

The concept of prohibited waste

The central idea in existing regulation is the prevention of certain specified occurrences defined as wastes. Predominantly, the wastes to be prevented represent physical losses without beneficial use of the substances oil and gas. Physical waste prevention usually stops short of working an unreasonable economic hardship on individual operators or requiring supplementary or secondary techniques to increase recovery; but subject to these qualifications, the aim of conservation regulation in practice is to maximize the physical recovery and beneficial use of discovered oil and gas.

The concept of waste underlying existing regulation is a useful one—because physical losses are objectively measurable, and many of them represent genuine wastes—but it is deficient in several respects. (a) It is without benefit of an abstract definition of waste. Consequently, the wastes statutorily "defined" by classification or example often are indefinite, and the effective concept fails to convey that waste prevention is intended to protect or add to human welfare. (b) The effective concept gives no recognition to the waste (of value or satisfactions) that may arise from a faulty time-distribution of use. Such waste may occur without involving any physical loss; and, indeed, it may be the result of inflexible efforts to prevent all physical loss. (c) The prevailing concept of waste reflects no appreciation of the connection between the manner of exploiting the known stock of petroleum resources and the rate of exploration for additions to that stock. Exploration, a voluntary endeavor undertaken entirely for economic reasons, is necessarily affected by anticipated controls over the use of discovered deposits. Such controls therefore have an economic effect, for good or ill, even though they are based on a noneconomic concept of waste. (d) The concept of waste underlying existing regulation lacks a frame of reference that would assure that the costs and benefits that regulators consider relevant to conservation decisions are those of society at large. The premise of regulation is independent pursuit of profit by each operator in a reservoir. Therefore, at the one point at which economic considerations enter the present concept of preventable waste—the test of reasonableness— it is the costs and benefits of individual operators that are considered relevant.

Control of external damages

All of the states regulating petroleum operations for conservation purposes undertake incidentally to prevent damages to resources other than oil and gas. This activity is highly commendable for two reasons: it implicitly recognizes the desirability of conserving all productive resources, and it tends to force the production of oil and gas to bear its full social costs. Furthermore, the regional differences in regulation and the lagged adjustment to modern needs suggest that legislators and regulators crudely weigh costs against benefits in designing and enforcing regulations to prevent external damages. Existing regulation may be mildly criticized because a lag in adjustment to current needs persists, and because there is no systematic cost-benefit analysis in the regulatory process.

Control of production and well spacing

Control of production and regulation of well spacing are closely interrelated tools that go to the heart of petroleum conservation. In different states reservoir production rates are limited by permitted well density, by the maximum rate consistent with no significant loss of ultimate recovery (MER), or by a depth-acreage well allowable schedule adjusted for market demand. Well drilling is constrained by minimum spacing regulations and is affected also in the states where applicable by the incentives embodied in MER production control or by depth-acreage allowable schedules conditioned by market demand.

The regulation of production rates and well spacing has made valuable contributions to oil conservation: (a) Both limitation of well density and control of production on the basis of MER or a depth-acreage allowable schedule preclude the grosser physical losses (including waste of real capital) associated with unrestrained drilling and production. (b) Regulation of production on the basis of market demand also tends to avert some socially unnecessary costs resulting from inefficient reservoir drainage, arbitrary allocation of production among reservoirs, and excessive surface storage. (c) The depth-acreage allowable schedule is a workable administrative device that provides an element of certainty in exploration and induces far wider spacing than would prevail without regulation.

On the other hand, the existing system of production and well spacing control is subject to criticism on a number of grounds: (a) Statewide minimum spacing rules are essentially arbitrary—no well density is singularly appropriate to all reservoirs on the grounds of conservation. (b) Regulation of production on the basis of MER is less than ideal, since the MER as usually conceived does not necessarily coincide with the optimum rate of production from a reservoir. (c) The depth-acreage allowable schedules employed in the major market-demand states are largely without foundation in conservation principles. They do not, except by coincidence, induce the optimum well spacing and rate of output in any reservoir; and they are not justified on conservation grounds in according greater allowables to deep or offshore wells. (d) The mixed pattern of spacing-production regulation distorts the allocation of exploration and production among states, both as between market-demand states and other states and among the several market-demand states. (e) The various exemptions from market-demand production restriction distort the allocation of productive activity within the affected states. (f) The regulatory adjustment of output to quantity demanded, regardless of the price, prevents the mutual adjustment of quantity supplied, quantity demanded, and price, and therefore deprives the economy of the market-clearing and satisfactions-maximizing functions of a free, competitive price. (g) The system of regulation in the major market-demand states, in association with industry pricing practices, tends to produce and perpetuate excess capacity, which burdens the industry with unnecessary costs, artficially discourages exploration, and shortens the resource life of oil and gas.

Unitization and unit operation of reservoirs

Unitization strikes directly at the root cause of the conservation problem in oil and gas by eliminating the multiplicity of competing interests in a common reservoir. It is a fundamental tool of conservation that permits or facilitates the realization of numerous benefits. In at least partial recognition of these benefits, the petroleum producing states encourage unitization, many of them exercising a degree of compulsion to effect it.

The states' encouragement of unitization, particularly the enactment of involuntary unitization laws, represents a critical advance in the progress of petroleum conservation. Yet there are weaknesses in the use of this tool: (a) A number of the more important producing states, of which Texas is the outstanding example, still lack involuntary unitization laws. (b) Even the states with such laws apply unitization with less force than other instruments of conservation, requiring consent by a substantial majority of interest owners before compulsion may be exercised. (c) Involuntary unitization laws seem to anticipate only one type of benefit—increase in ultimate recovery—thus unduly limiting the growth of unitized projects. And (d) the approach of the states reveals no understanding that unitization is a conservation tool that may be substituted for other kinds of regulation, except those addressed to the control of external damages.

Other forms of regulation

Several forms of regulation briefly discussed in the survey that begins chapter 3 have not been intensively analyzed because their incidental treatment has appeared to be adequate. However, it may be useful to say a few additional words about them here: (a) Penalties for excessive gas-oil ratios and limitation of associated gas flaring are valid and often useful supplementary tools of conservation under the conditions I have called "constrained competitive extraction." It should be clear, however, that gas flaring at a reservoir should not be prohibited when the cost of some beneficial use exceeds the value of the benefits to the affected operators as a whole. Furthermore, as seen in chapter 10, regulation of either gas-oil ratios or gas flaring is unnecessary, and may be harmful, under unitized operation of the affected reservoir. (b) The protection of correlative rights and the regulation of purchaser and pipeline practices to prevent inequities among producers stand on their own merits as legitimate government activities. This is not to say, however, that all conceivable methods are equally effective or equally consistent with conservation. The analysis in chapter 9 indicates that those methods associated with market-demand proration are complex, cumbersome, and not entirely consistent with conservation; while the analysis in chapter 10 shows that those methods associated with unitization are simple, direct, and entirely consistent with conservation. (c) The grant of the power of eminent domain to facilitate private acquisition of underground gas storage facilities requires no more analysis than that provided in chapter 3. It was explained there that such use of the states' powers furthers gas conservation by indirectly reducing flaring and extending the margin of profitable exploration and development. There appears to be no countervailing objection, so this conservation device merits approval and encouragement.

Outlines of an ideal approach to petroleum conservation

I want my positive proposals to represent improvements within the existing framework of conservation regulation, and at the same time to further the process of transition to an ideal scheme. So that both aims may be kept in view as specific proposals are discussed, I shall begin with a sketch of what I regard as ideal.

The whole may be divided into four parts, each corresponding to a separate functional purpose:

Part 1 consists of laws and regulations designed to prevent or limit external damages during the entire life of a reservoir, from the initial exploratory well to final abandonment. The laws and regulations contemplated in the IOCC models are essentially adequate for this purpose, although I shall suggest an expanded role for explicit cost-benefit analysis.

Part 2 consists of laws and regulations designed to govern reservoir development and operation during the period from discovery to unitization. These would cover tentative well spacing, maximum reservoir production rate, allocation of allowable production among wells or leases, permissible gas-oil ratios, and disposition of produced associated gas. The purpose would be to direct an orderly development and systematic collection of reservoir data, while conserving reservoir pressure and protecting correlative rights, with a view to unitization at the earliest reasonable date. To protect correlative rights and avoid reservoir damage caused by unequal access of producers to markets or pipelines, it may be useful during this phase to restrict each reservoir's aggregate output to the market demand for that reservoir's production, allocating the total equitably among all producers.

Part 3 consists of the basic involuntary unitization law and related regulations designed to govern reservoir development and operation during the remainder of its economic life. Entirely voluntary unitization would be encouraged; but after a reasonable period of data collection (which would vary from one reservoir to another), unitization would be mandatory regardless of the percentage of ownership interests consenting, unless it could be shown that unitization would confer no net benefits on the operators as a whole. After unitization, all regulation by the conservation commission of well spacing, reservoir production rate, allocation of output among wells or leases, gas-oil ratios, and disposition of produced associated gas would cease, these matters being left to the free choice of the unit management. Correlative rights would be protected by the terms of the unitization agreement covering relative shares in net benefits, and aggregate reservoir output would as a matter of course be limited by the unit management to no more than the quantity that could be marketed or transported. Profit-motivated management would thus be substituted for regulation, except that pertaining to external damages, during the unitized phase of reservoir life.

Part 4 consists of supplementary laws and regulations, chiefly designed to prevent inequities among producers. These would cover protection of correlative rights generally, prohibition of discriminatory purchasing or pricing, mandatory extension of pipelines to new reservoirs where economically feasible, and designation of major transporters as common carriers. Also included in the supplementary laws would be statutes authorizing the grant of the power of eminent domain to private companies to facilitate their acquisition of underground gas storage capacity.

In principle, the outlined scheme would apply equally to oil reservoirs, oil-and-gas reservoirs, and gas reservoirs. In practice, however, the unitization aspect of the scheme would probably be less significant or valuable in the case of nonassociated (dry) gas reservoirs. In most of these reservoirs wells can be appropriately spaced during initial development, the efficiency of recovery is unrelated to the location of wells within the reservoir or to the rate of production, fluid injection for pressure maintenance is uneconomical, the rate of production is constrained by the requirements of a long-term contract with a pipeline purchaser, waste disposal is a minor problem, and correlative rights can be protected by simple allocation of reservoir output among regularly spaced wells. The net benefits of unit operation of such reservoirs may be zero or negative. Therefore, existing regulation of nonassociated (dry) gas reservoirs, which centers on well spacing and allocation among wells of the reservoir's market demand, may in most instances be quite adequate to satisfy the requirements of our ideal scheme. Our proposals are directed primarily to regulation affecting oil, oil-and-gas, and retrograde condensate reservoirs.

Specific proposals

A broader definition of waste

The definition of waste in conservation statutes should be broadened in two ways. First, by adding "waste in the time-distribution of use of oil or gas" to the usual enumeration of more or less indefinite types of prohibited wastes. This type of waste—i.e., losses of net present value, whether the result of a physical loss (of ultimate recovery) or not— should be placed on a parallel with the general category of "physical waste" to emphasize the distinct recognition of nonphysical losses. Second, the enumeration of types of wastes should be supplemented with an abstract definition of the term "waste" itself. As indicated in chapter 7, I suggest: *Waste is a preventable loss the value of which exceeds the cost of avoidance.* To this the explanation should be added that both value (the saving of which is benefit) and cost refer to the appraisal of society at large, and not merely to the appraisal of individual operators immediately affected. The suggested abstract definition should make it clear that waste need not reflect a physical loss and that a physical loss need not be a waste. Waste, the definition emphasizes, is an economic concept, always involving a cost-benefit comparison. The application of the proposed definition to the development and management of discovered reservoirs would serve to integrate this level of the conservation problem with the second level—the allocation of resources to exploration—which also involves a cost-benefit comparison.

In order to implement all the implications of the proposed definition of waste, particularly with reference to the time-distribution of use, some other changes in conservation regulation would be required. These will be proposed below. But even without changes, the definition has useful applications in regulatory decision making, as three examples will show.

Question	*Answer*
1. When is gas flaring to be prohibited?	When the value to society of some beneficial use exceeds the cost to society of putting it to that use.
2. When is the use of gas to manufacture carbon black to be prohibited?	When the net present value to society of the gas in some other use would exceed that of the gas in carbon black manufacture.

| 3. When is the current rate of oil production in a reservoir to be reduced in order to increase ultimate recovery? | When the present value to society of the anticipated increment to recovery exceeds the cost to society of the required sacrifice of current satisfactions. |

Note: In each of these cases, if the affected reservoirs were unitized the operators as a whole would capture all the social benefits as income and bear all the social costs as expenses; as a matter of self-interest, then, they would make the proper decisions from society's point of view.

Cost-benefit analysis in control of external damages

As already indicated, legislators and regulators appear to have made crude cost-benefit analyses in designing and enforcing measures to prevent or limit external damages. Imperfect as it is, this area of control is one of the brighter ones in conservation regulation. I can only suggest more detailed, more precise cost-benefit analysis with a view to identifying (a) "damages" that have no value to society and therefore are not to be prevented at a cost, (b) damages that have a lower value to society than the cost of prevention and therefore are to be remedied by compensation of those damaged by those causing the damages, and (c) damages that have a greater value to society than the cost of prevention and therefore are to be prevented altogether. The oil and gas industry should be forced to bear its full social costs, but no more. I doubt (but cannot disprove) that this end is adequately served by, for instance, blanket prohibition of surface salt water disposal pits over an area as large and varied as the state of Texas. I recognize, on the other hand, that detailed local cost-benefit analysis is itself costly and perhaps unjustified by prospective benefits. Beyond these indefinite observations I am unprepared to go. The important point is that at whatever level a decision is made, that decision should be based on a pertinent and explicit comparison of costs and benefits.

More flexible minimum spacing rules

Statewide minimum spacing rules as applied are of questionable value for two reasons. First, the *appropriate* spacing varies widely from reservoir to reservoir as a function largely of recoverable reserves per acre and of well costs, the latter depending primarily on depth of reservoir and accessibility of well sites. Exceptions to the rules are common, and many reservoirs are developed on wider spacing than required. Second, such rules approach the problem of controlling the density of well drilling independently of the related problem of controlling the rate of reservoir production; they therefore do not adequately serve the aim of ultimately finding the optimum combination of well density and production rate.

Ideally, minimum spacing rules should be designed and enforced to permit spacing close enough to define new reservoirs and their characteristics, but wide enough to allow ultimate adjustment toward the optimum in each reservoir by means of in-fill drilling. These objectives may be mutually inconsistent in some instances, of course, in which case the former must govern. But for maximum realization of both objectives, spacing rules during the definition phase of development should be flexibly adapted to each situation, wider spacing being required in deep reservoirs or where discovery data indicate low reserves per acre. This suggests that a regulatory policy pronouncement should be substituted for a statewide minimum spacing rule. If the definiteness of a rule is considered administratively desirable, however, minimum spacing requirements should at least vary with depth and by location onshore or offshore.

Revision of the MER concept

The MER concept, as usually interpreted, is a product of the view that conservation consists of the prevention of physical waste. We have shown, however, that conservation requires not maximization of ultimate recovery but maximization of the value of each reservoir. The MER concept should therefore be revised to reflect the cost of time. It would then coincide with the *optimum* rate of production—that rate which in association with planned future rates of production promises to maximize the present value of expected income from the reservoir in question. The value of increased ultimate recovery would then be weighed against the value of current production that must be sacrificed to acquire it. Like the MER, the optimum rate of production would be subject to revision from time to time as new pertinent data develop.

This raises the question of how a regulatory commission can select an appropriate discount rate and estimate the future prices and costs required for determining a present value. Briefly, it can be done in exactly the same way that individual operators regularly do it in planning investment outlays and appraising properties for purchase and sale. But for that reason, it is unnecessary for commissions to make independent findings. As with most reservoir data currently employed in regulation, commissions can use the financial data supplied by the affected operators, who have a business interest in selecting a discount rate which accurately reflects the cost of capital and in estimating future prices and costs with all humanly possible accuracy. I do not suppose that all operators would agree on any particular point—this does not happen on the physical matters relating to MER—but the range of their views should be narrow enough to permit a commission to make a reasonably representative finding. As noted, the finding can be revised from time to time as the future unfolds.

Revision of depth-acreage allowable schedules

The allowance for depth in the typical depth-acreage allowable schedule is so large that, despite the wider spacing induced by greater depth, the permitted rate of production per unit area (or per unit of recoverable reserves per acre) increases steeply with depth. For example, at the preferred spacings under the 1965 Texas Yardstick, assuming recoverable reserves of 12,500 barrels per acre and a market-demand factor of 30 percent, allowable production per year rises from 1.4 percent of recoverable reserves at 2,000 feet to 5.5 percent of recoverable reserves at 14,000 feet. Higher offshore allowables at every depth similarly raise reserve depletion rates offshore above those onshore, given the same recoverable reserves per acre. As we have already observed, there is no basis in conservation principles for favoring deep or offshore production with higher effective allowables. The differential allowables simply provide an economic incentive to extend exploration into greater depths and less accessible locations before the naturally superior opportunities at shallower depths onshore are absorbed. Real social costs per unit of production are consequently raised—reflecting in part the burden of excess capacity imposed on rich shallow reservoirs—and the anticipatable resource-life of petroleum is shortened.

On the general principle of either the MER or the optimum rate of production, scheduled well allowables should be based at least in part on recoverable reserves per acre.[1] The allowable per acre should be

---

[1] Before Arizona repealed the portion of its law authorizing market-demand regulation, a factor for recoverable reserves per acre was included in its allowable formula. Arizona Oil and Gas Conservation Commission, *General Rules and Regulations* (February 1962). The province of Alberta, Canada, has recently instituted a plan under which well allowables are based in large part on recoverable reserves per acre. Alberta Oil and Gas Conservation Board, *Report and Decision on Review of Plan for Proration of Oil to Market Demand in Alberta* (Calgary, July 1964).

Table 21. Initial Depletion Rates and Net Present Values at Preferred Spacing: 160-Acre Tracts

Depth	Texas 1965 Yardstick		Initial 10 percent of recoverable reserves	
	Initial depletion rate	Present value	Initial depletion rate	Present value
(*thousand feet*)	(*percent*)	(*thousand dollars*)	(*percent*)	(*thousand dollars*)
2	1.4	358	3.0	709
4	1.6	392	3.0	692
6	1.8	415	3.0	668
8	2.1	449	3.0	640
10	2.8	572	3.0	597
12	4.0	718	3.0	529
14	5.5	871	3.0	447

Note: Recoverable reserves, 12,500 barrels per acre; 30 percent market-demand factor.

some fraction of estimated recoverable reserves per acre. Ignoring short-falls of well capacities below well allowables, this would tend to produce similar depletion rates and times in all reservoirs; and to the extent that reservoirs and their contents were otherwise similar (e.g., as to rock permeability and oil viscosity), it would tend to produce similar degrees of ultimate recovery. The annual allowable fraction of recoverable reserves to be produced could be selected so as to approximate an average MER for all reservoirs. Furthermore, given the relation of well costs to depth in the major market-demand states, basing allowables on recoverable reserves per acre would tend to discourage deeper relative to shallower exploration, as should be the case on the grounds of conservation.

To illustrate this last point, I have calculated the net present values at preferred spacings of 160-acre tracts overlying reservoirs at different depths, assuming recoverable reserves of 12,500 barrels per acre and a 30 percent market-demand factor, under two different assumptions as to the basis of allowables: (a) the 1965 Texas Yardstick and (b) an initial annual rate of 10 percent of recoverable reserves (3 percent under the given market-demand factor). The actual production rate is assumed to decline over time at a constant percentage rate until it reaches one barrel per well per day.[2] The results are given in table 21. It can be seen that under the 1965 Yardstick net present values rise from lesser to greater depths, while under the reserves-based allowable they decline

---

[2] This and the other assumptions employed in the present calculation are the same as those employed in the calculations reported in chapter 9 (see especially the section on "Spacing Incentives in Depth-Acreage Allowable Schedules.")

from lesser to greater depths. After subtracting exploration expense, the remaining differences in net present values would chiefly affect lease bonuses; but on marginal prospects the differences would induce a different distribution of exploration effort by depth, the reserves-based allowables favoring relatively shallow exploration.

To summarize, if scheduled well allowables were based at least in part on recoverable reserves per acre, conservation would be promoted in two ways. First, extremes in reserve depletion rates among reservoirs would at least be reduced, to that extent precluding depression of present values from either excessive loss of ultimate recovery or excessive lengthening of depletion time. Second, a more economical allocation of exploration outlays would be induced among prospects of different depth and accessibility, so that production would tend to move from lower-cost to higher-cost sources over time as technology improved or prices rose. In both ways costs would be lowered (the long-run supply curve would shift downward on the price scale) and thus the prospective resource-life of oil and gas would be lengthened.

Elimination of exemptions from market-demand regulation

Given market-demand regulation of output in several of the more important producing states, at least some of the special exemptions should be eliminated. Such action would improve the allocation of effort among different types of production (e.g., primary versus secondary) and help to eliminate unwanted excess capacity.

The most questionable special exemptions pertain to new discoveries, secondary recovery, and statutorily defined "marginal" wells. If they should receive any special treatment at all, discovery wells and other wells drilled during the definition stage of reservoir life should, in order to conserve reservoir pressure and protect correlative rights, be given lower-than-ordinary initial allowables. By helping enhance the long-run value of each reservoir, such allowables would encourage, not discourage, exploration. Secondary recovery operations and low-capacity wells should be treated neutrally in order to allow real social costs and benefits to determine the margin at which abandonment of production occurs.

Admittedly, neutral treatment is difficult to define when production in general is constrained by a depth-acreage allowable schedule adjusted for market demand, and when the capacity of some classes of wells is below the basic schedule allowable. One approach is to treat the capacity of a well, when that capacity is below the basic schedule allowable, as the basis of its allowable, so that the market-demand factor would apply to whichever was lower, schedule allowable or capacity. But besides being administratively expensive (requiring frequent, universal capacity tests), this approach is not necessarily neutral, since schedule allowables bear no particular relationship to the capacities of affected wells. Another approach is to allow a well to produce at the lower of the market-demand-adjusted schedule allowable or capacity.[3] This approach has the virtue of administrative simplicity (requiring no capacity tests), and it renders the production rate of every well at least potentially subject to the market-demand factor. For these reasons we prefer the latter approach, although it, too, fails to comply perfectly with the neutrality ideal, since the lowest-capacity wells would in practice be sheltered from market-demand restraint.

The difficulty of achieving neutrality among wells would be reduced (but not completely eliminated) if allowables were based on recoverable reserves per acre according to a scheme, say, of basing one-half of the allowable on initial recoverable reserves per acre and one-half on remaining recoverable reserves per acre.[4] The basic allowable would thus decline over the life of a well (or reservoir), but would never fall below the component based on initial recoverable reserves per acre. If, then, wells were permitted to produce at whichever was lower, reserves-based allowable adjusted for market-demand or capacity, some, but usually only the very lowest-capacity wells, would be sheltered from market-demand restraint. It seems likely that under this scheme most secondary recovery projects would be subject to restraint, particularly at low market-demand factors.

Reduction of differences among states

Widespread adoption of the foregoing proposals would improve the conservation quality of regulation in each adopting state, and would further promote conservation nationally by reducing the interstate differences in regulation that distort the allocation of exploration effort among states. This conclusion would hold especially for the several market-demand states. As for the differences between the market-demand and other states, they can only be eliminated, obviously, either by the universal adoption of market-demand regulation or by dropping such regulation in the present market-demand states. Since market-demand regulation is inimical to conservation in several ways, I strongly prefer the latter course.

[3] This is the procedure followed in Louisiana, which has no special allowables for discovery wells, secondary recovery projects, or "marginal" wells.
[4] This is the scheme of the Alberta plan referred to in footnote 1 of this chapter.

But the very excess capacity which market-demand regulation (in association with industry pricing policies) tends to produce stands as a barrier to the desired reform. Elimination of market-demand restraints in the face of substantial excess capacity would sharply reduce prices, creating hardships and massive abandonments in the weaker sectors of the industry, and would make it more difficult to prevent discriminatory purchasing and pricing. These consequences would be aggravated—and to a socially undesirable degree—by limited short-run pipeline and refinery capacity on one hand and by a highly inelastic short-run supply of crude oil under constrained competitive extraction on the other hand. To be politically feasible, the elimination of market-demand restraints must either be preceded by substantial reduction of excess capacity or be accompanied by the adoption of some more acceptable supply-control device. I shall make some suggestions later for reducing excess capacity. First, I shall consider the ideal substitute supply-control device.

Phased adoption of universal unitization

As indicated in the "ideal approach" to petroleum conservation outlined earlier in this chapter, essentially all reservoirs should be unitized at a reasonable time after discovery, their managements thereafter being free to make profit-motivated choices regarding well spacing, production rate, and other matters usually covered by production regulation. I need not recite again the great benefits that would flow from this reform, but will deal here with the manner of its introduction.

My purpose is to substitute unitization with free choice for both MER and market-demand regulation in a manner as little destabilizing as possible. Three phases of the transition are visualized. In the first phase only new reservoirs would be subject to mandatory unitization, and then only after a reasonable period of development to define their limits and characteristics. From discovery to unitization, new reservoirs would be subject to the package of controls described in part 2 of my "ideal approach." Unitization of other reservoirs during this phase would remain as voluntary as at the time of commencing the plan. In the second phase, which might begin four or five years after the first, other reservoirs of an age up to, say, ten years would become subject to mandatory unitization, the unitization of still older reservoirs remaining as voluntary as at the beginning of the phase. Finally, in the third phase, which might begin four or five years after the second, the remaining reservoirs would become subject to mandatory unitization. Regardless of the phase, unitization would not be required in reservoirs where it could be shown that no benefits would accrue to the operators as a whole.

As each reservoir became unitized, whether voluntarily or involuntarily, it would be freed from well spacing, production, and related regulations. Ununitized reservoirs would remain subject to the usual regulations; provided that, pending determination of MERs (or, better, optimum rates of production), production in such reservoirs would be limited in each year to some fraction of recoverable reserves. After determination, MERs (or optimum rates) would limit production until unitization occurred. Regulation of the market-demand type would be restricted to individual reservoirs for the purpose of protecting correlative rights and preventing a pattern of drainage harmful to ultimate recovery.

Even if excess capacity were negligible at the outset of the proposed plan, it is to be expected that prices would fall (or would fail to rise as much as otherwise) as the plan became fully operative. Prospective unitization would stimulate exploration (by raising expected values of discoveries), and short-run supply would grow at a faster pace than demand. The weakness in prices would be greater, of course, if there were some initial excess capacity that would be partially released by removal of market-demand restraints. In any case, introduction of the plan would cause some marginal secondary recovery projects and stripper wells to be abandoned at a date earlier than otherwise. This simply must be accepted as the inevitable price of greater realized efficiency in primary recovery. The decline in prices and adjustment in marginal production would be moderated, however, by the additional elasticity of short-run supply acquired through unitization of highly productive reservoirs. Such elasticity would increase as unitization became more prevalent. Thus, the substitution of unitization and free choice for market-demand regulation need not be excessively destabilizing, even if some initial excess capacity should exist.

Regarding unitization, we have used the word mandatory, indicating that operators of affected reservoirs would have no choice. In practice, we believe, that this would apply only in a few hard cases. Unitization would be required only where operators as a whole would benefit, and in such cases, assuming reasonable distribution of benefits, a majority of operators would have motivation to consent. Indeed, some experienced oil operators have told me that they believe that it is entirely possible that an involuntary unitization law of the presently prevailing type, if enacted in all producing states, would be adequate to assure unitization of every reservoir whose operators as a whole would benefit significantly. This view is strengthened by consideration of the fact that under my proposal unitization would substitute for most other regulation, operators acquiring freedoms that they do not now enjoy. In any case, I mean to imply that unitization would become a routine event in the early life of nearly every reservoir.

The power of conservation commissions to compel unitization ought to carry with it special responsibilities. First, as already indicated, a commission with this power should determine that unitization will bring net benefits to the operators of a given reservoir as a whole. Such determination is the equivalent of finding that unitization will benefit society at large. Second, such a commission should require that the unitization agreement adequately protects the correlative rights of all the parties. I can think of no better rule than that underlying the definition of "protect correlative rights" in the IOCC model statute. According to that definition, the term means "that the action or regulation by the Commission should afford a reasonable opportunity to each Person entitled thereto to recover or receive the Oil or Gas in his tract or tracts or the equivalent thereof, without being required to drill unnecessary wells or to incur unnecessary expense to recover or receive such Oil or Gas or its equivalent."[5] This implies that an acceptable unitization agreement should in effect remove structural advantage or disadvantage. Third, a commission with power to compel unitization should require that the unitization agreement insure each operator a proportionate voice in unit management and, if desired, a proportionate participation of his own personnel in drilling and extractive operations. Finally, in both voluntary and involuntary unitizations, the affected commission should oversee operations to assure that output policies serve the interests of the operators as a whole and not the exclusive interests of the operator designated unit manager.

To summarize, our proposal is to substitute unitization with free choice for other forms of production regulation gradually and with safeguards for minority and public interests. The gradual approach, beginning with new reservoirs, would minimize the destabilizing effects of the transition and hold the administrative task to manageable dimensions. At the same time, it would allow earliest realization of the larger benefits of unitization, including control of well density, optimum utilization of primary recovery mechanisms, and stimulation of exploration. The greatest practical difficulty would lie in coping with excess capacity during the transition. In this regard, the federal government is in a position to help.

[5] IOCC, *A Form for an Oil and Gas Conservation Statute*, p. 2.

A positive role for the federal government

As explained in chapter 3, the federal government contributes to petroleum conservation in the United States by supporting the states' regulatory efforts in various ways; by subjecting production on federal lands to the market-demand restrictions of the states in which (or, on the outer continental shelf, contiguous to which) these lands lie; and by otherwise cooperating with state conservation agencies in the regulation of drilling and operating practices on federal lands. The Department of the Interior's regulations applying to federal lands reflect a concept of waste and require operating procedures similar to those of the immediately surrounding or adjacent states.[6] In effect, the federal government reinforces and supplements state regulation of oil and gas operations and in no way seeks to undermine or shape it.

Undoubtedly the historical role of the federal government in petroleum conservation reflects (a) official approval of the states' efforts and (b) the view taken by the Federal Oil Conservation Board in 1926 that the federal government is constitutionally powerless to regulate petroleum operations outside the public domain, except in a national defense emergency. In this light, the federal government's contribution to petroleum conservation must be adjudged constructive and substantial. But, even if the constitutional interpretation is accepted uncritically—and I have no competence to challenge it—the federal government might well assume a more positive role in assisting the further evolution of state regulation toward the ideal.

First, Congress might well clarify the legality of certain operations under unitization agreements. It is clear that such agreements per se, and operations under them to prevent waste as officially conceived or to increase ultimate recovery, are not in violation of federal antitrust laws. A question remains, however, concerning operators' free control of the rate of production (to maximize present value) and cooperative marketing.[7] Both, in my opinion, should be explicitly sanctioned. The typical economic entity created by unitization is insignificantly small in

---

[6] U.S. Department of the Interior, Geological Survey, *Oil and Gas Operating Regulations* (30 C.F.R., part 221); and *Leasing and Operating Regulations for the Submerged Lands of the Outer Continental Shelf* (30 C.F.R., part 250 and 43 C.F.R., part 3380). It is interesting to note that waste is defined to include production in excess of "reasonable market demand" in the outer continental shelf regulations (part 250, §250.2) but not in the regulations applying to other federal lands.

[7] This question is raised in Richard J. Gonzalez, "Progress in State Petroleum Regulations," *IOCC Compact Bulletin*, vol. 24 (December 1965), pp. 17–18.

relation to the market for oil and gas. If unit operators are designated on the basis of leading interest in the affected reservoirs, concentration of control over producing capacity should not be increased by universal unitization. Where nonintegrated producers are involved, free control of the rate of production and cooperative marketing would increase bargaining power in relation to major buyers and improve both the flexibility and the competitiveness of oil and gas markets. For these reasons, universal unitization with free choice is entirely consistent with the spirit of federal antitrust laws and should be expressly recognized as such.

Second, the federal government might take the lead in mandatory unitization by exercising its power to require lessees of federal lands to enter and operate under a reasonable unit plan, including, if necessary, one prescribed by the Secretary of the Interior.[8] Such action, particularly if combined with the grant of free choice to unit managements, would improve conservation on the public lands. Just as importantly, perhaps, it would generate a fund of experience from which the individual states might profit in considering the merits of mandatory unitization. The outer continental shelf lands would be the most appropriate location for such an experiment, since there, in contrast with the onshore public domain, no private or state lands are interspersed with federal lands. The production freed from market-demand restraint would not be so great as to depress prices seriously (or, alternatively, to reduce allowables on other lands markedly), partly because allowables there are already so high. It is conceivable, even, that optimum rates of production selected by unit managements would be lower than recent reservoir allowables.

Third, the federal government might help reduce excess capacity in

---

[8] U.S. Department of the Interior, Bureau of Land Management, *Mineral Leasing Statutes*, 1962, ch. 3, §226(j). This power of the Secretary of the Interior, which dates from the Mineral Leasing Act of 21 August 1935, has never been exercised. Nonetheless, in 1962 approximately half of the oil and a third of the gas produced on federal lands was covered by unit agreements. (John A. Anderson, "Conservation Activities of the Geological Survey as They Pertain to Leasable Minerals," *IOCC Compact Bulletin* (June 1962), p. 3.) A strong inducement to voluntary unitization on federal lands onshore, often prior to exploration activity, is provided by the exclusion of unitized acreage from the total subject to the maximum that may be held by any given lessee. (U.S. Department of the Interior, *Mineral Leasing Statutes*, ch. 3, §§184(d) and 226(j). See also Ross L. Malone, "Oil and Gas Leases on U.S. Government Lands," *Second Annual Institute on Oil and Gas Law and Taxation* (New York: Matthew Bender and Co., 1951), p. 345.) No such inducement operates offshore, since no acreage limitations apply there.

the industry by slowing down the leasing of new lands for exploration in the outer continental shelf, except, perhaps, on the Pacific coast.[9] Except where unleased federal lands might be drained by productive wells on adjacent state lands, there is no compelling financial reason why new tracts should be put up for lease at past rates. Nor is there a reason rooted in resource-use efficiency, since the relative inducements to explore onshore versus offshore are arbitrarily affected by varied allowable schedules and market-demand factors. It is to help remove these arbitrary elements in the allocation of exploration effort that the present proposal is made. Once they are removed, the lands in the outer continental shelf should be allowed to compete for the attentions of explorers on the same basis as all other lands.

Finally, and perhaps most important of all, the federal government might help reduce excess capacity in the industry by purchasing developed reservoirs to create an explicit national defense reserve. Such a reserve would be superior to the typical excess capacity carried by the industry in several respects. It would be definite as to quantity and quality. Its parts could be located optimally with respect to pipelines and refineries, so that it could have maximum effectiveness in an emergency. And it would place the financial burden of reserve defense capacity where it belongs—on the taxpayer rather than on the consumer of oil products. In association with a program of gradual unitization of all reservoirs, it could be accomplished without raising prices or inducing the creation of new excess capacity in the industry.

There would, of course, be problems associated with purchasing and maintaining an explicit national defense reserve. First, it would be expensive. For example, if we assume an average purchase price of $1.25 per barrel of reserves and the aim of buying capacity equal to 25 percent of current demand (about six billion barrels of reserves), the necessary outlay would be $7.5 billion. There would be an annual implicit interest cost of about $400 million (at, say, 6 percent) and an additional maintenance cost of the idle wells and equipment. Second, problems would be associated with procedures of selecting and valuing reservoirs to be purchased. Negotiations with numerous operators and royalty owners would be cumbersome, pressures from interested groups would be strong, and corruption would be difficult to avoid. Third, the existence of the reserve would create uncertainties for the industry concerning

---

[9] To stop new leasing indefinitely would work a severe hardship on companies with large investments in specialized offshore exploration and drilling equipment which would become unemployed. Similar hardship might be suffered by affected personnel.

the conditions under which the reserve would be activated and deactivated. These uncertainties might seriously dampen exploration incentives.

There are other possible approaches to creating an explicit national defense reserve. For example, we might subsidize the private maintenance of reserve productive capacity, or we might tie import quotas to the maintenance of similar reserve capacity. But these approaches, too, involve problems, not the least of which would be the policing of private operators to insure their performance.

Although the creation of an explicit national defense reserve would facilitate the transition to a more ideal program of conservation regulation, its valid primary purpose should be to enhance the nation's defense capability. Without such a purpose, its benefits probably would not exceed its costs. With such a purpose, the benefit-cost ratio depends heavily on the weight assigned to the defense contribution. The judgment is not one for an individual to make; I leave the matter with the observation that if the United States sufficiently values reserve capacity as an instrument of defense, it can have both this and a better program of petroleum conservation too.

Thus, by clarifying the law, exerting the leadership of example, and helping reduce the excess capacity that stands as a barrier to reform, the federal government can facilitate the transition to an ideal program of petroleum conservation.

Some objections considered

My proposals finally focus on universal unitization with managerial freedom thereafter. Such an approach to conservation would represent a major change from present practice. It is not surprising, then, that doubts and objections arise. I shall consider here those that seem most important.

Market-demand regulation serves a vital conservation function. The conservation argument for market-demand regulation goes as follows: If output exceeds quantity demanded, buyers are placed in a position to discriminate among producers within given reservoirs and among reservoirs. Discrimination within reservoirs allows some producers to drain oil (or gas) from their neighbors' property, not only violating correlative rights but also creating a pattern of withdrawal that may cause loss of ultimate recovery. Discrimination among reservoirs by some buyers, other buyers taking as usual or discriminating in a different pattern, also results in drainage across property lines with damage to both equities and recovery efficiency. The injured producers can only protect themselves by producing for surface storage (in hopes of future purchases), which is itself hazardous and wasteful. In addition, an excess of output over quantity demanded tends to depress prices, causing the premature abandonment of stripper wells and perhaps permanent loss of the reserves under them. Thus restriction of output to a level equal to quantity demanded is necessary to protect correlative rights and prevent physical waste in petroleum production.

Although some important producing states have never considered this form of regulation necessary to protect correlative rights and prevent physical waste, the argument has merit if the assumed alternative is unrestrained extraction. But it has no merit if the assumed alternative is universal unit operation. Under unit operation, it is impossible for purchasers to affect the pattern of withdrawal from a reservoir (hence recovery efficiency), and impossible for them to force surface storage upon any operator. A unit management can always adjust reservoir output to match quantity demanded from the reservoir. If prices fall, as they should when there is excess supply at the going price, unit managements can respond by reducing output if they expect prices to be higher again in the future. If some reservoirs lose sales relatively, their managements can either adjust output accordingly or attract purchasers with lower relative prices. Competitive buyers cannot long afford to discriminate in favor of higher-priced oil, even if it is their own.[10] Thus unit operation and price competition prevent waste and protect producers' access to markets.

As for the matter of preventing premature abandonment of stripper wells, since there are always some marginal wells at any price level this argument amounts to a rejection of any price reduction at any time, which is absurd and unacceptable.

Market-demand regulation serves the national defense by creating spare capacity. We have seen that market-demand regulation in association with purchasers' past price policies does indeed tend to create excess capacity. But the amount and location of this capacity are unplanned and possibly ill-adapted to requirements in probable emergencies. Moreover, excess capacity is a burden on the industry that discourages exploration and shortens the resource life of oil and gas. Both defense and conservation aims would be better served by creating an explicit national defense reserve at the expense of the federal treasury.

Compulsion is abhorrent. Most, if not all, operators would agree that

---

[10] If market prices fall relative to their expected future level, it pays owners of oil to postpone production, even if that means that as purchasers such owners must buy greater quantities currently from other producers.

unitization is a valuable tool of conservation, but many object to *compulsory* unitization. Natural as this objection seems, it is a strange one in the context. For all regulation involves compulsion, and regulation per se is no longer an issue. The question is, *What* will be compelled? In the prevailing system of regulation, compulsion centers on well spacing, the rate of production, gas flaring, and similar matters. In what I propose, compulsion would center on unitization. Free operations under unitizations would substitute for specific, detailed kinds of regulation. I interpret my proposal as a net grant of freedom—a step back toward free enterprise in petroleum production, which unitization makes compatible with conservation. Others may interpret it differently, of course; but they cannot validly reject my proposal on grounds of objection to compulsion per se.

Free operations under unitization would be in conflict with antitrust laws. As indicated above, I recognize the possibility that joint management of output and cooperative marketing by operators in a unit might be held to be in violation of federal antitrust laws. They should not, however; for, if anything, they would improve the quality of competition in petroleum markets. But to remove all doubts and fears, federal law should explicitly sanction these activities by operators within individual units.

Unitization agreements are very difficult and time-consuming to effect. Apparently it is true that agreements are difficult and time-consuming to effect where initiative must be assumed by some interested operator, where consent is entirely voluntary, and where owners can protect themselves only by careful bargaining. As we have seen, some of the difficulties are reasons for the enactment of involuntary unitization laws. But the situation would be significantly different if initiative lay with the conservation commission, if unitization were routinely mandatory, if law and regulations contained guidelines and safeguards to protect correlative rights, and if operators would acquire valuable freedoms upon consummation of an agreement. Under these circumstances, it would be a rare case indeed where the expense of unitization exceeded the prospective benefits of unit operations.

Operators would disagree on key matters. It is not to be expected that all operators would continuously agree on matters affecting unit management, from reservoir characteristics to the rate of discount to be employed in planning investments or the time-distribution of output. Nor is it to be assumed that the majority would always be "right." It is possible that a unit management would make mistakes that would preclude or offset the potential benefits of unit operation. But these are difficulties common to all group endeavors, including all business partnerships and corporations. The best we can do is protect the right of the individual operator to a proportionate voice in management, provide the flexibility to allow correction of perceived mistakes, and hold out rewards for good management. These things would be accomplished in my proposal.

Operators might have contrary interests. It is possible that two or more integrated operators in a unitized reservoir would, as transporters, refiners, or marketers, have conflicting competitive interests bearing on reservoir operating policies. One of these operators as unit manager might be able to inflict competitive damage on the others. It is for such reasons that I have included two safeguards in my proposal: (a) Reservoirs should not be unitized when the operators as a whole would not benefit; and (b) conservation commissions should oversee unit operations with power to intervene in the interest of minority operators or the public. Regarding both simple disagreements and conflicting interests, it should be borne in mind that commission regulation and allocation of output, which is the alternative to freedom under unitization, also may not equally satisfy the opinions or serve the interests of the several operators in a reservoir.

The transition to universal unitization would, in the face of excess capacity, unduly depress prices. This would be true if the transition were attempted abruptly or without specific attention to the excess capacity problem. Consequently, I have proposed a gradual, phased transition accompanied by direct measures to remove the overburden of excess capacity. The major practical difficulty would lie in trying to coordinate the required revisions of state law with federal steps to create an explicit national defense reserve.

Free operations under unitization would result in unstable prices. The correct statement is that prices would freely fluctuate in response to uneven growth of supply and demand. Indeed, one of the purposes of my proposal is to return to free competitive prices the function of equating quantity supplied with quantity demanded—the function that prices are supposed to have in a free enterprise economy. The instability that results from, say, erratic rates of discovery should be accepted as one of the risks inherent in the industry, to be appraised along with other risks by prospective investors. But instability would not be nearly as great as it was in the pre–market-demand days. For one thing, the market is now much larger relative to the likely variation in annual new discoveries. For another, well spacing and production controls during the definition stage of new reservoir development tend to stretch out and moderate the impact of new reserves on capacity. Most important, perhaps, universal unitization would impart significant elasticity to short-run supply, which, as we have seen, reduces the degree of price instability associated with relative shifts in either supply or demand schedules.

So only a few of the objections to my proposal have substantial merit, and these objections can be met with ancillary proposals. I conclude that my "ideal approach" to petroleum conservation is within the realm of feasibility.

A final word

The resource life of oil and gas must inevitably end some day. Inescapably, as we continue to push out the margins of exploitation to ever leaner, ever less accessible deposits, the prices of these materials must rise in relation to the prices of close substitutes. The quantities of oil and gas demanded must then grow more slowly, eventually shrink, and finally dwindle to nothing. Thus oil and gas will cease to be resources as lower-priced materials are substituted for them.

We can effectively delay the inevitable and thus derive greater satisfactions from the remaining natural stock of oil and gas in two ways. The first, of course, is through further technological progress in exploration, production, and conversion to usable forms. Undoubtedly, such progress will continue for a long time. But it is not costless: it requires the application of productive resources, and a satisfactory return is not guaranteed. The other way is through further gains in the efficiency with which we exploit our oil and gas resources. Conservation regulation to date is responsible for major advances in efficiency, without which the petroleum industry as we know it might already be on the verge of extinction. But substantial inefficiencies remain as a threat to the optimum resource-life of oil and gas. Happily, no great expenditure of labor and capital is required to devise the means of removing them. Essentially all that is required is a fresh conception of efficiency and a will to innovate further in the regulatory institutions of the industry. The potential rewards, to the industry and to society at large, are very great.

APPENDIX

A Chronology of Major Legislative Acts and Court
Decisions Affecting Petroleum Conservation, 1948–67

This chronology is not intended to be exhaustive. It is confined to those acts and decisions that, in my opinion, have significantly affected the substantive nature of conservation regulation. Its purpose is to reveal the principal trends in conservation regulation in the United States during the period covered.

Year	State	Act or decision
1948	Mississippi	Comprehensive regulatory act on IOCC model, lacking provision for compulsory unitization or restriction of production to market demand. Miss. Code Ann. (1942) 1952 Recompilation, tit. 23, §§6132–01 to 51.
	Federal	Act extending the program, initiated under the Synthetic Liquid Fuel Demonstration Plants Act of 1944, of constructing and operating demonstration plants to produce synthetic fuels from, among other substances, oil shales. 62 Stat. 79; 30 U.S.C. §321.
1949	Kansas	Act authorizing the Corporation Commission to replug abandoned wells causing fresh water pollution. Kan. Stat. Ann. (1964) §55.139.
	Louisiana	Only case on question of validity of unit operating agreements under federal antitrust law. Suit under §§1 and 2 of Sherman Act, directed at cooperative refining and exclusive marketing rather than unit operation of reservoir, dismissed on procedural grounds. *United States* v. *Cotton Valley Operators Committee*, 77 F. Supp. 409, 339 U.S. 940 (1948).

Year	State	Act or decision
	New Mexico	Basic act (1935) extended to cover gas as well as oil, protection of correlative rights, and supervision of secondary recovery. N.M. Stat. Ann. (1953) §§65–3–2 to 37.
	Texas	Act authorizing the Railroad Commission to approve voluntary unitization agreements upon certain findings and exempting approved agreements from state antitrust laws. Vernon's Rev. Civ. Stat. of Texas (1962) tit. 102, art. 6008b.
	Texas	Commission order shutting down oil wells until flared gas could be put to beneficial use upheld by Texas Supreme Court. *R.R. Comm'n.* v. *Sterling Oil and Refining Co.* 147 Tex. 547, 218 S.W.2d 415 (1949).
	W. Virginia	Act authorizing use of power of eminent domain to acquire underground gas storage reservoirs. W. Va. Code Ann. (1961) §5362(c).
1950	Arkansas	Commission held powerless to compel unitization to prevent waste without specific statutory authority. *Dobson* v. *Arkansas Oil and Gas Comm'n.*, 218 Ark. 160, 235 S.W.2d 33 (1950).
	Oklahoma	Commission orders fixing minimum gas price upheld by U.S. Supreme Court as valid means of preventing economic and physical waste of gas. *Cities Service Gas Co.* v. *Peerless Oil and Gas Co.*, 340 U.S. 179 (1950).
	Virginia	Limited regulatory act prohibiting waste and controlling drilling through coal seams. Code of Va. (1950) 1967 Repl. Vol., §§45.1–106 to 144.
	Wyoming	Act prohibiting gas flaring as wasteful. Wyo. Stat. (1957) §30–232.
1951	Arizona	Comprehensive regulatory act on IOCC model, lacking provision for compulsory unitization. Ariz. Rev. Stat. Ann. (1956) §§27–501 to 527.

Year	*State*	*Act or decision*
	Arkansas	Act authorizing compulsory unitization of all or part of a reservoir under certain conditions. Ark. Stat. Ann. (1947) 1969 Supp., §53–115.
	Colorado	Comprehensive regulatory act on IOCC model, lacking provision for compulsory unitization or restriction of production to market demand. Colo. Rev. Stat. (1963) §§100–6–1 to 22.
	Illinois	Comprehensive regulatory act on modified IOCC model, lacking provision for compulsory unitization or restriction of production to market demand. Smith-Hurd, Ill. Ann. Stat. (1935) 1970 Supp., ch. 104, §§62–88.
	Illinois	Act authorizing use of power of eminent domain to acquire underground gas storage reservoirs. Smith-Hurd, Ill. Ann. Stat. (1935) 1970 Supp., ch. 104, §§104–12.
	Indiana	Amendment of basic regulatory act of 1947 providing for, among other things, authority of commission to study feasibility of and to order unitization of all or part of a reservoir; and regulation of drilling through coal seams. Burns' Ind. Stat. Ann. (1965) §§46–1714 to 1715, 1717 to 1720, 1722 and 1724.
	Kansas	Act authorizing use of power of eminent domain to acquire underground gas storage reservoirs. Kan. Stat. Ann. (1964) §§55–1201 to 1205.
	Michigan	Act authorizing supervisor of wells to enter private property to plug an abandoned well. Mich. Stat. Ann. (1967) §13.138(12).
	Michigan	Act regulating the plugging of abandoned wells and test holes. Mich. Stat. Ann. (1967) §13.139(18a).
	Ohio	Act placing drilling and plugging of wells under control of Div. of Mines, Dept. of Industrial Relations. Ohio Rev. Code Ann. (1965) §4159.02.

Year	State	Act or decision
	Oklahoma	Amendment to compulsory unitization statute of 1945 to reduce limitations on commission power to compel unwilling owners. Okla. Stat. Ann. (1969) tit. 52, §§286 to 287.
	Oklahoma	Act authorizing use of power of eminent domain to acquire underground gas storage reservoirs. Okla. Stat. Ann. (1969) tit. 52, §§36.1 to 36.7.
	Oklahoma	Constitutionality of compulsory unitization law upheld through appeal to U.S. Supreme Court. *Palmer Oil Corp.* v. *Phillips Petroleum Co.,* 204 Okla. 543, 231 P.2d 997 (1951).
	Tennessee	Act regulating drilling of wells through coal seams. Tenn. Code Ann. (1968) §§58–616 to 617.
	Washington	Comprehensive regulatory act on IOCC model, including provision for compulsory unitization and restriction of production to market demand. Rev. Code of Wash. Ann. (1962) §§78.52.-001 to 920.
	Wyoming	Comprehensive regulatory act on IOCC model, lacking provision for compulsory unitization and restriction of production to market demand. Wyo. Stat. (1957) §§30–216 to 238.
1953	Kansas	Act regulating disposal of wastes in wells and requiring State Board of Health to maintain certain related records. Kan. Stat. Ann. (1964) §55–1004.
	Kansas	Amendment of 1949 act prohibiting pollution of fresh water supplies. Kan. Stat. Ann. (1964) §§55–139 to 140.
	Kansas	Amendment of 1949 act more comprehensively regulating drilling and abandonment of wells. Kan. Stat. Ann. (1964) §§55–128 to 132.

Year	State	Act or decision
	Missouri	Act authorizing use of power of eminent domain to acquire underground gas storage reservoirs. Vernon's Ann. Mo. Stat. (1949) 1969–70 Supp., §§393.410 to 510.
	Montana	Comprehensive regulatory act on IOCC model, lacking provision for compulsory unitization or restriction of production to market demand. Rev. Code of Mont. (1947) 1970 Repl. Vol., §§60–101 to 148.
	Nevada	Comprehensive regulatory act on IOCC model, lacking provision for restriction of production to market demand. Nev. Rev. Stat. (1967) §§522.010 to 150.
	N. Dakota	Amendment of basic regulatory statute so as to make it conform more closely with IOCC model, but lacking provision for compulsory unitization. N.D. Century Code Ann. (1960) §§38–08–01 to 18.
	Oregon	Comprehensive regulatory act on IOCC model, lacking provision for compulsory unitization or restriction of production to market demand. Ore. Rev. Stat. (1969) tit. 43, §§520.005 to 991.
	S. Dakota	Amendment of basic regulatory statute authorizing formation of spacing units and pooling of tracts to form units of minimum size. S.D. Compiled Laws (1967) §45–9–20.
	Texas	Act authorizing cooperative construction and operation of facilities for conservation and utilization of gas, including liquids extraction. Vernon's Rev. Civ. Stat. of Texas (1962) tit. 102, art. 6066c.
	Texas	Texas Supreme Court held invalid commission orders shutting down all wells in a reservoir to halt gas flaring when some operators using gas beneficially.

Year	State	Act or decision
		Railroad Comm'n. v. *Rowan Oil Co.,* 152 Tex. 439, 259 S.W.2d 173 (1953).
	Federal	Act permitting regulated pipelines to cross public lands without incurring obligation to become common carriers. 67 Stat. 557, 30 U.S.C. §185.
	Federal	Act deeding to states title to lands beneath tidal navigable waters seaward of states' historical boundaries. 67 Stat. 29, 43 U.S.C. §1301.
	Federal	Act authorizing the Secretary of the Interior to prescribe rules and regulations for leasing offshore lands beyond state boundaries. 67 Stat. 462, 43 U.S.C. §1331.
1954	Federal	U.S. Supreme Court held that under Natural Gas Act of 1938 the Federal Power Commission has jurisdiction over the rates of all wholesales of natural gas in interstate commerce. *Phillips Petroleum Co.* v. *Wisconsin,* 347 U.S. 672 (1954).
	Federal	Act permitting simultaneous development of public lands under mining claims and oil and gas leases. 68 Stat. 707, 30 U.S.C. §521–a.
	Federal	Act relaxing requirements for extension of leases on public lands and providing for extension of leases committed to cooperative or unit plan of development. 68 Stat. 583, 30 U.S.C. §226.
	Federal	Act amending Mineral Leasing Act of 1920 to increase the number of acres of public lands that may be held under lease in one state by a person or company. 68 Stat. 648, 30 U.S.C. §184.
1955	Alaska	Comprehensive regulatory act on IOCC model, but lacking provision for restriction of production to market demand. Alas. Stat. Ann. (1962) tit. 31, ch. 05, §§010 to 170.

Year	State	Act or decision
	California	Act declaring the MER recommendations of the Conservation Committee of Calif. Oil Producers in the interest of conservation and making voluntary compliance lawful. West's Ann. Calif. Codes, Public Resources (1956) art. 8, §3450.
	Colorado	Colorado Supreme Court held commission order halting all flaring in a reservoir invalid as not restricted to "unreasonable" flaring; and observed that no-flare order is illegitimate means of compelling unitization, lacking specific statutory authority. *Union Pacific R.R.* v. *Oil and Gas Conservation Commission*, 131 Colo. 528, 284 P.2d 242 (1955).
	Montana	Act authorizing use of power of eminent domain to acquire underground gas storage reservoirs. Rev. Codes of Mont. (1947) 1970 Repl. Vol., §§60–801 to 805.
	Oklahoma	Act giving broad powers to commission relating to disposal of salt water and other oil field wastes and prevention of fresh water pollution. Okla. Stat. Ann. (1969) tit. 52, §139.
	Oklahoma	U.S. Supreme Court held that commission orders fixing minimum gas prices invalid because in conflict with Natural Gas Act of 1938. *National Gas Pipeline Co. of America* v. *Corporation Comm'n.*, 349 U.S. 44, 99 L.Ed. 866 (1955).
	Pennsylvania	Act authorizing use of power of eminent domain to acquire underground gas storage reservoirs. Purdon's Pa. Stat. Ann. (1966) tit. 52, §2401.
	Utah	Comprehensive regulatory act on IOCC model, lacking provision for compulsory unitization or restriction of production to market demand.

Year	State	Act or decision
		Utah Code Ann. (1953) 1970 Repl. Vol., §§40–6–1 to 17.
	W. Virginia	Act giving the Dept. of Mines power to regulate operation of gas storage areas near active coal mines.
		W. Va. Code Ann. (1961) §§2493(9) to (20).
	Federal	Trade Agreements Extension Act authorizing president to limit imports of an article when the volume of imports is such as "to threaten to impair the national security."
		69 Stat. 169, 19 U.S.C. §1351–2.
1956	Alabama	Act relaxing restrictions on size of drilling units at depths over 9,990 feet.
		Code of Ala. (1958) tit. 26, ch. 3, §179 (35-B).
	Maryland	Limited regulatory act on modified IOCC model, lacking provision for any limitation of production or compulsory unitization.
		Ann. Code of Md. (1957) 1967 Repl. Vol., art. 66C, §§675 to 689.
	Mississippi	Act vesting responsibility for preventing soil or water pollution from petroleum activities in Oil and Gas Board.
		Miss. Code Ann. (1942) 1968 Supp., tit. 23, §6132–10.
1957	Alabama	Act authorizing compulsory unitization of all or a part of a reservoir under certain conditions.
		Code of Ala. (1958) 1969 Supp., tit. 26, ch. 3, §§179(72) to (74).
	Arkansas	Act authorizing use of power of eminent domain to acquire underground gas storage reservoirs.
		Ark. Stat. Ann. (1947) 1969 Supp., §§53–901 to 907.
	Arkansas	Act authorizing compulsory formation of salt water disposal units under certain conditions.
		Ark. Stat. Ann. (1947) 1969 Supp., §53–115.

Year	State	Act or decision
	Arkansas	Act prohibiting disposal of salt water into any stream, lake, or pond. Ark. Stat. Ann. (1947) 1969 Supp., §§53–211 to 212.
	Indiana	Act prohibiting injection of potable ground water into strata containing nonpotable water without a permit. Burns' Ind. Stat. Ann. (1960) §27–1315.
	Kansas	Act to prevent fresh water pollution by requiring that oil or gas well surface pipe be cemented in place below fresh water strata. Kan. Stat. Ann. (1964) §§55–136 to 137.
	Kansas	Act removing limitation of commission power to restrict production in pools of low average production per well. Kan. Stat. Ann. (1964) §55–603.
	Kansas	Act relaxing minimum allowable per well on small tracts. Kan. Stat. Ann. (1964) §55–604.
	Ohio	Comprehensive act regulating underground gas storage. Ohio Rev. Code Ann. (1965) §§4161.01 to 99.
	Ohio	Act providing for plugging of wells abandoned prior to enactment of 1951 well law. Ohio Rev. Code Ann. (1965) §4159.12.
1958	California	Act authorizing compulsory unitization under certain conditions for the purpose of facilitating repressurization of reservoirs beneath subsiding lands. West's Ann. Calif. Codes, Public Resources (1956) 1970 Supp., art. 5.5, §§3315 to 3347.
	Kansas	U.S. Supreme Court held commission orders fixing minimum gas prices invalid on grounds of exclusive jurisdiction of Federal Power Commission under Natural Gas Act of 1938. *Cities Service Gas Co.* v. *Corporation Comm'n.*, 355 U.S. 391, 2 L.Ed. 355 (1958).
	Texas	U.S. Supreme Court upheld state common

Year	*State*	*Act or decision*
		purchaser act despite conflicting private contractual agreements.
		Permian Basin Pipeline Co. v. *R.R. Comm'n.*, 302 S.W.2d 238, 358 U.S. 37, 3 L.Ed. 43 (1958).
	Federal	Act authorizing leasing of oil and gas lands beneath nontidal navigable waters in Alaska under Mineral Leasing Act of 1920.
		72 Stat. 322, 48 U.S.C., §456a.
1959	Arkansas	Act allowing credit against severance tax to apply against cost of underground salt water disposal system.
		Ark. Stat. Ann. (1947) 1969 Supp., §84–2113 to 2120.
	Illinois	Act authorizing Mining Board to order wide spacing of wells at depths over 4,000 feet, and to form drilling units of small tracts.
		Smith-Hurd, Ill. Ann. Stat. (1935) 1970 Supp., ch. 104, §82a.
	Indiana	Act authorizing use of power of eminent domain to acquire underground gas storage reservoirs.
		Burns' Ind. Stat. Ann. (1968) §§3–1729 to 1733.
	Kansas	Act authorizing reduction of minimum well allowable when attributable acreage less than that in spacing order.
		Kan. Stat. Ann. (1964) §55–604.
	Kansas	Act authorizing commission to consider factors other than purchaser nominations in determining market demand for gas.
		Kan. Stat. Ann. (1964) §55–703.
	Michigan	Act authorizing compulsory unitization of all or part of a reservoir under certain conditions.
		Mich. Stat. Ann. (1967) §§13.139(101) to (144).
	Nebraska	Comprehensive regulatory act on IOCC model, lacking provision for compulsory unitization or restriction of production to market demand.
		Rev. Stat. of Neb. (1968) §§57–901 to 921.

Year	_State_	_Act or decision_
	Oklahoma	Act relaxing limitation on size of spacing unit at depths under 9,990 feet. Okla. Stat. Ann. (1969) tit. 52, §87.1(c).
	Federal	Presidential proclamation establishing mandatory restrictions on imports of crude oil and products. Pres. Proc. No. 3279, 24 Fed. Reg. 1781.
1960	Kentucky	Limited regulatory act providing chiefly for spacing and plugging controls. Ky. Rev. Stat. Ann. (1969) §§53.500 to 720.
	Louisiana	Act authorizing compulsory unitization of all or part of a reservoir under certain conditions. La. Rev. Stat. (1969) tit. 30, §5–C.
	Federal	Act relaxing restrictions on maximum acreage of public lands a person or company may hold under lease or option in one state. 74 Stat. 781, 30 U.S.C. §184.
	Federal	Act authorizing Secretary of the Interior to purchase and extract helium from natural gas under long-term contracts with private parties. 74 Stat. 918, 50 U.S.C. §167.
1961	California	Declaration of policy that a lease, in the absence of contrary provisions, implies authority of lessee to use secondary recovery techniques when approved by oil and gas supervisor. West's Ann. Calif. Codes, Public Resources (1956) 1970 Supp., art. 2, §3106.
	New Mexico	Oil Conservation Commission given jurisdiction over disposition of salt water produced in connection with oil and gas operations. N.M. Stat. Ann. (1953) 1969 Supp., §65–3–11.
	Oklahoma	Supreme Court of Oklahoma held that commission is without authority to require crude oil purchasers to buy more than they desire. _Gulf Oil Corp._ v. _State of Oklahoma_, 360 P.2d 933 (1961).
	Oregon	Act authorizing compulsory unitization of all or part of a reservoir under certain conditions.

Year	State	Act or decision
		Ore. Rev. Stat. (1969) tit. 43, §§520.260 to 330.
	Pennsylvania	Comprehensive regulatory act on IOCC model, lacking provision for compulsory unitization or restriction of production to market demand.
		Purdon's Pa. Stat. Ann. (1964), tit. 58, §§401 to 419.
	S. Dakota	Comprehensive regulatory act on IOCC model, lacking provision for restriction of production to market demand.
		S.D. Comp. Laws Ann. (1967) §§45–9–1 to 72.
	Texas	Supreme Court of Texas held invalid an order of commission allocating gas and condensate production so as to give well on small tract grossly more than its fair share. *Atlantic Refining Co.* v. *R.R. Comm'n of Texas*, 36 S.W.2d 801 (1961).
	Texas	Act regulating injection wells to prevent water pollution and giving Railroad Commission jurisdiction over injection wells relating to oil and gas production.
		Vernon's Rev. Civ. Stat. of Texas (1962) 1969–70 Supp., tit. 128, art. 7621b.
	Texas	Act prohibiting water pollution and creating Water Pollution Control Board.
		Vernon's Rev. Civ. Stat. of Texas (1962) 1969–70 Supp., tit. 128, art. 7621d.
	Utah	Act withdrawing certain state lands from oil and gas leasing to preserve them for potash development.
		Utah Code Ann. (1953) 1968 Repl. Vol., §§65–1–99 to 100.
	Federal	U.S. Supreme Court upheld F.P.C. denial of certification to a pipeline on grounds that transported gas would be used for an "inferior" purpose (firing boilers) in an area where other, more plentiful, fuels (coal) available.

Year	State	Act or decision

		Fed. Power Comm'n. v. *Transcontinental Gas Corp.*, 365 U.S. 1 (1961).
1962	Arizona	Act authorizing compulsory unitization of all or part of a reservoir under certain conditions. Ariz. Rev. Stat. Ann. (1956) 1969–70 Supp., §§27–531 to 539.
	Arizona	Act requiring purchasers of oil and gas to take ratably from producers. Ariz. Rev. Stat. Ann. (1956) 1969–70 Supp., §§27–507.01 and 508.01.
	Arizona	Act repealing authority of commission to restrict production to market demand. Ariz. Rev. Stat. Ann. (1956) 1969–70 Supp., §27–507 repealed.
	Louisiana	Act authorizing commissioner of conservation to prescribe rules and regulations governing underground storage of gas. La. Rev. Stat. (1969) tit. 30, §22.
	Texas	Supreme Court of Texas again held invalid an order of commission allocating production so as to give well on small tract grossly more than its fair share. *Halbouty* v. *R.R. Comm'n.*, 357 S.W.2d 364 (1962).
1963	Indiana	Act eliminating maximum spacing restrictions. Burns' Ind. Stat. Ann. (1965) §46–1709.
	Kansas	U.S. Supreme Court overturned commission ratable take order (as to gas in interstate commerce) as an invasion of F.P.C. jurisdiction. *Northern Natural Gas Co.* v. *State Corp. Comm'n. of Kansas*, 372 U.S. 84 (1963).
	Nebraska	Act authorizing use of power of eminent domain to acquire underground gas storage reservoirs. Rev. Stat. of Neb. (1968) §§57–601 to 609.
	New Mexico	Act authorizing use of power of eminent domain to acquire underground gas storage reservoirs.

Year	*State*	*Act or decision*
		N.M. Stat. Ann. (1953) 1969 Supp., §§65–9–1 to 8.
	New York	Comprehensive regulatory act on IOCC model, lacking provision for restriction of production to market demand.
		McKinney's Consol. Laws of N.Y. Ann., Conservation Law, art. 3–A, §§70 to 97.
	Ohio	Act authorizing chief of Div. of Mines to make and enforce rules governing permits to drill oil and gas wells.
		Ohio Rev. Code (1965) §4159.03.1.
	Washington	Act authorizing use of power of eminent domain to acquire underground gas storage reservoirs.
		Rev. Code of Wash. Ann. (1962) 1969 Supp., §§80.40.010 to 920.
1964	Mississippi	Act authorizing compulsory unitization of all or part of a reservoir under certain conditions.
		Miss. Code Ann. (1942) 1968 Supp., ch. 8, §§6132–101 to 112.
	Ohio	Act increasing the power of the chief of the Div. of Mines to prevent water pollution and to make rules governing disposal of salt water and other wastes.
		Ohio Rev. Code (1965) §4159.031.
1965	Arkansas	Act providing that compulsory unitization law of 1951 applies to any pool in the state, regardless of date of discovery.
		Ark. Stat. Ann. (1947) 1969 Supp., §53–115.
	Colorado	Act authorizing compulsory unitization of all or part of a reservoir under certain conditions.
		Colo. Rev. Stat. (1963) 1965 Supp., §100–6–16.
	Georgia	Act authorizing use of power of eminent domain to acquire underground gas storage reservoirs.
		Ga. Code Ann. (1958) 1969 Supp., §§93–801 to 813.
	Kansas	Act authorizing commission to grant tempo-

Year	*State*	*Act or decision*
		rary bonus discovery allowables to wells drilled in new sources of supply.
		Kan. Stat. Ann. (1964) 1969 Supp., §55–603.
	Nebraska	Act authorizing compulsory unitization of all or part of a reservoir under certain conditions.
		Rev. Stat. of Neb. (1968) §§57–910.01 to 910.12.
	New Mexico	Act conferring jurisdiction on commission to prevent waste of potash in connection with petroleum operations.
		N.M. Stat. Ann. (1953) 1969 Supp., §65–3–5.
	N. Dakota	Act authorizing compulsory unitization of all or part of a reservoir under certain conditions.
		N.D. Century Code Ann. (1960) 1969 Supp., §§38–08–09.1 to 09.16.
	Ohio	Comprehensive regulatory act on IOCC model, lacking provisions for restriction of production to market demand and compulsory unitization.
		Ohio Rev. Code Ann. (1964) 1969 Supp., §§1509.01 to 1509.99.
	Oklahoma	Act authorizing volunteers, with commission approval, to enter private lands with immunity from prosecution for the purpose of plugging or replugging leaking wells causing water pollution.
		Okla. Stat. Ann. (1969) tit. 52, §§309 to 17.
	Oklahoma	Act broadening power of commission to control oil field pollution, particularly with respect to salt water disposal in earthen pits.
		Okla. Stat. Ann. (1969) tit. 52, §§139, 140 and 142 amended.
	Texas	Act providing for compulsory pooling of tracts to form drilling units of minimum size.
		Vernon's Rev. Civ. Stat. of Texas (1962) 1969–70 Supp., tit. 102, art. 6008c.
	Utah	Act removing limitations of 160 acres for oil and 640 acres for gas wells on maximum size of drilling units.

Year	State	Act or decision
		Utah Code Ann. (1953) 1971 Repl. Vol., §40–6–6 amended.
1966	Kentucky	Act amending the Oil and Gas Conservation Act of 1960 to require surety bond to insure proper well plugging upon abandonment. Ky. Rev. Stat. Ann. (1969) §353–590.
	Missouri	Act creating the State Oil and Gas Council and granting to it power to regulate drilling, spacing, and production. Vernon's Ann. Mo. Stat. (1959) 1969–70 Supp., §§259.010 to 230.
1967	Kansas	Act authorizing compulsory unitization of all or part of a reservoir under certain conditions. Kan. Stat. Ann. (1964) 1969 Supp., §§55–1301 to 1315.
	New Mexico	Act providing for the prevention of water pollution in the state, giving Oil Conservation Commission exclusive authority over prevention in connection with oil and gas operations. N.M. Stat. Ann. (1953) 1968 Repl. Vol., §§75–39–1 to 12.
	Texas	Act granting to Railroad Commission exclusive responsibility for prevention of water pollution arising from oil and gas activities. Vernon's Rev. Civ. Stat. of Texas (1962) 1969–70 Supp., tit. 128, art. 7621d–1.

Index

Alabama: carbon black regulation, 53; production control, 41*n,* 50, 151*n*; unitization, 51, 52, 225

Alaska: carbon black regulation, 53; production control, 50, 151; salt water disposal, 141; unitization, 51, 219–21, 225; water damage control, 135

Alaska Department of Natural Resources: 141*n*; Division of Mines and Minerals, 135*n*

Allocation of resource: decisions, 6; dimensions of, 60–61; optimum, 62–63, 74, 67–68 *passim*; and price system, 64, 67–70 *passim*; steps involved, 160–61

Allowables: basic state, 48–49, 50, 151, 160; discovery, 160, 161, 162*t*, 163*t*, 185; under market-demand restriction, 37, 160–63, 240–41; recoverable reserves as basis, 238–39, 241. *See also* Depth-acreage schedules

Anticlinal trap: 11

Antitrust laws: and unitization, 210, 213, 245, 250

Arizona: allowable formula, 238*n*; purchaser practice, 52*n*; unitization, 51*n*, 225

Arizona Oil and Gas Conservation Commission: 50, 238*n*

Arkansas: carbon black regulation, 53; production control, 50, 51, 151; salt water disposal, 145, 146; statute, 40; unitization, 51, 221–22, 225

Arkansas Board of Conservation: 147

Blow-out preventer: 53, 125

Buckley, Stuart E.: 9*n*, 10*n*, 16*n*, 19, 20*n*, 22*n*, 23*n*, 24*n*, 25*n*, 35*n*, 184*n*, 200*n*, 213*n*, 215*n*

Burner oils: 94, 95*n*

California: early regulation, 36–41*n passim*; production control, 50, 151; reserves, 43*t*; subsidence regulation, 142; unitization, 51, 225, 226; well spacing, 45

California Oil Producers, Conservation Committee: 40*n*, 50

Canada, Alberta Oil and Gas Conservation Board, 238*n*

Capital: defined, 59

Carbon black: manufacturing restriction, 53, 116, 117, 119, 120, 126; regulation based on abstract definition of waste, 235

Checklist: regulation, forms of employed by states, 54*t*

Clark, Norman J.: 9*n*, 10*n*, 16*n*, 18*n*, 22*n*, 24*n*, 35*n*

Colorado: gas-oil ratio, 46; mine damage control, 134; output to capacity ratio, 167*t*; production control, 50, 151; purchaser and transport practices, 52; statutory definition of waste, 119; unitization, 51, 219, 225; waste disposal, 141; well plugging, 138

Common carrier. *See* Pipelines

"Common purchaser." *See* Purchasers

Companies: integrated, 27, 193*n*, 194*n*

Conservation: defined, 30, 61, 62, 70–73

Continental shelf: exploration, 247

Coolidge, Calvin: 36

Correlative rights: protection, 52, 53; 119, 120, 128, 198, 203–10 *passim*, 217, 232, 240, 244, 249

Cost-benefit: allocation formulas, 5; analysis, 148, 230, 233, 235, 236; ratio, 224